The Heart of Development

The Heart of Development

Gestalt Approaches to Working
with Children, Adolescents
and Their Worlds

Volume II: Adolescence

**Edited by
Mark McConville & Gordon Wheeler**

A GestaltPress Book

**The Analytic Press
Hillsdale, NJ**

Copyright © 2001 by The GestaltPress
66 Orchard Street
Cambridge, MA 02140

Distributed by: The Analytic Press, Inc.
101 West Street
Hillsdale, NJ 07642

Library of Congress Cataloging-in-Publishing Data

ISBN: 0-88163-350-X

Table of Contents

Acknowledgements   8

Preface   9

Part I: Toward a Theoretical Framework

Chapter 1.   Lewinian Field Theory, Development,
                and Psychotherapy
                        Mark McConville   26

Chapter 2.   Enlarging the Field: African-American Adolescents
                in a Gestalt Context
                        Deborah Plummer and Darryl S. Tukufu   54

Chapter 3.   Late Adolescence: A Gestalt Model of
                Development, Crisis, and Brief Psychotherapy
                        Robert Ferguson and Charlie O'Neill   72

Chapter 4.   The Self in the Eye of the Father: A Gestalt
                Perspective on Fathering the Male Adolescent
                        Gordon Wheeler   122

Chapter 5.   A Field of Difference: A Gestalt Consideration
                of Learning Disabilities
                        Marlene Moss Blumenthal   153

Part II: Applications in the Field

Chapter 6.   Coming Out of the Shadows: Supporting the
Development of Gay, Lesbian, Bisexual, and
Transgender Adolescents
Allan Singer   172

Chapter 7.   A Gestalt Approach to the Treatment of
Adolescent Eating Disorders
Beverly Blaney and John Smythe   193

Chapter 8.   Assertiveness and Conflict Resolution:
An integrated Gestalt/Cognitive Behavioral
Model for Working with Urban Adolescents
Iris G. Fodor and J. Christopher Collier   214

Chapter 9.   Shame and Support: Understanding an
Adolescent's Family Field
Robert G. Lee   253

Chapter 10.   Anorexia and Contact
Nicole de Schrevel   271

Chapter 11.   Shame, Interiority and the Heart-Space
of Skateboarding: A Clinical Tale
Mark McConville   286

Chapter 12.   Sex, Lies and Audio Tape: A Conversation
about Adolescence with Sonia Nevis
*Mark McConville, Mary Ann Kraus,
and Gordon Wheeler*   299

Acknowledgements

There are several people whose support and contribtuion to the successful completion of this collection. First and foremost, my thanks go to Gordon Wheeler and Sonia Nevis, who conceived the original Heart of Development Conference, the inspiration for this volume. It is largely their vision and encouragement that has prompted others, myself included, to begin thinking about the intersection of Gestalt field theory and developmental psychology. Whatever we achieve in this volume, and indeed in the larger enterprise of articulating a Gestalt field approach to children and adolescents, is their invention.

I would also like to thank Paul Shane for his very competent production supervision of this volume. There is a great sense of reassurance and relief that comes with knowing that someone this knowledgeable and thorough is vetting the finished product.

And, finally, I wish to acknowledge once again my fellow traveler, Joanne, my wife, for her twin gifts of perspective and ground, and for the companionship and inspiration she brings to my life.

Mark McConville
January 2001

Preface

Mark McConville

For as long as I've known Gordon Wheeler, the two of us have been engaged in an ongoing conversation about the relationship of child development and Gestalt therapy theory. Each of us deeply committed to the vision and framework of Gestalt therapy, with its basis in phenomenology and field theory, and each of us engaged in professional practice with children, adolescents, and their families, we have struggled with the integration of these two worlds. What would a Gestalt theory of development look like? we asked each other. What does Gestalt theory have to say about development that isn't already being said? I knew in my bones that my Gestalt training and background shaped my day to day clinical work, that it helped me to see my clients and appreciate their situations more compassionately, and that it supported me to use myself more fully as an intervener. But this support was largely intuitive, very much in the ground of my clinical thinking and practice. And whenever I wrestled with making this ground explicit, I found myself at a loss. And so, my conversation with Gordon Wheeler has continued, each pushing himself and the other to articulate, to find words and images, for what we, and so many other child and adolescent practitioners, seem to already know viscerally and intuitively. What does Gestalt therapy have to say about child development? And what guidance does it have to offer practitioners who attempt to support and influence that development?

Gordon and I have, over the years, brought slightly different emphases to this conversation. I noted that existing psychotherapy frameworks tend to specialize in some limited portion of the wider field. Some writers focus on the private world of thoughts, feelings and impulses; whereas others focus on the public world of peer groups, family process, or academic performance. Further, some approaches address the child/adolescent as an individual entity, whereas others view the child within a context, say, a family, or a classroom. And for practitioners who work with children, of course, this is all relevant, with the net result that we must, if we hope to work with the complexities of real life, jump between different theories and models as the presenting issues and circumstances seem to dictate. My faith in the Gestalt approach has been that it holds the potential to frame and address the whole--inner and outer, individual and context--within a unified field theory of experience, behavior, and development.

To this conversation, Gordon Wheeler has brought a clear and unwavering answer to the question, "What is it that develops?"--the question which, according to Patricia Miller, anchors any theory of human development. Gordon answers this question from the heart of Gestalt theory: our focus must be the development of the self--not the intrapsychic self of object relations theory, or the conceptual-linguistic self of cognitive/behavioral approaches--but the self of Perls, Hefferline and Goodman, the self as "integrator of the field," as the"system of contact process" that organizes the interpenetration of subject and world.

The implication of this view, as Wheeler has pointed out repeatedly, is that we must look at the child or adolescent's development always with an eye to the environmental conditions--the wants and needs and personalities of others in the developmental milieu, as well as the wider social and political context--in short, the system of supports (and non-supports) that are intimately a part of the developing field. And on this point, Wheeler has insisted, any Gestalt developmental theory must hang its hat, namely, that it is not strictly speaking an individual child whose development we trace, but the field of which the child is an interactive constituent. In the present volume, Wheeler states this view eloquently:

> Over and over we see that the child or adolescent develops along the paths that are supported--both by inner capacities and creativity, and by outer receptivity in the social/relational field.

If this seems like a truism, Wheeler notes:

> It is one that violates the basic terms of the traditional models of self ... [and we would add, of development generally] handed down in our individualist cultural and clinical tradition. The Gestalt model, with its insistence that the self can and must integrate and create itself out of the whole field, outer and inner, is in a better position to show us how it is that the relational conditions of the child's environment are not just the environment of the self, but themselves become a part of the self, part of the stuff out of which the self weaves its own unique integration *(From "The Self in the Eye of the Father" in Chapter 4 of this volume).*

Of course, Gordon Wheeler and I were not by any means the first Gestalt therapists to turn our attention to the subject of children and their development. This laurel falls to Violet Oaklander, who has been writing and teaching on the subject for more than 20 years. The importance of Oaklander's work, for Gestalt therapy, for child therapy generally, and as a foundation for our project in particular, can hardly be overstated. Her book, *Windows to our Children*, published in 1978, was unlike anything that had come before, and perhaps since. She demonstrated there, and in her subsequent writing and teaching, what it means to engage a child fully within the framework of the child's own phenomenology, and how to support the child's contact functioning in the service of healing and development. While not primarily devoted to theory development, Oaklander's work does sketch out certain essentials of a Gestalt approach to development. For example, she shows that the symptomatic behaviors that children present clinically can best be understood as creative (albeit self limiting) adaptations to environmental conditions, thus foreshadowing Wheeler's contention that development is essentially a field process. Perhaps more than any other Gestalt writer, Oaklander's work has become accepted among the standard pillars of general clinical practice, and it is difficult to imagine a child therapist today who is not familiar with, or at the very least influenced by, her ideas and methods.

But Oaklander's work presents us with a model that might properly be described as more clinical than developmental, and we are committed here to the belief that child/adolescent practitioners need a model that is both. In the late 1980s, encouraged principally by Gordon Wheeler and James Kepner, and most certainly inspired by the writing of Violet Oaklander, I began to write about my clinical work with adolescents and their families. The result was *Adolescence: Psychotherapy and the Emergent Self* published in 1995. Picking up on ideas implicit in Oaklander, this book attempted to describe adolescent development in terms of the evolution and growth of contact, showing how the field of contact process, in both its interior and interpersonal dimensions, is transformed over the course of adolescence. Of course, I also attempted to describe some of the ways that a therapist can insinuate him or herself into that field so as to promote its unfolding. At the time, I was very satisfied with my effort. Looking back on it now, however, I can see that it didn't go nearly far enough, particularly in its attempt to articulate a distinctly field orientation to the issues of development and intervention.

The present two volume set takes us, I believe, quite a ways farther on this road toward a Gestalt developmental model. It began with a simple observation by Gordon Wheeler--an observation that revealed the obvious. "There are plenty of us out here," he began, "child/adolescent therapists, teachers, physicians, who are trying to integrate our Gestalt orientation with our work. But *we're all doing it alone*. We haven't found each other, and so we're all under-supported. We have no community of voices!" From this beginning, and with the confident support of Sonia Nevis, we organized a community of voices in the form of the Heart of Development Conference in 1996 in Cleveland, Ohio. For the first time, practitioners who were struggling just as Gordon and I were struggling, to bring the wisdom of Gestalt to their work with children, came together to teach and learn and discuss and scratch our heads together. The present volumes represent largely the collective efforts of those conference participants.

We have divided this volume into two major sections. Part I, Toward a Theoretical Framework, presents pieces that push toward a more clearly conceived and articulated model of adolescent development. True to the spirit of the Gestalt approach, these contributions are studded with clinical examples, but in my view, their greatest value lies in the direction of expanding our theoretical vision. Part II, Applications in the Field, presents the thoughtful and provocative contributions from an assembly of master practitioners, touching upon a wide variety of issues and problems related to adolescent development.

In the opening chapter of Part I, I show that this project of charting a Gestalt developmental-clinical model really began with the work of Kurt Lewin, over sixty years ago. In particular, Lewin understood that development is not simply a matter of the individual acquiring new potentials and abilities over time, but of an evolving re-organization of the organism-environment field, or "life space." In Lewin's framework, my 1995 model of emergent and evolving adolescent contact process finds a more solidly grounded theoretical base, and points more clearly to a philosophy and method of clinical intervention. This is illustrated by two brief case histories which are somewhat contrasting in nature, but which demonstrate that psychotherapeutic work--even individual therapy--needs to address the wider field of the adolescent's development.

Following this, Deborah Plummer and Darryl Tokufu demonstrate the applicability of the Gestalt model of contact boundary development to African American adolescence, and at the same time push that model to fulfill its potential as a radical field approach to development. They summarize recent work on racial identity development, and describe this development as a reorganization of the self in the field, showing how the adolescent must come to terms with the meaning of his or her Blackness at intrapsychic, interpersonal, and social-cultural levels. It is imperative, they point out, for therapists--black or white--to appreciate this comprehensive reorganization of experience for African-American youth. They argue convincingly that therapeutic intervention based upon a field model must go beyond the constrained forms of traditional individual and family therapy, and become truly *contextual* in character. In this connection they describe a variety of interventions, such as Rites of Passage, that address and directly impact the social and cultural ground in which the adolescent 'selfing' process unfolds. While this chapter is most certainly an important contribution of the subject of adolescent African-American development and therapy, it also points the way for Gestalt developmental theory and therapy in general, if it is to fulfill its promise as a radical field model.

Rob Ferguson and Charlie O'Neill present a model of late adolescent development, and document the unique challenges of doing brief individual psychotherapy with this age group. Their chapter makes a substantial contribution to Gestalt developmental theory, and at the same time offers a virtual manual for brief psychotherapeutic work with college age individuals. On the theoretical side, in addition to their meticulously constructed model of late adolescent development, the authors offer an important elaboration of the Gestalt theory of contact. They contend that "...a more complex theory of contact is necessary to fully appreciate the perspective and common needs of late adolescent clients in developmental crisis." The authors then expand and elaborate the Gestalt theory of contact style (particularly as articulated by Wheeler, 1991), taking it one step further in its evolution as a utilitarian model of clinical assessment and intervention.

Next, Gordon Wheeler examines the relationship form of father and son in Western societies, showing the critical role this relationship plays in male adolescent development. In examining this legacy, Wheeler exposes the paradigm of hyper-individualism which so thoroughly saturates Western culture in general, and certainly our dominant traditions of developmental theory and psychotherapy in particular. Counterposing the traditional individualist model with a Gestalt field model, Wheeler identifies and clarifies the meaning and role of *support* (and its opposite, shame) in the developmental field of the fathering relationship. He does this within the context of three highly detailed clinical vignettes, and in so doing offers us not only an important descriptive model of male development, but also a highly practical guide to clinical assessment and intervention in father-son dynamics.

Preface

In the final chapter of Part I, Marlene Blumenthal reflects on the nature of learning, approached from a Gestalt perspective. Focusing on the problem of learning disabilities, Blumenthal de-constructs the conventional notion of learning as a process occurring within the child, describing it instead as a process occurring within a highly charged social field. Blumenthal examines the influence that field conditions of connection and disconnection have on a child's ability to learn in a school situation. She contends that the acts of identifying and diagnosing learning disabilities in children and adolescents are themselves contact episodes, and as such can influence the field conditions of learning. She draws upon the work of Wheeler and Lee (1996) to show the role of shame in school learning, and shows at least some diagnosable learning disabilities to be "creative adjustments to a learning disabled field."

Part II opens with Allan Singer's moving description and illumination of the hardships and challenges faced by gay, lesbian, and bi-sexual adolescents. First through the lens of his own growing-up, and then through the lens of Gestalt developmental theory, Singer shows us how the emergence and strengthening of self is impacted by field conditions of danger and non-support. He leaves us with an articulate description of the work which must be done--the developmental work of adolescents themselves, the work of support that falls to the adults in their lives, and the work for all of us in making society at large a more hospitable milieu for the emergence and celebration of uniqueness and difference.

Following this are two chapters that present the application of Gestalt developmental principles to structured adolescent intervention programs. In the first of these, Beverly Blaney and John Smythe document their development of a Gestalt based inpatient treatment program for adolescent anorexia nervosa. Blaney and Smythe note their early dissatisfaction with conventional psycho-educational and behavioral treatment methods, and describe their search for an approach that would address more the felt experience of the disorder and its amelioration. "If new learning is to be fully integrated into one's sense of self," they write, "the conflicts generated by our culture of thinness must be clearly perceived as a sensed experience." The authors document their efforts to create a treatment program that incorporates an emphasis on awareness and ownership of first person experience, and their utilization of Gestalt developmental theory in accomplishing this enterprise. The results of their efforts underscore the clinical utility of the Gestalt model as a framework for designing comprehensive intervention strategies.

14

Preface

Iris Fodor and Christopher Tollier similarly describe their efforts in creating a school based conflict resolution program for a selected group of inner city, pre- and young adolescent boys. The authors argue that assertiveness and social skills training, which have come from the cognitive-behavior therapy tradition, can be more effectively conceived and implemented when integrated with Gestalt objectives and methods. Adolescents, as Fodor and Collier point out, are natural experiential learners, and hence their model "adopts a Gestalt lens to highlight the self awareness process and awareness of contacting in interpersonal interactions as a foundation for assertive and conflict management skills." The result is an important reminder of the richness that a Gestalt perspective brings to any educational or clinical intervention.

These two chapters on programmatic intervention are followed by a trio of clinical tales that together provide and intimate and richly nuanced portrait of Gestalt psychotherapy with adolescent clients. In the first, Bob Lee gives us the story of his work with an acting-out, fifteen-year-old boy and his family. In doing so, he explores how family field conditions can underlie problem behavior in adolescents, and shows how shame is often the organizing dynamic of troubled family fields. His case history reveals the deft hand of a master practitioner as he follows the traces of hiding and avoidance in a family's interaction, back to shame experiences that keep them from fully engaging one another. Lee extends here his earlier articulation of a Gestalt theory of shame (Lee, 1996), showing us what a powerful force shame can be in shaping and obstructing the developmental course of adolescence. The description of his concrete treatment strategies also provide a good example of how Gestalt field theory supports interventions at multiple levels of a system as he combines individual, couple, and family work in his pursuit of a single, unifying treatment theme.

In the second clinical tale, Nicole de Schrevel tells us the compelling story of her individual therapy with Denise, a fourteen-year-old anorexic girl. In this case history, which stands both in contrast and complement to Blaney and Smythe's chapter on anorexia, de Schrevel demonstrates careful attention to the subtleties of therapeutic contact process. Her attention and receptivity lead her to a deeper understanding of Denise's world, and ultimately, to a successful treatment of her anorexia. de Schrevel shows us that the essence of individual psychotherapy with an adolescent client lies in understanding the symptom picture itself as a mode of contact, and then utilizing the contact process, as it occurs in the therapeutic relationship, to mediate the emergence of new possibilites. And the "method" de Schrevel uses is also quintessentially Gestalt, as she goes to work on herself as a way of opening the field of her client's experience. "If she was anorexic," de Schrevel describes poignantly at a critical point in the therapy, "I disciplined myself not to be 'bulimic' with my words, not to spew out my own ideas and questions and curiosity." Her description of the therapeutic process is both touching and instructive.

A final clinical vignette is entitled "The Heartspace of Skateboarding," in which I describe my therapeutic work with Jeff, a thirteen year-old boy diagnosed with Attention Deficit Disorder. This chapter provides a concrete clinical complement to Blumenthal's analysis of learning, as I explore the profound role that shame played in shaping the learning experience for Jeff. The chapter details my entry into Jeff's world through the window of his skateboarding; a preoccupation that turned out to be many things at once--diversion, defense, identity, metaphor, language, and interiority. This case history illustrates the *"therapist-as-anthropologist"* dimension of one-to-one clinical work, and underscores the developmentally healing power of therapeutic resonance and support.

This collection is capped by an important interview with Sonia Nevis, the co-founder of the Center for the Study of Intimate Systems at the Gestalt Institute of Cleveland. In this interview, we are treated to the qualities so familiar to her clients and students - playful provocation, penetrating analysis, and unexpected twists of insight and observation that leave you with a sense of seeing the obvious for the first time. Sonia Nevis has become a legend to generations of students in Cleveland and Cape Cod by virtue of her uncanny ability to see quickly to the heart of the matter, and to see with such depth and clarity as to sometimes take your breath away. We are lucky indeed to include this delightful interview in the present volume.

This is our collection, proudly presented. But in all honesty, this is pride mixed with regret; regret that there are important topics that are not addressed, such as chemical dependency and drug use, adolescent sexuality, violence, and risk-taking behavior. Regret that we have only two contributions addressing the intra and inter-cultural diversity of adolescent experience. Regret that we have not included directly the voices of any adolescents themselves. These omissions are not so much oversight, as they are testimony to the infancy of the Gestalt developmental model. For most of our authors, the contribution to this volume required some degree of groundbreaking, some painful pushing to deliver the words for what they knew already in intuition and praxis. Our hope is that ground broken will become ground reorganized, ground that supports this project of dialoging, articulating, debating, writing, and reading. Our hope is that this volume supports the emergence of a community of voices invested in inventing and speaking a Gestalt language of development.

Mark McConville
Shaker Heights, Ohio

Dedicated to my teachers

John Margrett, M.D.

and

Sonia Nevis, Ph.D.

The Editors

Mark McConville, Ph.D. is a clinical psychologist in private practice in Shaker Heights, Ohio specializing in adolescent and family psychology. He is a senior faculty member at the Gestalt Institute of Cleveland, and has lectured widely on the subjects of child development, parenting, and counseling methodology. In addition to his practice, Mark consults regularly with Hathaway Brown School and University School, both in the Cleveland area. His book, *Adolescence: Psychotherapy and the Emergent Self* (Jossey-Bass, 1995) was awarded the Nevis Prize for Outstanding Contribution to Gestalt Therapy Theory. Together with other faculty members at the Gestalt Institute of Cleveland, Mark is involved in the development of a post-graduate training program in Gestalt approaches to working with children and adolescents.

Gordon Wheeler has written extensively on the Gestalt model as the basis of a new integration of evolutionary psychology, developmental constructivism, and intersubjective understanding. In particular his writings in the field have focused on self and developmental theory, intimacy and relationship, shame and support, narrative theory, gender studies, men's issues, and child and adolescent therapy. A longtime member of the teaching faculty of the Gestalt Institute of Cleveland, Gestalt International Study Group, the Esalen Institute, and a number of training institutes overseas, he also serves as Director and Editor of GestaltPress, where he has overseen the editing and production of some twenty-five books on Gestalt topics by other authors. He is the father of five children and three stepchildren, and together with his wife Nancy Lunney Wheeler, divides his time between Cambridge, Massachusetts and Big Sur, California. His recent books in the Gestalt field include *Beyond Individualism: Toward a New Understanding of Self, Relationship & Experience* (GestaltPress/The Analytic Press, 2000) and *Reading Paul Goodman: Gestalt Therapy, Essays & Commentary* (in press).

The Contributors

Beverly Blaney, M.A. received her post-graduate training in Gestalt therapy at the Gestalt Institute of Cleveland. In addition, she is a certified Behavior Therapist. Beverly conducts a private practice in Kingston, Ontario, where she is also on the staff of the Hotel Dieu Hospital, Department of Psychiatry. Beverly is also an instructor at St. Lawrence College where she teaches a course on body image and self esteem.

J. Christopher Collier, Psy.D. is a psychologist at New York Presbyterian Hospital in the Special Needs Clinic and at the Incarnation Children's Center in New York City. He is also the director of the SNC's After-School Program which provides group psychotherapeutic experiences for children ages 5-13. His current areas of interest include: psychosocial and pain-management aspects of children and families dealing with chronic and terminal illnesses; crisis intervention with survivors of child sexual abuse, violence and other traumas; and forensic issues related child sexual abuse allegations and youth who commit violent crimes.

Robert Ferguson, Ph.D. is a psychologist in private practice in Durham, North Carolina. He combines cognitive, Gestalt, and developmental frameworks in his work with adolescents, adults, and couples. He also works with businesses as a consultant and executive coach. Dr. Ferguson is a professional speaker and co-author of *Mastering Team Leadership: 7 Essential Coaching Skills*.

Iris G. Fodor, Ph.D. is a Professor of Applied Psychology at New York University where she trains graduate students in School Psychology in Cognitive, Gestalt, and Integrative Therapy. She has done workshops and written about the integration of Cognitive and Gestalt therapy. Among her extensive writings are: "Awareness and Meaning Making: The Dance of Experience," *Gestalt Review* 1998; "Making Meaning of Therapy: A Personal Narrative of Change over Four Decades" in M. Goldfriend (Ed.), *How therapists change: Personal and professional reflections*, APA Books; "A Cognitive Perspective for Gestalt Therapy," *British Gestalt Journal*, 1996; and "A Woman and Her Body: The Cycles of Pride and Shame" in R.

Lee and G. Wheeler (Eds.) *The voice of shame: Silence and connection in psychotherapy*, 1996.

Mary Ann Kraus, Psy.D. is a clinical psychologist specializing in consultation and training with individuals, couples, groups, and organizations. She is a member of the Professional Staff at the Gestalt Institute of Cleveland (GIC) where she co-chairs the Gestalt Training Program and teaches in the specialization tracks Working With Individuals and Working With Groups. She is also a member of the faculties of the Organization and System Development Program and Becoming A Better Intervener Program through the Organization and System Development Center at GIC. Her interests include the expansion of integral and holistic theory, and the creation of the capacities for more full-spectrum developments in individuals, groups, and organizations. She has particular interests in gender issues and women's development across the life span.

Robert G. Lee, Ph.D. is a clinical psychologist working with children, adolescents, couples, and families in private practice in Cambridge and Newton, Massachusetts. He is also a member of the visiting faculty of the Gestalt Institute of Cleveland. He has written extensively on the phenomenon of shame and its interconnection with Gestalt theory, and co-edited The Voice of Shame: Silence and Connection in Psychotherapy. His ongoing interests include exploration of the field conditions of support and shame, and the implications of this knowledge for solutions to modern problems. Bob is currently working on a book on ethics and Gestalt therapy.

Marlene Blumenthal, Ph.D. is a psychotherapist and school psychologist working in family practice in Shaker Heights, Ohio. She is a member of the Professional Staff of the Gestalt Institute of Cleveland where she teaches in training programs and facilitates workshops on Gestalt approaches to conflict management. She has extensively studied mother-daughter conflict with regard to the Gestalt resistances, conflict handling modes, and mutuality. Her professional work is anchored by a peaceful life with her husband that includes special times with adult children, learning from grandchildren, and traveling.

Charlie O'Neill, Ph.D. is a licensed psychologist in the state of Kentucky and Associate Director of the Counseling Center at the University of Kentucky. He has worked his entire professional life in higher educational settings where late adolescents and emerging adults have been the primary focus of his work. He has taught extensively on late adolescent issues. Charlie was trained by Bob Harman, and has practiced Gestalt therapy throughout his career.

Deborah Plummer, Ph.D. is a practicing psychologist and Associate Professor of Psychology at Cleveland State University, where she is the Director of the graduate level Diversity Management Program. As a researcher and author, Deborah has published numerous articles and book chapters on racial identity attitudes of adults and adolescents, and on diversity consultation. As a consultant, Deborah specializes in diversity and organizational change management for corporations and non-profit organizations. In addition, she maintains a small private practice in counseling individuals, couples, and families. Deborah is a graduate of the Post-Graduate Training Program at the Gestalt Institute of Cleveland, and holds a Diversity Management Certificate from NTL Institute for Behavioral Sciences.

Nicole de Schrevel is Founder and Director of the Gestalt Institute of Belgium, with programs in Brussels and France. She teaches the Gestalt model widely in French-speaking countries, with special emphasis on adolescent and adult groups, women's issues and development, and eating disorders. She is the mother of five children and grandmother, to date, of eight.

Allan Singer, LICSW is in private psychotherapy and consulting practice in Boston, Massachusetts specializing in gay, lesbian, bi-sexual, and transgender (g/l/b/t) issues. Allan serves as chairperson of several national and regional organizations, including the Massachusetts Chapter of the NASW, influencing and shaping policy concerning g/l/b/t issues. In addition to his extensive experience in training educational and mental health professionals, he has written several chapters and articles on g/l/b/t issues, in which he has explored themes of shame, intimacy and relationship, and development. In recent years, he has served as a visiting teacher at Esalen Institute in California, and has immersed himself in the seemingly interminable renovation of his new home.

John Smythe, MD, FRCPC, is Associate Professor of Pediatrics and Associate Dean of Student Affairs for the faculty of Health Sciences at Queen's University in Kingston, Ontario.

Darryl Tukufu, Ph.D. holds Diversity Management Certificates from both Cleveland State University and from the NTL Institute of Applied Behavioral Science. Currently, he is an adjunct member in the Department of Psychology at Cleveland State University, and is President of the Tukufu Group, a Cleveland, Ohio human resource consulting firm specializing in personal growth and development, organizational development, and diversity management. As a consultant and public speaker, he has more than 30 years of work experience in both public and private sectors throughout the United States. He is author of *A Guide Toward Successful Development of African-American Males* and *R to the 3rd Power: Reflection, Regeneration and Revitalization in the New Millenium.*

Part I:

Toward a
Theoretical Framework

1

Lewinian Field Theory, Adolescent Development, and Psychotherapy

Mark McConville

"It is... this relatedness-at-the-boundary, this system of contacts, whose development we wish to trace..." (Gordon Wheeler, 1990)

Introduction

In the lived world of adolescent clinical practice, we are presented in most instances, initially at least, with a *situation*, more than an individual client. There are anxious adults, strained relationships, and a story line unfolding toward an unfulfilled and unfulfilling future. And somewhere in the drama, we encounter the adolescent, a child who is no longer exactly a child, but also not yet self-organized or directed enough to make a viable life on his or her own. Such was the case with Nora, a depressed, self-mutilating sixteen-year-old referred to me by her school counselor. In fact, the counselor used this exact expression when she first telephoned me: "We've got a *situation* here," she said, "and we'd like you to get involved." And a situation it was, indeed, a piece of real-life drama unfolding in her office, its characters including scared classmates, "uncooperative" parents, frustrated and alarmed school officials, and of course, Nora herself, a bright, attractive girl who had sadly come to the conclusion that growing up was impossible, and life itself some sort of curse.

Todd, also sixteen, had come (apparently) to a somewhat different conclusion--something more along the lines of 'life is a party, and growing up is irrelevant.' And like Nora, Todd was introduced to me as part of a larger situation, a *field* in the language of Gestalt theory, which included Juvenile authorities, n'er-do-well friends, and parents who were divorced but still at war.

26

The question with both Todd and Nora, and in fact with most adolescent clinical referrals--the question that virtually defines the interface of clinical practice and developmental/psychotherapy theory--is *where* in the situation to insinuate ourselves, with whom, and in what fashion. We will return to Nora and Todd later, but first we must address this critical question: how is the clinician to assess and catalog the possibilities for intervention. Do we meet with the individual adolescent him or herself? Do we include the parent or parents? And what about the wider field, the adults and peers beyond the family who have become part of the adolescent's unfolding drama? And whomever we engage therapeutically, do we address the subjective phenomena of experience and meaning-making? Or do we intervene to influence the external environment in an effort to increase or decrease the likelihood of specific behaviors? And beneath these questions, another question: how are we to make these determinations? What are the criteria, and what is the model that organizes our understanding of the adolescent's development and the clinical difficulties that have solicited our involvement?

This array of questions is partly a reflection of the nature of adolescent development. For one thing, this development is mediated largely by interpersonal relationships, such that the adolescent self is intrinsically part of a wider social field. And as this self evolves through the teen years, adolescents spontaneously begin to segregate "inner" and "outer" worlds of experience and behavior, which sometimes seem indeed, almost as parallel, non-intersecting universes. The upshot, for the clinician who works with adolescents, is that sometimes we are called upon to engage our adolescent clients as singular beings, and at the most intimate level of subjectivity. At other times we are shut out of that world entirely, and can only intervene to influence and shape the social environment in which our clients behave, and in which their subjective experience takes shape.

Clinical theory and practice has evolved in corresponding fashion. There are approaches which attend almost exclusively to the nuances of the adolescent's private, subjective experience--such as Blos' (1979) Psychoanalysis, Kaupenhauer's (1990) Jungian analysis, Wexler's (1991) Cognitive Behavior therapy, or Oldfield's Mythic Journey therapy (Peay, 1990)--and there are approaches which essentially disregard subjectivity and manipulate the environment--Glasser's (1965) *Reality Therapy*, Minuchin's (1974) and others' family therapy approaches, and most behavior management methods--in order to shape behavioral outcome. And on both sides of the line, the adolescent's first person experience is marginalized, relegated to epiphenomenal status, subjected to interventions which are either interpretive or manipulative, but which for the most part lack a rationale for authentic encounter and dialog.

In actual clinical practice, therapists who work with adolescent clients find themselves in an unenviable position. Those who practice strictly within the confines of a particular approach, say orthodox analysts, or strict family therapy practitioners, are limited to maps which cover only part of the total field, rendering them effective only with certain "types" of cases. Eclectic practitioners, by contrast, find themselves shuttling between models depending upon the presenting clinical profile. They are guided in this process by their intuitive grasp of where in the total field the 'action' is, and what sort of involvement on their part will most effectively promote the cause of development. One situation seems to call for parent guidance, another for family therapy, another for intervention in the school, and still another for individual work with the adolescent herself.

In other words, effective adolescent practitioners seem to develop their own intuitive field model of adolescent development and intervention, creatively adjusting to the insufficiencies of existing theoretical models. Gestalt therapy theory, in our view, provides the necessary theoretical base for developing a model of adolescent development and intervention that is both comprehensive and utilitarian--a model that allows us to understand adolescents on their own terms, in all their inward and outward complexity, and which supports interventions in all regions and levels of the field.

Field and Development

Developmental theories, according to Patricia Miller (1989), differ most essentially according to their implicit answer to the question, "What is it that develops?" Each developmental theory, she points out, makes assumptions concerning the proper unit of analysis. Gestalt therapy theory, as laid down in Perls, Hefferline and Goodman's (1951) classic text, *Gestalt Therapy*, holds that the dynamic, interactive field of organism and environment is the only proper unit of psychological investigation. They write:

> In any psychological investigation whatever, we must start from the interacting of the organism and its environment. Every human function is an interacting in an organism/environment field, socio-cultural, animal and physical. No matter how we theorize about impulses, drives, etc., it is always to such an interacting field that we are referring..." (1951, p. 228).

Traditional approaches to development, even in their most current articulations, generally fail to incorporate the central insight of field theory, namely, that all phenomena are *of-a-field*. According to developmental theorists Cathy Dent-Read and Patricia Zukow-Goldring (1997), "prevailing theories generally attempt to explain the changes in form, function and complexity observed during development by seeking causes in the child, or in the environment, or in some combination of the two." But this sort of dualistic thinking is breaking down in the face of recent research and thinking, they point out, even in such fields as cellular biology. In a voice reminiscent of Perls, Hefferline, and Goodman, Dent-Read and Zukow-Goldring (1997) conclude that "...organisms and their environments do not 'interact' or cause each other... Rather, organisms and environments form reciprocal wholes, in which each plays a complementary role: Organisms act and adapt, environments support and surround" (p.7).

The implication of a field approach to development is that utilitarian psychological constructs, such as "self","symptom", and "personality," and even developmental constructs such as "adolescence," must be defined in field terms, as integrators of the overarching field of experience, and as organizers of the contact boundary of the child and her environment. Symptoms, personality traits, and even adolescence itself, traditionally viewed as phenomena of the encapsulated self--the self conceived in isolation--must be understood as creative adjustments to conditions of the field.

The *meaning* of emergent language, for example, in an 18-month old child, and more specifically, the meaning of this emergence *for development* is co-determined by the ground structures and environmental conditions of the overarching field in which the child finds himself. The value and utilization of language in a particular parent-infant dyad, and the role of language in a particular family, in a particular socio-economically indexed subculture, and at a certain time of the family history--these are integral reciprocals of the child's emergent information-processing strategies. How this emergent potential is received may well determine its significance in the child's overall development, and whether or not this or any emergent set of phenomena come to define a "stage" of the individual's development.

Kurt Lewin's Theory of Development

Twenty years before the publication of *Gestalt Therapy*, Kurt Lewin answered the dominant developmental theories of his day--psychoanalysis and American behaviorism--with a field theory of adolescent development and behavior (Lewin, 1997). In contrast with other approaches, which tended to partialize development according to biological, psychological, or social causality, Lewin proposed a model that integrated these dimensions. Most theories of human development tend to emphasize one dimension of functioning--say, intellectual operations (Piaget, 1950), psycho-sexual maturation (Freud, 1962), social learning (Bandura, 1977), or cognitive information processing (Siegler, 1986). Most theories, in other words, are theories of a part, and accordingly tend to reduce the growth of the whole to the development of some part function.

Lewin saw the biological, psychological, and social as dimensions of an integrated field, which he called the *life space*; and it is this field, the life space, that Lewin envisioned as the proper subject of developmental theory and research. The life space represents a map of the developing person's phenomenological field. It incorporates, in the words of Ernest Hilgard (1948), "the space in which I live psychologically...[and] corresponds in many ways to the world around me... [but is also] a space that somehow exists within me."

In this concept of the life space, in other words, we have a model that undercuts the dualistic split of inner and outer, and brings to our attention that ground of experience and behavior from which "inner" and "outer" emerge. It includes the genetic and physiological givens, the familial, social, cultural, political and geographical contexts of development, and the experiential domains of thought, need, fantasy, feeling and personality organization.

In Lewin's conceptualization, the field, or life space, is continuous in space and time. "Using the field approach one thinks of living, moving, changing, energetic interacting ... the forces of a field are of a whole and *develop over time*" (Yontef, 1993, p. 301, emphasis added). In other words, because the psychological field is dynamic and evolving, a field approach to human behavior is by definition an implicit model of development. The child-environment system is in a state of temporal dynamic tension, a tension of movement or *becoming*. The researcher or clinician is presented fundamentally with an unfolding (or the interruption of an unfolding) that magnetizes the field of the child and her environment and orients that field in a certain developmental direction.

Having established the psychological life space as the proper unit of analysis, Lewin identified three major parameters of its development. These are:

(1) the extension of the life space;

(2) the increased differentiation of the life space;
(3) the change in organization of the life space.
We will consider each in turn, with special attention to the power of Lewin's theory for illuminating the phenomena of adolescence.

Extension of the Life Space

"The psychological world which affects the behavior of the child seems to extend with age," (Lewin, 1997, p. 242). And this expansion shows itself in several ways. First, there is throughout development a general increase in the scope and range of the life space. In the psychological present, as it evolves over time, there is an increase in the "space of free movement"--the region, both geographical and psychological, that the child finds accessible. This trend reflects both the emergence of new abilities and potentials for the developing person as well as an evolution of the mix of environmental supports and prohibitions related to these emergent behaviors. A client of mine, age fifteen, would occasionally, without his parents' knowledge or approval, take the train from his suburban neighborhood into the center of downtown Cleveland. There, he would buy a pack of cigarettes in one of the shops and smoke as he wandered the city streets. Often, he would sit in one of the outdoor malls, smoking and reading a paperback, usually William Boroughs or Friedrich Neitzsche. With this ritual, he pushed beyond the constraining boundaries of his familiar life space--geographically, behaviorally, intellectually, and relationally, by taking himself beyond the boundary of parental cognizance and approval. And at the same time, he was exploring new "internal" space, in the sense of becoming 'a person who does such things.' Developmental change, in other words, subtends the child-environment system, and requires new environments (in this case, an urban center where little is thought of a fifteen year-old buying cigarettes, and where his various modes of wandering were treated with an accepting indifference) as much as it requires new interests and impulses bubbling up within the adolescent himself.

Lewin points out that this expansion of the life space is anything but linear and orderly for the adolescent. For one thing, as some areas are made available (driving a car, for example), others are closed off (e.g., turning to adults for protection when being teased by a bully). Furthermore, the areas of the life space that are opening up are at best unfamiliar and vaguely determined and, in many cases, ambiguously permitted and prohibited at the same time. For example, many adults expect adolescents to experiment

31

with tobacco and alcohol, and precisely because of these expectations, intensify their efforts to discourage and prohibit such behavior.

Lewin contends that many of the characteristics traditionally understood as a function of the adolescent as a *self-in-isolation*, (and ascribed in most theory to "internal" causes such as hormonal change or archaic superego function), are best understood as expressions of a disequilibrating field. It is, to take a familiar example, as much a social field which is frightened and intensely ambivalent concerning adolescent sexuality, and which accordingly provides little coherent support and structure for the emergence of sexual experience, as it is the adolescent's surging hormones that co-construct the phenomenon labeled "sexual impulsivity."

The second extension of the life space cited by Lewin is temporal, as its "psychological time dimension" expands to include increasingly more distant representations of past and future. This aspect of development is nowhere more dramatic than in adolescence when the field of experience becomes polarized between the all too familiar ways and means of childhood and the daunting expectations and possibilities of becoming grown up. Time seems to open up for the adolescent, not merely as a cognitive construct, but as an existential reality, but as a force-field which alternatively pulls in opposite directions. This is probably most salient as adolescents approach the end of high school or near their eighteenth birthday. The protracted future, which seems relatively insubstantial to the younger adolescent, becomes a palpable organizer of the older adolescent's reality. When my downtown sojourner passed his seventeenth birthday, his wanderings gradually lost their satisfying allure, and he would find his dreamy trances interrupted by troubling observations and thoughts. "What do these people *do*," he found himself wondering as he walked the busy streets; "How will I make it out here in this world?"

Differentiation of the Life Space

Lewin's description of the differentiation of the life space represents one of his most important contributions to developmental theory, and he spells out the nature of this process with careful precision. Differentiation means, first, that the child's behavior displays greater variety over time. New actions are added to the motor repetoire, emotional expression becomes more variegated, and social behavior becomes more articulated in its forms of relatedness. In short, the number of dynamic "parts" within the dynamic whole of the life space increases with development.

In addition to the greater variety of experience and behavior, differentiation also refers to the relations between the emerging parts of the life space. He writes: "...the term differentiation can refer to relations of dependence and independence between parts of a dynamic whole. In this case increasing differentiation means that the number of parts of the person which can function relatively independently increases; i.e., that their degree of independence increases" (1997, p. 243). As a simple illustration, Lewin describes the development of motor skills in the young child. When first attempting to grasp an object, the infant simultaneously mobilizes arms, legs, mouth and eyes, "grasping" as it were, with its whole body. Over time, movement loses this globally unified character, as the motor system sub divides into parts capable of operating more "independently," i.e. in more differentiated fashion. Arm and hand extend while the rest of the body remains quietly anchored; hand and fingers rotate the object while the arm remains motionless and the gaze explores, and so on, as more articulated sequences emerge from the "mass action" of infancy.

The developmental principle of life space differentiation is easily observed in adolescence. The world of the adolescent opens up like a cell structure sub-dividing, corresponding to new awarenesses, activities, and interests, and yielding newly distinguished regions of both the environment and the self. And these regions have the quality of relatively differentiated parts, segregated or bounded from one another in their differentness. For example, the landscape of peers opens up into a spectrum of social identities, "types" of people who, in the adolescent's experience at least, seem very different from one another. The classifications have changed historically, and vary somewhat from one part of the world to another, but the effect is the same. There are the straights and the punks, the brains and the jocks, the straight-edgers and dopers, as well as nihilists, hippies, gang members, skaters, preps, and so on. Similarly, activities and areas of interest take on more a quality of separate areas of life: sports, schoolwork, family life, weekend party life, on-line role playing, church youth group, private fantasy life, theater, sex and/or romance, and so on.

As the social landscape opens up, so also the adolescent's sense of self becomes more variegated, diversifying into multiple, relatively independent (in Lewin's sense of the word) sub-parts. These parts, or "self-gestalts" (McConville, 1995), allow the adolescent to develop a broader repertoire of personality traits and contact skills. One of the signs of this differentiation of experience is the emergence of phenomenological opposites, or polarities, in the topography of adolescent experience. Both in the self and

33

in the environment, salient distinctions emerge that are charged like repelling magnets: childlike and grown-up, masculine and feminine, compliant and rebellious, goal oriented and playful, and so on. These budding polarities, which may play out between the self and others in the environment, or between parts of self, reveal the emergence of charged boundaries, testifying to this developmental differentiation of the phenomenological life space.

An important expression of life space differentiation, and one which Lewin considers especially characteristic of adolescence, is that between the "subjective" and the "objectively real." Adolescents, Lewin points out, become increasingly realistic in their assessment of the world around them, factoring out the subjective coloring of fantasy from the "real world" of their perceptions (Muuss, 1982). The fluid interplay of fantasy and reality during childhood gives way to an experiential field where these domains are, relatively speaking, more clearly differentiated from one another. We observe this development in a variety of ways. Teenagers become increasingly accurate in the assessment of adults, beginning to see their parents in particular more as ordinary personalities and less as paragons of power and authority. So too, their teachers and their peers come to be viewed more in terms of their objective qualities than their subjective impact. And in general, throughout the course of adolescence, we see the individual gradually letting go of unrealistic assumptions and projections, as he or she synthesizes an understanding of how the "real world" works.

Adolescent Interiority. This increasing objectivity of adolescent experience is a reflection of the growing segregation of "inner world" and "outer world" dimensions of the life space. And as this distinction gains phenomenological salience for the individual, the heightened objectivity and realism of which Lewin speaks is counter-posed by a growing *interiority* of experience (McConville, 1995). The adolescent becomes aware, sometimes acutely and painfully, of a growing region of affectively charged "inner space." Poignant feelings, fantasies of love and glory, dreamy, abstract wonderings, all intensify to fill up hours of daydreaming, copious journal and diary entries, and late night, heart-to-heart conversations with intimate friends. Parents may become aware of their child's disengagement from ordinary family intercourse, and may sense the depth and weight of hidden experience accumulating behind the barriers of silence, detachment, or anger. And all of this represents the phenomenological expression of what Lewin calls the differentiation of the life space, the emergence and segregation of relatively bounded regions of behavior and experience.

34

And this differentiation, it is important to realize, is not a segregating of the self from the environment, but an emergence of meaningful boundaries of inner and outer *throughout* the field. Interiority, in other words, does not refer to an isolated inner domain of the subjective self, but to an emerging dimension of the field taken as a whole. Thus, the adolescent is aware of private experience as an emergent possibility everywhere, becoming acutely attuned to the potential discrepancies of private experience and outward expression in others as much as self: are adults being truly sincere, and can they be trusted? Is my friend's behavior genuine or phony? What does this girl *really* feel about me? Does anyone really know the "real me," and so on. The point is that interiority and objectivity, as emergent phenomena, refer not to subject and object, but to dimensional qualities of the life space--to others as well as self--taken as a whole.

Self Gestalts and Compartmentalization. Lewin's description of differentiation is important to us because it clarifies some of the more mystifying nuances of adolescent experience and behavior. One of these is the quality of compartmentalization that is so common in adolescence. As the range of adolescent involvements extends to include multiple peer subgroups, school work, job, athletics and extra-curriculars, extra-familial adults, and so on--the expansion of the life space, in other words--the adolescent's self experience correspondingly diversifies. The organization of self experience, or "self gestalt," which attaches to school work may be radically different from the self who goes out with friends on weekends, or the romantic self of an intimate dating relationship, or the self that arrives at the dinner table for a family meal. And furthermore, these variations of self-organization may be highly compartmentalized, even to the point of mild dissociation. The boy who leaves an after-school conference with his English teacher and joins his friends in the school parking lot for a ride home, may undergo a dramatic mutation of self-organization in a few short minutes, leaving behind one set of thoughts, feelings, memories, values, in fact one entire contact style, for another.

Clinically, this phenomenon is important because youths who present for consultation so frequently do so in a compartmentalized fashion. The polite, thoughtful boy who sits today in my office, hardly resembles the explosive and abusive older sibling of several days previous that his parents describe. The angry, defiant girl who faces me seems a far cry from the frightened, teary child who required her mother's tender support just last night. And what's more, neither of these teenagers seem quite able to grasp the divergencies in their experience, and when asked about it, even once we

35

have managed the business of rapport and connection, seem themselves mystified by the spontaneous shifts in their own behavior. In other words, the topography of adolescent awareness directly mirrors the dis-unification and differentiation of the developing life space. For as Lewin said of differentiation, the regions of the field begin to display greater degrees of relative independence, and this independence shows itself in the conspicuous gaps and overall lack of integration in the adolescent's awareness of self. And perhaps most important of all is the fact that in light of Lewin, we can see this compartmentalization, these segregations of self experience, not as pathology nor even as "defenses," but as a necessary expression of a differentiating, which is to say developing, life space.

Again the point to be emphasized is that differentiation, including the attendant phenomena of compartmentalized self-gestalts and furcated awareness, is a feature not of an encapsulated self but of the field taken as a whole. Accordingly when we work with adolescents we find this phenomenon not only in the adolescent's experience of self, but throughout the environment as well. People in the adolescent's social world are much more segregated from one another than in earlier childhood. Teachers may have little of no interaction with parents; parents are likely not to know their son or daughter's newer friends; and sub-sets of friends my exist who have little knowledge or commerce with one another. Furthermore, the specific compartmentalizations of a given adolescent's experience are commonly mirrored by people in his environment. The teenage boy who does not seem able to integrate his 'shoulds and his 'wants' (for example, his goals for academic success and his desires to 'party' and play), typically has parents who themselves have not mastered this integration of opposites, and populates his social world with allies who line up on one side or the other of this compartmentalized polarity. The differentiation and the "independence of parts" described by Lewin, in other words, is a field development first and foremost, characterizing the individuals social environment as much as his private world of attachments and impulses.

Lewin's description of differentiation of the life space is important because it sets the stage for his theory of developmental organization. He introduces this line of theorizing with the following seemingly paradoxical observation: as the life space differentiates into functionally independent regions, and precisely because it differentiates in this fashion, it decreases the unity of the child. He writes: "the older child does not always show a more harmonious personality or a personality more strictly governed by one center. One has, rather, to expect ups and downs in the *degree of unity* of the person, whereby differentiation tends to decrease the unity from time to time..." (1997, p. 248). As the life space diversifies, in other words, there is the inevitable emergence of dissonance, dis-connection and conflict (which of course, brings us to mind of adolescence), and this leads Lewin's developmental theory to the problem of organization.

Change in the Organization of the Life Space

The third parameter of life space development described by Lewin is its organization, the way in which regions of the field are integrated to form an organized whole. According to Lewin, the nature of this organization changes as the field develops. Initially, the different parts of the child's field are integrated by a principle that he calls *"simple interdependence"* and over time this gives way to a higher order form of integration which he calls *"organizational interdependence."* This shift is necessitated by the progressive differentiation described above, the process by which the child's experience and behavior becomes more diversified, and by which regions of the life space become functionally more independent of one another.

By "simple interdependence," Lewin means that neighboring regions of the life space--and this might refer to the boundary between portions of the motor system, the boundary between felt needs and motoric actions, or the boundary between the child's "ego" and his immediate social environment--are connected in a fluid and direct fashion. Lewin characterizes this mode of contact as follows: "first, it is based on a process which has the character of 'spreading' from one part to neighboring regions according to proximity. Second, the change of the dependent part usually occurs in the direction of equalizing its state and the state of the influencing part" (1997, p. 253). Thus, in younger children, feeling and need states spread relatively unchecked into action (i.e., tension spreads readily from the regions of felt need and affective arousal to the region of the "motor system") and, similarly, the child's ability to resist or "filter" its interpersonal environment (to "chew" in Perls' language) is relatively undeveloped.

In younger adolescents, this "spreading" between regions of experience is commonly observed. In junior high school age students, for example, the learning functions of attending, comprehending, and problem solving are often dramatically affected by the affective-interpersonal functions of feeling known and accepted. How commonplace it is to find students this age who demonstrate academic and intellectual competence when they feel liked by a particular teacher, and who become demonstrably "learning disabled" or intellectually vacuous when they sense a break in emotional support. Older adolescents are far more able to maintain the "independence" of these functions, organizing them in effect as differentiated regions of the life space. "I expect my math teacher to teach me math," one high school senior commented to me recently, "I don't need him to be my buddy."

The Maturation of Contact

What Lewin speaks of under the heading of organization--the conditions of connection between regions of the life space--Gestalt therapy theory addresses with its notion of *contact*. The meaning of all psychological constructs according to Perls, Hefferline and Goodman (1951) lies in their relation to the phenomena of contact. And contact, in this view, refers to the whole of the processes of connection--engaging, joining, separating, adjusting--which describe the meeting of an experiencing organism and its environment. These processes are precisely what Lewin implies by his term "organization," and thus lie at the heart of a Gestalt approach to human development.

In a Lewinian-Gestalt developmental theory, adolescence is understood as a progressive unfolding of the comprehensive field, an unfolding that includes de-structuring of childhood unity, expansion and differentiation of the life space, and transformation of the boundary processes that organize and integrate the field. In a process that unfolds both recursively and progressively throughout adolescence, the field of the child's experience evolves from its pre-adolescent status of relative *embeddedness*, through a disembedding process of *differentiation*, toward a reorganized *integration* of the field. And this developmental process represents, in the language of Gestalt therapy, the emergence of the capacity for contact, the mature engagement of person and environment. In the course of this developmental process, we witness the loss of childhood cohesiveness, the "*sturm und drang*" of rapid and dramatic change, and the transformation of boundaries and, correspondingly, of the modes of relatedness which come to characterize the evolving field. Let us briefly examine each aspect of this process more closely.

Embeddedness and Disembedding. The life space of the pre-adolescent child exhibits a state of relative unity. That is, relative to the adolescent development that will follow, it exhibits a "simple interdependence" of parts of the field. Contact in such a field is characterized by confluent boundary process, and this characterization holds throughout the life space, whether between subparts of the child's mind-body system, between components of self experience, of between the child and his social environment. I have previously described this character of childhood experience, and the fluid boundary processes which organize it, as *embeddedness* (McConville, 1995). In Gestalt therapy terminology, embeddedness means to be immersed in a context--family, society, culture--with permeable boundaries and relatively confluent, introjecting boundary processes. Embeddedness is what allows the family and cultural environment to shape the child as it does, and so by definition sets the stage for the developmental *disembedding* of adolescence.

The life space differentiation described by Lewin has the effect of disembedding the early adolescent child from the enveloping contexts of childhood experience. In addition to the phenomena described above, we find the adolescent generally reorganizing contact boundaries, such that the "simple interdependence" of neighboring regions--for example, at the boundary of the adolescent and his parents, or more generally, of adolescent culture and adult culture--is replaced by a heightened sense of difference and independence. Where formerly the child felt fluidly immersed in the family, and comfortably available to adult influence, she now begins to stand apart and turn to peers instead, creating a differentiating boundary within the field. Adults may be held at arms length, and the child may hold back information about her personal feelings and thoughts, heightening this boundary through her emergent concern for privacy.

The same sort of organizational transformation occurs in the "intrapsychic" dimension of the child's developing experiential field. In less developed fields, where parts are related in the fashion of "simple interdependence," different needs, wants, and feelings tend to "spread" and interpenetrate one another. This is easily observed in adult psychotherapy when exploring conflicted, underdeveloped aspects of a client's self experience. In Perls' formulation of "top dog-underdog" dynamics, for example, portions of the psychological field were described as strangling and interrupting one another, such that neither portion can develop the intregrity of its own expression.

In children, needs for approval and needs for self-expression are often "bundled" in the fashion of simple interdependence, such that each evokes the other, and the contact potential of neither is realized. But as adolescence gets under way, we tend to see a differentiating of these portions of the field, such that each is held longer and with more integrity, perhaps in the form of a polarity which may be played out in different ways across the broad field of experience. The adolescent, for example, may adopt a posture of "counter dependency" with parents, highlighting his sense of autonomy and self-support. And at the very same time, with friends he may enter a bond of intense loyalty and unqualified support and acceptance. The net effect, across the broad field, is a more clearly bounded and fulsome development of each of these experiences.

Developmental Integration. As the adolescent life space differentiates, losing its former coherence and unity, there is simultaneously, according to Lewin, a developmental push toward a higher order integration of the life space, and this integration is characterized by an "organizational interdependence" of parts. For Lewin, organizational interdependence describes a more evolved boundary process that the simple interdependence of less mature fields, one where portions of the field are brought more into a *relationship of contact* with one another, and where that relationship achieves a coordination and working together for some purpose. In adolescent development generally, we witness this developmental-organizational process at work, both in the child's diversifying interiority, and in the realm of interpersonal relationships. As regions of the life space differentiate, and even as they compartmentalize, there is also at work a tendency to bring them into contact with one another, to establish coherence and connection throughout the life space. Thus, the same adolescent who was so counter-dependent with his parents, and so intensely confluent with his friends (and who, no doubt refused to bring these friends home to fraternize with his parents), now experiments with contact between these regions of the life space. His relationship with parents becomes warmer and more connected, while his personal friendships allow for more difference and assertiveness. And, at the same time, he becomes interested in having his friends and parents establish contact with one another.

As an evolving system, the organism-environment field is oriented toward this achievement as a sort of *developmental Pragnanz*, a state of dynamic organization that constitutes the "best" organization that the field is capable of attaining. The field where full and satisfying contact is possible is one in which a dynamic balance is achieved between the organism's organizational integrity and its need to interact with various regions of the field. This maturation of contact process is the goal of development, the dynamic equilibrium toward which the life space is tending. Elsewhere, I described the emergent "organizational interdependence " of the adolescent life space under the heading of *integration*.

As the adolescent self matures, it becomes literally

more of a *con-figuration*, an assemblage of figures, a gestalt formation that assumes into its structure the fragments and partial organizations--impulses, prohibitions, introjects, attributions, wants, polarities, and partial self gestalts--of childhood and earlier adolescence. In this way, the self emerges progressively through adolescent development as a *higher-order gestalt* that integrates increasingly diverse aspects of self and promotes an ever-growing sense of ownership of experience (1995, p. 117).

It is certainly no mistake that adolescents themselves describe this kind of developmental movement as "getting it together."

Clinical Implications of Developmental Field Theory

What we find in the writings of Kurt Lewin, then, is a highly specific description of the developmental process which at the same time is broad enough to capture the full range of developmental phenomena. It allows us to conceptualize the developing child's emotional, social, intellectual, and familial evolution as dimensions of a larger whole, and it traces clearly the processes by which this whole transforms itself over time. It is significant that Lewin views development not as a succession of discrete stages following one after another, but as a process of recursive unfolding of the comprehensive field--differentiation and reorganization, followed by further differentiation and further reorganization. This is development conceived as process rather than defined by content, defined by evolving organization rather than by developmental "milestones." And this is part of what makes Lewin so strikingly contemporary and applicable, for the actual children who come to our attention rarely fall neatly into any chart or timetable. Rather, they present all the ambiguities of real human existence, the fits and starts, the progressions and the regressions, the asynchronies and inconsistencies of human beings adjusting to changing circumstances, both visible and invisible, where conditions of support and structure are continually emerging, continually changing.

For the clinician, this conceptualization of development points toward some very specific principles of therapeutic intervention when working with adolescent clients. We will describe several of them here.

1. Developmental Process Organizes the Work

Children and adolescents are typically referred to us with specific issues brought to our attention. It may be a ground issue, such as a divorce or the death of a family member. Or it may be a more figural symptom behavior, such as obsessive-compulsive rituals, or oppositional defiance, or self-mutilating behavior. With children and adolescent clients, the content of the problem--the specific disruptive behaviors and diagnosable symptom patterns--typically has an extremely high salience for those adults advocating treatment, and typically a large amount of pressure is brought to bear upon the therapist, either implicitly or explicitly, to solve the problem at a content level. Parents are not inclined to recognize the developmental value of their teenager's argumentativeness or experimentation with forbidden behavior; they want the therapist to make it stop, and fast.

Similarly, managed care and mandated treatment plans require that therapists target specific behavior change as treatment goals, and identify specific therapeutic intervention strategies tied to specific goals. And while this approach makes a certain kind of "common sense" and has a certain logical appeal it quite severely misses the boat concerning the essential nature of developmentally effective psychotherapy.

From a Gestalt developmental perspective, the primary datum presenting itself to the therapist is not an individual child, and certainly not a "symptom picture" per se, but a field that is laced with some degree of developmental tension. "What sort of growth is trying to happen here," I ask myself throughout my assessment process. It may be the "What's gone wrong" that first catches my eye--the disruptive acting out, the depressed withdrawal, the bingeing and the purging--but these figures reflect a field whose development has been disrupted or interrupted in some fashion. The work of psychotherapy with adolescents is essentially a work of supporting and unblocking the developmental process. And this process, as we saw earlier, involves a recursive reorganization of fields, of experience, of behavior, of relationships. The work is to shake this process loose, to move it along.

In the case of Nora, a just-turned fifteen-year-old girl, the therapeutic work was to support the natural developmental process of life-space differentiation. Nora was referred by her school guidance counselor following a crisis conference with her parents, precipitated by an "anonymous" report to the counselor by several of Nora's classmates. As a new ninth grader, Nora was, in the guidance counselor's words, "both striking and invisible" all at once. Indeed, her skin had a dramatic, porcelain-white cast to it, and her long, strawberry, red hair was held perfectly in place with tortoise shell barrettes. Her downcast gaze and retiring manner made her seem not quite present and her china doll look gave one the impression that she might be too fragile to fully engage. When she did engage; it was often with a smile that was sweetness itself, a smile that neither invited nor discouraged contact, and seemed more a pose than an expression.

Several of Nora's classmates became concerned when they observed a ladder of razor cuts running up her forearm, at which point they sought out the guidance counselor. Nora herself had little to say about her cutting, other than to acknowledge that she was embarrassed at all the attention it had generated. Nora's feelings about therapy, and her difficulty formulating and expressing them, were very characteristic of the way she moved through her life generally. "You seem like a nice man," she said to me in our third individual meeting, "I don't really mind being here." And certainly, "being nice" herself seemed to be the organizing principle for her being in the world. Nora's relationship history was one of *being-for-others*. As a younger child, she had been overweight, and this fact, as she remembered it, was more an embarrassment to her parents than to her. Nonetheless, she bought into their anxiety and, by junior high school, had developed a mild but persistent obsession about her weight.

During this period, however, she had begun to pull away from her parents in ways that aroused their concern without ever quite escalating into conflict. She dropped off the swimming team, a decision that disappointed her father, himself an accomplished competitive swimmer as a young man. Her academic performance went from superior to average triggering heightened attention and supervision from her parents which she resisted in a fashion commonly described as "passive-aggressive." By her own recollection, she became depressed and unhappy. By her parents' recollection, she became moody and uncommitted.

Nora viewed me, initially at least, as one more adult to contend with; one more set of expectations, one more source of potential hurt feelings and disappointments. This was Nora's world: expectations, disappointments, hurt feelings, wants for her to be something other than herself, though what it meant to truly be herself she had hardly a clue. In the field of our budding relationship, I sensed an unformed voice of objection, a resistance to this business of talking about her problems. "Your cutting," I suggested, "we need to talk about it." "There's nothing to say," she countered. And again, "You seem like a nice man..." "But what?" I asked, and the silence that followed pointed the way for our work together. I spent an entire month helping Nora to complete that sentence, and after that, several more working with her to articulate and understand the disappearance of her voice in similar engagements.

"But I don't want to talk about it," she eventually offered, tentatively, almost under her breath. "Tell me that again," I encouraged her, "only try saying it like you mean it, like you have a *right* to refuse my request." "Well..." gathering herself, "I *really* don't want to talk about it," she finally asserted. "And how is it standing up to me this way?" I asked. "Scary," she said adding "I don't want you to think..." but not finishing her thought. "You don't want me to think you disagree with me?" I suggested. "I guess that's right," she conceded, hanging her head as if waiting for the inevitable disapproval.

The blueprint of Nora's reluctance, I learned in the weeks that followed, was a blueprint of a differentiating life space just as Lewin had described it. For Nora, the need and desire to comply with adult expectations, at least superficially, was a well-defined need, a well-developed region of her life space in Lewin's terms. The need and capacity to resist expectations on the other hand, was new and still tentative, but nonetheless strong enough that it could not be denied. It had been, in fact, times when she left this piece of self-experience unspoken that she ended up cutting herself, in a gesture that welded her want to rebel and her anger at herself for "wimping out."

Nora's budding polarity--her desire to please and her desire to stand by her personal wants--was itself under-differentiated in Lewin's sense, such that neither experience could hold its integrity in the presence of the other. As separate experiences, or regions of the life space, each "spread" across its boundary and flooded the other: she could not comply without feeling disgusted with herself; she could not object or rebel congruently without being flooded by guilt. The work in our sessions together therefore, was to support Nora to speak with her own voice, and to do so with sufficient "independence of parts" as to bound off, temporarily at least, her wishes for approval.

I encouraged Nora to name these parts of self and, once she had named them, to begin writing about them in separate voices. She began to keep a journal, again with my encouragement, and over the course of several sessions we did a protracted piece of "two-chair" work, heightening and supporting each end of the polarity, and then bringing them into more differentiated contact with each other. In this way, Nora began to cultivate an interior life where her sense of herself as a center of experience grew deeper and more vivid.

As therapy unfolded over time, Nora's voice grew, and as it grew, her ability to find support for it out in her world grew correspondingly. She discovered an Internet "Bodies Under Siege" chat group where she talked with others about her and their experiences, and subsequently developed more conventional supportive peer relationships at her school. At home, not surprisingly, (with the help of some joint family therapy sessions that I will describe below) her relationship with her parents began more and more to resemble ordinary adolescence as intra-family boundaries began to differentiate much in the same fashion as Nora's intra-psychic boundaries had in her individual therapy work.

In contrast to Nora, sixteen-year-old Todd came into therapy with a well-developed voice for his personal wants and needs, and a correspondingly differentiated sense of his rebellious, adolescent self. Todd's divorced parents, citing a pattern of deteriorating school performance and escalating brushes with the law, had together mandated that he see a therapist. It was the first thing they had agreed upon in the three years since their divorce. In separate intake sessions with each parent (they declined to come together), Todd exhibited widely different persona. With his father, who took a strong stand on issues of accountability, responsibility, and preparing for adulthood, Todd presented a face that was correspondingly reasonable and future oriented. With his mother, a soft and solicitous woman, he was aggressively manipulative, lobbying persuasively for expanded freedoms and second chances.

And with me, at least after we had spent some time together, and once he had come to trust my relative neutrality and objectivity, he was strikingly straightforward and candid. "My mother's a piece of cake," he assessed and, on the other hand, "My father's not so easy; he makes me uncomfortable." But Todd lived with his mother, and so was able to avoid his father's confrontations, and the uncomfortable issues his father raised, for the most part. Todd was like many of the adolescents I see in his conscious devotion to "things adolescent:" hanging out with friends, avoiding and conning adults, strategizing for the next concert or the next party, experimenting with and abusing alcohol and marijuana. And all of this was carried out behind a façade of "good kid" dissimulation. Except for report card time, or the occasional phone call from the police department's Juvenile Officer, Todd attracted little attention and concern from the adult world.

At these uncomfortable moments, a different side of Todd emerged, a side that only his father could access with any regularity. This was the part of Todd that indeed could see the larger picture, and acknowledged guilt and worry about the viability of his "endless summer" philosophy of life. "Yeah, school's important," he would allow in principle, "but it's just such a pain." And as for his two speeding tickets, two curfew violations, and pending possession of alcohol charge, "That was stupid" he conceded; "I'm being much more careful now."

Unlike Nora, Todd had accomplished the initial developmental work of disembedding from the world of child-self experience and adult supervision. He could stand apart from this world and oppose it; he had become expert at bounding it off and minimizing its power to "spread" across the boundaries of his newly fashioned life space. But like so many adolescents, Todd accomplished this task by compartmentalizing his life space, keeping dissonant regions of his experience (both intra-psychically and interpersonally) out of contact with each other.

Dictated by this developmental status, my relationship with Todd needed to become a vehicle of integration, a place where disparate parts of self could be held together, and where their relationship could be worked out. Clients like Todd, I have learned, instinctively attempt to organize therapy in the same dissociative fashion that they organize the rest of their life space. Friend or foe? They seem to ask their therapists. Are you one of those adults who's "cool," who winks and confirms my adolescent experimenting? Or are you another one of those disapproving adults who's going to lecture me about responsibility? And the challenge, of course, is to be neither, to become instead a venue where these compartments no longer apply, where the developmental value of experimenting, and the wisdom of prudence and good judgement are both valued, where each is accepted as the completion of the other.

There are some therapists who seem to work very effectively with acting out experimenters like Todd. They are able to draw their clients into conversation about their secret escapades and do so with an interested neutrality that falls well short of conspiratorial approval. They are able to see the hidden developmental value of challenging the rules and finding a path of ones own, even when that path comes precariously close to the cliff's edge. But, at the same time, these therapists have a knack for bringing the adolescent's own capacity for caution and balance into the therapeutic dialog, transforming dissociation into contact and thereby supporting the developmental work of life-space integration.

This was the outcome of my individual work with Todd. And if this description sounds too simple to be true, that's because it is. Like much effective individual therapy work with adolescent clients, my work with both Nora and Todd was set up by field interventions that addressed the contextual ground of their individual behavior and experience. We will turn to this dimension of therapeutic intervention in the next section.

2. Assessment and Intervention are Field Based

When the clinician is confronted with a clinical situation, Gestalt theory dictates that we assess it precisely as a situation, i.e., a field. A presenting problem--say, a child's aggressive behavior toward siblings, or deteriorating school performance, or self-mutilation--can only be fully understood as belonging to a context, a relational field which includes contact boundaries as far as the eye can see. It includes the ground of the child's own first person experience, as well as social and historical context accessible only to others in the child's world. It includes the contact process of parent and child, child and peers, parent and spouse, family and school, as well as the contact processes that occur at the boundaries of community, ethnic group, and culture. It includes the relational histories of the child and important others in her environment, as well as the relational histories of those persons with each other.

And from this extraordinarily rich and complex array of influences, how are we to make order? How are we to query the field of the child's experience? What are we looking for? What are the conditions of the field, in other words, that help adolescents such as Nora and Todd to "get it together?" What is it that promotes the shift, in Lewin's language, from simple interdependence to organizational interdependence, from embedded to differentiated contact, across the spectrum of the developing psychological field? For developmentally-oriented psychotherapists, this is the critical question because the answers proferred constitute the basis for a theory of clinical intervention.

Malcolm Parlett, the psychological theorist most responsible for articulating contemporary field theory in Gestalt therapy, has recently drawn attention to Gestalt therapy's answer to this question (Parlett, 1997). Addressing the question of adult development, Parlett describes the integral role of the contextualizing field:

> If personal and situational are not divided but seen
> together as one realm, then changes in one part of the
> field will automatically lead to changes in other parts
> of the field as well. New conditions foster develop-

mental shifts. Changed circumstances and novel situations require the individual--challenging him or her--to experiment and extend his/her range (p. 24-25).

In other words, Parlett takes the question of human development immediately back to the epicenter of Gestalt therapy theory. For this describes exactly what Perls, Hefferline and Goodman call "creative adjustment," which, as Parlett points out, lies at the heart of Gestalt's notion of experiment. Development, from this point of view, is experiment writ large, and thus the field conditions for development and the field conditions for experiment must be one and the same. And what are these conditions? Parlett, again:

> As in life generally, changes in habitual patterns of behavior occur only if there is enough accompanying support in the field, linked to a compelling invitation to "risk doing something differently"... *Major shifts require a particular kind of callibrated support and challenge in the field* (1997, p. 25; emphasis added).

Developmental shifts therefore, and in adolescence to be sure, require field conditions of adequate challenge accompanied by conditions of adequate support. This is what enables adolescents progressively, from time to time, and certainly often in the throes of some degree of personal and situational crisis, to "get it together," that is, to integrate their fields at higher levels of organization and with richer modes of contact process. Clinically, Parlett's analysis yields two simple but powerful tools for making order of the developmental field, two questions which orient both our assessment of 'dysfunction' and our design of clinical strategy and intervention.

How is this child's environment providing, or failing to provide challenges to which the child must adapt and reorganize?

How is the environment providing, or failing to provide, supports for the child as he/she mobilizes to accept these challenges?

These questions--these queries of the field--are what organized my therapeutic work with both Nora and Todd. In Nora's case, I encountered a child whose emergent adolescent voice was insufficiently supported by her environment. And what was inhibiting such support, I wondered? When first referred to me her family was, like Nora herself, polite but guarded. They seemed as invested as she was in exiting therapy before it could begin. A brief history resolved this small mystery. In eighth grade, at her former school, Nora had come to the attention of the counseling staff. In the wake of an ugly scene at home, in which her father had lectured and berated her for her decision to quit the swim team and for her falling grades, Nora had locked herself in her bedroom. Then, in an implosive fit of rage and despair, she had beaten herself with her fists around the face and eyes. When she showed at school the next day, black and blue, the school psychologist refused to believe that her bruises were self-inflicted and, as required by law in such circumstances, reported the incident to Child Protective Services. The ensuing mandatory visits by the county social worker and the brief abortive therapy "suggested" by the County had enveloped this family is a shroud of shame and confusion. As is so often the case with irresolvable shame, they had "left the field" at the first opportunity, transferring Nora to a new school in September.

Nora's cutting, and their referral again to therapy, was clearly once more an occasion of family, and particularly parental, shame. Nora's father, a successful businessman, seemed to register Nora's symptomatic behavior as a testimony to parenting failures. As a father, he cared deeply about Nora's welfare and development but, like so many men, had been deprived of an adequate model for fathering an adolescent daughter. In particular, he had neither clue nor concept for the special business of providing support. He had been harangued and demeaned into behaving himself as a child, and covertly drove himself in similar fashion as an adult. He could hardly be faulted for expecting that I was going to take him to task for his parenting in similar fashion, and indeed this had been the net of his experience with previous "helping" professionals. He was a hard man, not easy to like, but he was also a man deeply committed to his daughter's welfare, and I told him so at every credible opportunity.

And so my first intervention with this frightened, retroflective family was to build a decidedly supportive relationship with Nora's parents and, in particular, her father. This paved the way for further field work, all of which was a necessary preamble to any sort of constructive individual work with Nora. For one thing, I offered to interface between the family and the school. This involved a joint meeting with Nora's parents and the school psychologist, the purpose of which was to create for them an underlying sense of collaboration. Schools, in my experience, have an odd tendency to blame parents when a child's behavior is problematic and resistant to the school's own best efforts to ameliorate the situation. Inevitably, these judgments, however implicit, serve unwittingly to become part of the problem. In this case, the interactive boundary of school and family had begun to replicate the same disturbed contact process--the accentuation of shame and the suppression of voice--that characterized the relations of family members.

Another contextual intervention was to tutor Nora's parents concerning the nature of adolescent development, helping them feel less personally responsible for her struggles and her choices. As Nora's parents learned to receive my support, and as she perceived their growing ability to support each other, she became more willing to use her fledgling voice in family interactions.

Nora's situation was a clear example of an individual's developmental struggles reflecting the developmental struggles of the wider social field. Absent attention to these wider field conditions, it seems unlikely that I would have succeeded in my efforts to support Nora's individual differentiation, and the emergence of interiority and voice that made that differentiation real.

Todd's situation presented a somewhat different set of challenges but, as with Nora, the utility of individual therapy work was predicated upon field interventions. While Todd's environment provided more than adequate support--from parents (his mother especially) and peers--it failed to provide sufficient structure to challenge Todd's growth. He was a classic example of a teenager for whom being a teenager was just too easy. Todd was charming, smooth talking, confident, and smart. He did pretty much what he wanted, and up until recently had been quite skilled at keeping adults off his back. He was far more clever and streetwise than his mother with whom he lived. He would negotiate agreements of every sort: curfews, privileges, consequences, grades, household chores, and so on. He rarely kept his full end of a bargain typically doing just enough to fuel his mother's fantasy that "things are starting to get better." Rule breaking and irresponsibility led to consequences, which as often as not were just politely ignored, though sometimes re-negotiated on the basis of empty reassurances of future change, which, of course, would never materialize. And all the while, Todd's partying and chemical use moved gradually toward the center of his life as his behavior devolved in an ever-tightening spiral of self-absorption and impulse gratification.

Attempts to treat adolescents such as Todd in isolation from their environment is sheer clinical folly. For Todd's compartmentalization of intra-psychic parts was mirrored in his family. His parents couldn't talk to one another. His father had becoming increasingly unsympathetic and unyielding in an effort to compensate for his ex-wife's softness. And she, of course, had become increasingly empathic in order to compensate for Todd's father's constant disapproval. Each undermined the other while Todd honed his intuitive skill for conquering by dividing. In order to gain leverage for engineering Todd's integration of dissociated parts, I needed first to created contact between the dissociated regions of his environmental life space. This sort of therapy work is simple in concept but difficult in execution. In this case, it required that I meet first with each parent several times, forming an alliance with each on the basis of their strengths, and persuading each, without shame, of the value of joining forces.

We became initially a "parenting threesome" as they learned the rudiments of contracting with Todd and compromising with each other. They accepted my rationale that it would be a waste of time and money to begin individual therapy with Todd before establishing environmental structure that would require some creative adjustment on his part. And so it was. When Todd's mother called me to report finding several empty beer bottles under his bed, and informed me that she and her ex had already conferred and agreed to call Todd on the carpet for this infraction, I pronounced that individual therapy with Todd could begin. Of course, in some sense, the real therapy with Todd had already ended. At the very least, it was a foregone conclusion, because therapy with acting out adolescents who are required to contend with competent and loving structure, is generally, to borrow Todd's words, "a piece of cake."

As with Nora and her family, the therapeutic work with Todd was to promote the continued evolution of the developmental field, in this case toward an integration of its parts at a higher level of organization. In practical terms, this meant to support the development of more sustained and respectful contact of the two compartmentalized positions (whether intrapersonal or interpersonal), and thus of a field where impulse and rationality, i.e., pleasure seeking and the cautions of reasonable authority, could coexist, interacting and influencing one another across a contact boundary. Again borrowing from Lewin, the work in such clinical situations is to guard against the devolution toward a field state of "simple interdependence," where one position overwhelms the other, and to promote instead an emerging field whose parts are integrated via "organizational interdependence."

For both Nora and Todd, the clinical situation was best understood as an expression of a comprehensive field, and more precisely, as an interruption or stalling out of the recursive processes that Lewin describes for the developing life space. In Nora's case, we saw that the natural process of life space differentiation so characteristic of adolescent development was under supported, with a resulting symptom picture that included depression and retroflective self-injury. In Todd's case, we encountered an adolescent life space that was more than adequately differentiated, but where the wider social field provided insufficient challenge in the form of limits. The result was that Todd's experience remained fragmented and compartmentalized, that is, until that wider field required his creative adjustment. This adjustment involved the development of contact between hyper-segregated portions of the life space, and promoted his organization of self at a higher level of integration. And, in both instances, the developmental-therapeutic process, the further articulation and organization of the field, required interventions that subtended the intra-psychic and the interpersonal, moving the entire field forward developmentally. Certainly, this is the essence of a Gestalt approach to development and psychotherapy, namely, that we must locate symptomatic behavior within a context of a developing field, and we must design our intervention strategies to address that field as an evolving whole.

Conclusion

In this chapter, I have attempted to show the power and viability of a Gestalt field model of adolescent development and psychotherapy. Drawing upon the timeless formulations of Kurt Lewin, we have seen that development itself is not simply an unfolding of individual potentials, but a process whereby the broader field of organism and environment evolves and is transformed. As practicing clinicians, we might say that we have always known this; but in Lewin's theory of the differentiating life-space, we have at last a language and a set of foundational ideas for describing the clinical situations we encounter, and a theoretically consistent rationale for the multi-faceted intervention strategies that are necessary to impact these situations.

References

Bandura, A. (1977). *Social learning theory.* Englewood Cliffs, N.J.: Prentice-Hall.

Blos, P. (1979). *The adolescent passage.* New York, NY: International Universities Press.

Dent-Read, C., & Zukow-Goldring, P. (1997). *Evolving explanations of development.* Washington, DC: American Psychological Association.

Freud, S. (1962). *Three essays on the theory of sexuality.* New York, NY:

Avon Books.

Glasser, W. (1965). *Reality therapy*. New York: Harper Collins.

Hilgard, E.(1948). *Theories of learning*. New York: Appleton-Century.

Kiepenheuer, K. (1990). *Crossing the bridge*. La Salle, IL: Open Court Publishing.

Lewin, K. (1997). *Field theory in social science*. Washington, DC: American Psychological Association.

Miller, P. (1993). *Theories of developmental psychology*. New York, NY: W.H. Freeman.

Minuchin, S. (1974). *Families and family therapy*. Cambridge, MA: Harvard University Press.

Muuss, R. (1982). *Theories of adolescence*. New York, NY: Random House.

Parlett, M. (1977). The unified field in practice. *Gestalt Review, 1*(1), 16-33.

Peay, P. (1990). The singing sword: images guide adolescents' journeys. *Common Boundary*, Jan.-Feb., 7-9.

Perls, F., Hefferline, R., & Goodman, P. (1951). *Gestalt therapy: Excitement and growth in the human personality*. New York. NY: Dell Publishing.

Piaget, J. (1950). *The psychology of intelligence*. New York, NY: Harcourt-Brace.

Siegler, R (1986). *Children's thinking*. Englewood Cliffs, N.J.: Prentice-Hall.

Wexler, D.(1991). *The adolescent self: Strategies for self-management, self-soothing, and self-esteem in adolescents*. New York, NY: W. W. Norton.

Wheeler, G. (1990). Self-in-contact: A gestalt developmental model. Working Paper III. Unpublished manuscript.

Yontef, G. (1993). *Awareness, dialogue & process*. Highland, NY: The Gestalt Journal Press.

2

Enlarging the Field: African-American Adolescents in a Gestalt Context

Deborah L. Plummer
and Darryl S. Tukufu

African-American Adolescents in the Larger Context: Gestalt Applications

Identity formation or establishing a coherent sense of individuality from one's personality traits and circumstances of life is an essential developmental task in adolescence. Formation of a personal identity has traditionally been viewed as a positive outcome of adolescence and the essential developmental task for this stage. For African-American adolescents another milestone embedded in the work of this life stage is racial identity resolution. In other words, for African-American adolescents, defining themselves as African-American or Black is an essential task to becoming an adult. Doing so requires a heightened awareness of what it means to be African American in today's society. With that awareness, a conscious decision is made to "become Black" and embrace African-American values. This is by no means a simple process for a teen considering the sociopolitical implications of race in our culture. In addition to the racial socialization process, African-American adolescents, like most adolescents, are faced with school completion and school-related problems, employability, police involvement, risky sexual behavior, alcohol and drug use, psychological symptoms, and suicide. Historically, African-American adolescents have been participants in many major social and health-oriented programs that were designed to promote healthy development. Today, increasing numbers

54

of African-American parents have sought out psychotherapy for their adolescent children as a resource for personality stability. Therapy as a preventive and protective mechanism for Black adolescents is a challenge particularly for the therapist. Traditional forms of therapy have been criticized for not considering the larger cultural and societal context. Thus, exploring racial identity as a core and critical aspect of personal growth remains unexamined. For the most part, clinicians are left without a conceptual framework that incorporates racial identity resolution and the appropriate skill sets to work with African-American adolescents during this developmental phase.

McConville (1995) presents a compelling developmental tasks model from a Gestalt perspective that offers a space for racial identity inclusion. A basic tenet of the model is that adolescents can be understood only as part of the larger field in which they live. According to McConville, it is the clinician's role to explore the adolescents' status within that field and assist them in finding meaning and a place for themselves. Gestalt theory, by embracing the whole context of the individual in a phenomenological stance, offers a framework for understanding adolescents in the larger context. Yet, do the tenets of Gestalt theory hold space for racial identity consciousness? How does the Gestalt therapist incorporate the racial socialization process into a therapeutic alliance? Could other indigenous cultural forms of healing be incorporated into the therapy process and be compatible with Gestalt interventions?

We seek to explore these questions by first examining the larger field of African-American adolescents and describing the current status of Black youth. Second, the concept of racial identity development is explored through the lens of the evolutionary phases of the contact boundary described by McConville. Third, racial socialization interventions in the African-American community will be examined, particularly Rites of Passage, as an alternative form of healing and a supportive function of psychotherapy. Lastly, in our concluding remarks, we will offer some recommendations for applying these concepts in therapeutic work.

Current Status of African-American Adolescents

Recent demographics for African-Americans indicate that there has been both progress and setbacks over the last twenty-five years. On the plus side, there are more Black middle-income families and more Black college students than at any other period in United States history. At the same time, the number of Blacks receiving public assistance has increased along with a number of severe problems that particularly face adolescents.

This current situation can be defined by a number of social indicators. Among them are education, delinquency and crime, substance abuse, teenage pregnancy, suicide, potential employability, and the development of self. To begin with, although there has been improvement in African-American educational attainment, many Black adolescents are not on the path to obtaining the necessary skills and training for most entry-level positions. This problem is exacerbated not only by those adolescents who have or are contemplating dropping out of school, but by those who will have to stand in line for training slots in welfare reform.

African-American juveniles continue to be arrested more frequently for robbery, rape, homicide, disorderly conduct, sexual misbehavior, and handling stolen property (Gibbs, 1989). It is striking that information compiled over fifteen years ago continues to read like yesterday's newspaper.

Some studies have suggested that African-American teens are most likely to be arrested, booked, remanded for trial and to receive harsher dispositions than Whites. It has also been suggested that Black youth may be arrested more frequently for minor offenses both because inner city neighborhoods are patrolled more intensively and because police overact to the negative attitudes and anti-authority demeanor of Black youth (Thornton, et. al, 1982).

Compared to other groups, particularly Hispanics and Whites, African American adolescents' substance use rates are lower in the following categories: marijuana, hallucinogens, cigarettes and alcohol, cocaine and crack-cocaine or freebase (National Institute of Drug Abuse, 1995). However, the use rates have to be watched closely because there has also been an overall increase in substance use. Furthermore, the National Institute of Drug Abuse (1995) reports "at high risk for drug abuse often are those whose lives are marked by poverty, malnutrition and other unhealthy environmental conditions"(p.1). As long as many African-American adolescents fall in this category, substance abuse will continue to foster additional problems.

Although current reports indicate that teenage pregnancy rates are decreasing among African Americans, it is too early to tell if this trend will continue. Black teenage pregnancy rates continue to run at least twice that of Whites, with more Black teens choosing to have their babies instead of terminating them. Teenage mothers, in general, may likely experience complications in pregnancy and associated psychological and physical problems.

The trends indicate the ongoing concern for possible effects on African-American families and Black communities.

In his 1969 book, *Black Suicide*, Herbert Hendin indicated that a sense of despair, stemming from a feeling that life will always be unsatisfactory, confronts Black youth at a much younger age than Whites. This work preceded the recent spotlight on the rising suicide rate among African-American male adolescents over the past fifteen years. Some writers indicate that rates exist and/or have increased because of the existence of family problems brought about by the absence of a father, difficult relations between the mother and son(s), and unemployment. Others cite a strain existing between mid-to-upper middle class African-American families as a byproduct of integration. It is believed that an association and an increase in buying power further support assimilation to larger society norms and values. Upwardly mobile African-American families adopt some of the behaviors of the larger society, including the ways of dealing with hopelessness and depression. Consequently, the problems experienced by the majority culture are subsequently experienced by the African-American subculture (Tukufu, 1997).

African-American youth unemployment continues to be deplorable. Overall, it has consistently run, comparable with Black adults, at least twice the rate of the general population. In large urban areas throughout the country, unemployment has consistently ranged between 40-50%. There are strong indications that many of these youths, particularly males, have become discouraged to the point of dropping out of the job-seeking market. Clearly, the educational and training gap that exists for African-American youth in a highly technological culture carries major implications and concomitant consequences for American society.

The final social indicator defining the status of contemporary African-American adolescents is the development of self. We stated previously that increasing numbers of African-American parents have sought psychotherapy for their children. Intricately linked to personal identity is resolution of racial identity. When working with African-Americans, it is imperative to acknowledge the importance of both. It is this ongoing problem with self and racial identity that must be understood by psychotherapists interested in effectively helping their African-American clients. In fact, some researchers believe that the racial resolution process is paramount to identity and self-esteem. It is this ongoing struggle with self and racial identity that must be understood by psychotherapists.

Yet, even for the most well-intentioned therapist working with

African-American adolescents, there has not been much offered that encompasses a cultural or racial framework. Traditionally, adolescent theorists have focused on the cognitive, moral, social, and personality aspects of this life stage. Transformation and growth occurs by successful completion of developmental tasks associated with each component of the self. For the adolescent, creating an identity is considered primarily an internal reorganization process. Within that framework, Erikson (1968) describes the central task as that of identity versus role confusion. The adolescent must give up the old identity of the child in order to become an adult. Likewise, Marcia (1966; 1980) proposes two key parts to any adolescent development formation: a crisis and a commitment. During the crisis period the adolescent re-examines old choices and old values. The outcome of this re-examination is commitment to a particular ideology or specific role. Both models, used extensively by researchers and practitioners, minimize the environment as a critical component in the search for identity.

McConville's (1995) Gestalt developmental model includes the critical component of environment by exploring the meaning and function of the contact boundary and contact process change during adolescence. His basic premise is that the essence of adolescent development is to reorganize the field of experience so that a "certain sort of relationship between self and environment becomes possible" (p.101). In McConville's model, what matures during adolescence is the contact boundary-the boundary that defines the self while simultaneously organizing and regulating the relationship with the environment.

This conceptualization of the contact boundary maturation process as the defining feature of adolescent development is a distinguishing component of McConville's model. It is this feature that allows for inclusion of the racial identity resolution process, thus enabling Gestalt therapy to address salient aspects of African-American adolescent development. We will continue to examine this point by first giving a brief summary of racial identity theory and its application to the adolescent life stage and then incorporating this theory to McConville's evolutionary phases of contact boundary.

Racial Identity Development

Over the past three decades, a major contribution to the understanding of the African-American personality has been the development of racial identity models. Racial identity development models, which include

Black, White, Asian, American Indian Hispanic/Latino, and Biracial, seek to delineate the process by which a person incorporates race with his or her understanding of self. Beyond a mere demographic categorization, racial identity refers to the psychological connection a person has with race. This connection occurs through a developmental process that begins with racial socialization in childhood and reaches resolution in young adulthood. Over fifty models have been conceptualized to characterize the process of racial identity resolution. Although each model defines each stage with different characteristics, the movement to resolution appears to be a similar process.

The first state for people of color is characterized by identification with majority culture, and for Whites the first state is an unawareness of self as a racial being. In this state, the focus is on conceptualizing life from a White frame of reference. Historically, for many African-Americans racial identity resolution took the form of denial or devaluation of Blackness. For most adolescents who have had the benefits of the civil rights movement, racial identity resolution takes the form of low-race salience. Age-related concerns, friends, music, religion, clothing, or sports may carry more importance than race, leaving many African-American parents wondering if their post-desegregation teen is "black enough."

A racial awakening process characterizes the next state. A catalyst for this awakening is often a critical incident that leads an individual to reconceptualize issues of race and to reorganize racial feelings. When experienced in adolescence, this is often a brutal experience for the African-American teen. The following brief case example will serve to illustrate this point. In a racially mixed high school with predominately white administrators and teachers, Angela, a fourteen- year-old ninth grader generally "hangs out" with Gail, her White best friend, in their favorite teacher's room after school. Together they assist this teacher with chores as they engage in adolescent-to-adult banter. On one occasion Angela and Gail decided to play a practical joke on the teacher by hiding in the room before he arrives. When the teacher discovers Gail, they laugh and joke about the prank. He asks about the whereabouts of Angela. Gail, still playing the game, states that she has no knowledge of Angela's whereabouts. As time passes the teacher in conversation with Gail makes an off-color remark about African-Americans and his lack of tolerance for what might be considered stereotyped behaviors. Angela overhears all of this and emerges from her hiding place, not only to the dismay of the teacher and embarrassment of her friend, but as a teen who now experiences herself very differently. She must now reorganize her world in a way that allows her to remain whole while incorporating the reality that her race is figural for many people.

This awakening experience generally leads to an ownership of one's race that is in many ways marked by a visible investment in racial identity. For African Americans, it may mean wearing ethnic clothing and hairstyles, choosing ethnic entertainment forms, and associating primarily with Blacks. For Whites, it may mean educating oneself to the notion of privilege and looking at the world through the lens of race. African-American adolescents often move from having racially mixed friends to exclusively Black friends. Their taste in music and films may also radically change.

The next movement of the racial identity resolution process is characterized by internalization. The heightened awareness of racial identity moves the individual to achieve a high degree of self-comfort as a racial being. In this period, the Black adolescents (usually late adolescent stage) insist on being acknowledged as African Americans but also recognize and appreciate other racial groups. They are aware of the sociopolitical implications of race and respond to the world in a way that their race and person cannot be separated. Choices about who to be friends with, what groups to join, music to listen to, where to go to college, and what career to pursue are all made with intention and awareness of oneself as a social, political, and racial being.

Some mature adolescents move to embracing a multicultural identity. A multicultural identity is characterized by healthy racial identity that is coupled with an understanding, both cognitively and experientially, of the interdependent aspects of the self's diverse dimensions. One can recognize and experience self as Black yet heavily influenced by White or Hispanic or Asian heritages. One experiences herself as female but also is aware that she possesses male traits. One understands chronologically that he is adult but also is in touch with his child side. One embraces heterosexuality but in touch with a gay/lesbian side. Developing and living out of a multicultural identity is culturally complex and is not the resolution status most individuals achieve. However, for an increasing number of biracial adolescents, this is the racial identity status they are compelled to develop and choose as the most whole and healthy expression of self they can achieve.

Adolescent Developmental Tasks and Racial Identity Resolution

In the course of adolescent development, the self-environment field passes through three evolutionary phases, each of which emphasizes a different aspect of reorganizing and developing the contact boundary. The first is disembedding, or differentiating both from ones own childhood and the world of parental adults; the second is interiority, or deepening the inner life and establishing ownership of self; and the third is integration, or establishing a stable organization of intrapsychic and interpersonal experience (McConville, 1995). All three phases can be integrated with the resolution process of racial identity. Disembedding encompasses the identification and awakening phase of racial identity. Interiority clearly reflects the ownership and investment status of racial identity. Likewise, integration embodies the internalization of racial identity status.

Disembedding, Identification and Awakening. In the stage of disembedding, the essential task of development is establishing a sense of boundary that can be clearly distinguished as different from childhood. This generally takes place externally (hairstyles, clothing, and entertainment choices) before it concretizes intrapsychically. During the racial identity process, African-American adolescents work to differentiate themselves as Black. This generally occurs as a result of an external event such as the one described for Angela in the previous section. The meaning of the experience must be incorporated intrapsychically, and the self must reorganize. Thus, while reorganizing themselves as "not children," they are also establishing themselves as "not being raceless" to the world. Dealing with the "ism" associated with race is a skill most adults have not mastered yet, in early adolescence, most African-Americans face this incredible task along with the disembedding process.

The interpersonal boundary becomes the focus of the disembedding process and is also the boundary where the first status of racial identity is experienced. Uncritical introjection of the environment's definition of self diminishes sharply. As the adolescent disembeds from an environment in which she formerly took for granted, she begins to see it more objectively, and to more authentically shape her response to it. In doing so, she begins to take ownership of her experience and definition of self. But as McConville points out, the field of adolescent self-experience is limited to what individuals can manage intrapsychically and/or what is of interest to them. Some unacceptable aspects of their experience are consequently disassociated from the figural sense of self and relegated to ground, while others may be projected out onto the environment.

An example of this theme is evident in the case of Angela. Realizing that her favorite teacher had racial biases and thus could possibly hold her in disregard was too much for her to manage intrapsychically. As

61

she relates this incident to trusted African-American adults in her world, they comfort her but clearly make her aware that this experience is only the tip of the iceberg. For Angela, race now becomes figural at the interpersonal contact boundary. She begins to see the world through the lens of race. With her trust in Whites seriously compromised, (her teacher now belongs to that social category, and she has thrown the baby out with the bath water), she can no longer manage a relationship with Gail, her former best friend. As this process of disembedding establishes itself, Angela begins to deepen her racial interiority while immersing herself in Black culture.

Interiority and Immersion. With the emergence of interiority, the individual begins to develop a heightened sense of the divergencies of inner, private experience from the outer world of social relatedness. Relationships become more complex, and the inner world of the adolescent becomes deeper (McConville, 1995). Similarly, African-American adolescents struggling to own their racial identity immerse themselves in everything that is considered Black. Sixteen-year-old Tiffany is a case in point. After being accused by school administrators of "stuffing the ballot box" when named the first Black prom queen in a suburban racially mixed school, Tiffany begins associating with only Black people, wearing distinctively African clothing, and braiding her hair with colorful beads. Even her parents believe that she is working to be "blacker than black."

McConville characterizes this middle phase of boundary development as a stage when adolescent inner life intensifies. The reflective journals that are kept, poetry that is written, and moral dilemmas that are raised and discussed during this stage of interiority are characteristically loaded with racial themes for African-American adolescents. They are not only vulnerable to feelings of alienation resulting from the differentiation of the intrapsychic from the interpersonal, but they are left hostage to the cultural and social context in which they have unwittingly been placed. It is during this period that parents often seek outside intervention, most often in the form of "Does anyone know any black therapist who can work with my teenager?"

Integration and Internalization. In late adolescence, the individual generally has moved toward an integrated sense of self that encompasses the diverse aspects of self and promotes an ever-growing sense of ownership of experience. This "higher-ordered gestalt" has obtained enough resilience and sturdiness to support mature contact with others. Older teens can engage in meaningful discussions with parents and adults. They are able to maintain their identity while withstanding external field forces. Likewise, the older adolescent who has achieved racial identity resolution experiences the self in a "higher-ordered gestalt" and exudes a comfort with race. Teens in this status make their own decisions about choice of friends, taste in music and entertainment, and are not concerned with ridicule from other Black friends about their choices. Teens who have established a multicultural identity are able to name and label racism and keep it in context while their racial self remains whole.

Felicia, a Black senior in a racially mixed high school, is upset and confused when she was not named valedictorian of her class. She is convinced that her grade point average exceeds the named valedictorian and seeks the support of one of the Black guidance counselors in the school to check her records. Together, she and the counselor re-calculate her grades, finding that her GPA does indeed exceed the White student named for this honor. The guidance counselor brings this mistake to the attention of the administration only to be interrogated about the discovery process. Felicia wonders whether the incident was really an "honest mistake," especially after she is left without an apology, and is isolated by the school administrators for "raising the issue." Yet, throughout the ordeal, Felicia's racial self remains whole despite her encounter with suspected racism. She is able to conceptualize the event as situational racism determined by the specific individuals and circumstances. She can complain and vent to both her Black and White friends about the incident with the understanding that racism is ever present in the world and therefore a part of the fabric of her life.

During this period the interplay of the intrapsychic and interpersonal contact boundary is critical to understanding the adolescent experience. In addition, the societal and cultural field must be incorporated for therapists to understand African-American adolescents. McConville states that the organizing theme of psychotherapeutic work with adolescents is the facilitation of the natural developmental process. The therapist is a visitor in the life of this client, and when working with African-American clients, the therapist must realize that the client's life includes the Black experience. The response to parents'cries for Black therapists who can work with their teens are not adequately heard by the relatively few qualified Black mental health professionals currently in practice. Nor do we propose that only African-American therapists can work effectively with Black adolescents. It is a case of building cultural competence on the part of all therapists engaging in any intervention with Black youth. Intervening in the field of African-American adolescents requires not only understanding the racial identity process, but in many cases, incorporating alternative forms of healing. We propose that supportive social structures and indigenous forms of healing presently in place within the community can enhance psychotherapy, particularly Gestalt therapy, with African-American adolescents. We turn attention to these forms in the next section.

Contextual Forms of Healing

We asked the question, could other indigenous cultural forms of healing be incorporated into the therapy process as a way of deepening and extending the breadth of Gestalt intervention? Gestalt theory, essentially a field model of human experience and behavior, is uniquely compatible with indigenous forms of healing and development currently active in the African-American community. The ways in which an individual connects to and forms his or her relationship with the surrounding world is of central importance to Gestalt theory (McConville, 1995). Likewise, African-American development models incorporate the cultural field. The very meaning of self for an African-American can only be derived in context of the cultural field.

Tukufu's African-American Development Model (1997) illustrated in Figure 1 is an example of the essential role of culture in models of African-American development. Successful youth and adult development emanates from six criteria: religious, philosophical and /or ideological orientation; positive mental attitude; the Nguzo Sabo (the seven principles of unity, self-determination, collective work and responsibility, cooperative economics, purpose, creativity, and faith practiced by African-Americans and celebrated at Kwanzaa); African/African-American culture and history; social development; and social capacity.

In traditional clinical work, most of these criteria would be considered ground by many therapists. What is usually figural is the client's presenting issue, generally conceptualized from an intrapsychic perspective. The presenting problem might be influenced or shaped by one's religion, social development and capacity, mental attitude, culture and history, but the problem itself is thought to be intrapsychic. When a client's history and cultural context are functional, they provide an accumulation of learning experiences that provide a rich ground; in this instance, the clinician can afford to focus instead on figural symptomatology. On the other hand, when a client's history and ground have been tainted by cultural and societal dysfunction, they need to become figural aspects of the clinical process. The very visibility of race for African Americans promotes that culture and history remain in the forefront simultaneously with the presenting concern. My problem as an African American can only be fully understood in the context of this larger field. This is why African-American parents first seek a therapist of the same race for their adolescent.

Figure 1
African-American Male Development Model

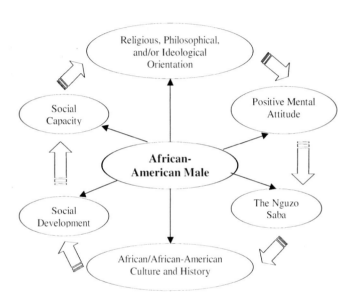

Religion is another contextual aspect of Black life that historically and currently holds salience. However, African-American religion must be understood in its context as a cultural form. In Black life, religion is grounded in the social and historical experiences of African-Americans. Thus, for many Blacks, the search for spiritual fulfillment includes both a definition of a meaning of their Blackness as well as a spiritual expression speaking directly to their individual needs.

If one were to visit many African-American Christian churches (Christianity being the predominant religion practiced by Blacks in this country), a great deal of comparison is made between the children of Israel and the plight of Blacks. Emphasis is placed on the discrimination, oppression, and subjugation of early followers of Christianity. These conditions are believed to be similar to issues and events affecting African-Americans today. Clinicians must understand that many of the past and current leaders of the civil and human rights movements have come from churches and mosques around the country. This approach to religion is largely a result of one theme of African religions, the balance between both one's personal identity and responsibility, and collective (race and culture) identity and responsibility.

Religion is a key component of development for Malik, a young high school senior who has been in trouble with the law. His mother is a drug addict and Malik himself sold drugs at one point. He always appeared to be angry. He was failing every subject in school, most of the time due to absence. He carried a small revolver and moved around from one place to another as often as he could. Many a night he found himself sleeping on the street. One of Malik's teachers, a male African-American, strongly and repeatedly encouraged Malik to accompany him to the church where he served as one of the associate pastors. It took a long time, but Malik committed to attend (particularly since he didn't have anything else to do and there was the extra incentive of spending more time with the teacher).

Malik began to attend church and found he liked it. One Sunday, to the delight of the teacher, he joined the church. His life began to change almost overnight. By the end of the school year, he was making the honor roll, he was given the opportunity to address the entire church during "Youth Sunday," and he was recognized on a national television program targeting youth who had changed their lives.

Malik's religious experience helped him to develop a positive mental attitude that enabled him to be whole. Positive mental attitude and knowledge of African and African-American culture and history have also provided instances of forms of healing for African-American adolescents. The former, already utilized by many clinicians, has a different connotation for African-Americans. To this group, positive mental attitude includes both self and race esteem. To a large extent, knowledge of African and African-American culture and history has played an important part of personal growth and development.

Take the case of Shaquita, a fourteen-year-old African-American teenager, somewhat obese and dark-skinned. All of her life, she recalled instances of other Blacks and occasionally Latinos and Whites, who lived on her street and/or attended the same schools, talking about her. Shaquita developed an overbearing personality, was quick to anger, and illustrated a dislike for anything related to Blacks. She used the "N" word quite frequently and had noted on more than one occasion that "Blacks ain't shit!

Shaquita began running with an all-girl gang whose members appeared to like her just as she was. She had two younger brothers, one who was light brown, the other medium brown. She despised them both because she felt that there was differential treatment by their parents based on skin color. Although Shaquita believed gender may also have played a role, she remained convinced that her darker skin caused her to be less loved. One day, the gang went to a community center in an adjacent neighborhood. The gang was intent on expanding their territory and so entered the center and proceeded to a nice-sized room where they heard voices and laughter. They entered what they found to be an African-American history course. There were about twenty-five other teenagers in attendance. Shaquita and her group planned to enter the center talking loudly and possibly even starting a fight. However, they were surprised there was no negative reaction to their presence by the members of the history class. All of the gang, except Shaquita, immediately left the room and headed toward the gym where they felt they could play out their intent. Shaquita stayed behind because on the overhead was a picture of Queen Ann Nzinga, a dark-skinned African woman who led her Zimbabwean troops to victory after victory over the Portuguese in a forty-year period. Shaquita was fascinated that Queen Nzinga was not only the ruler of a country but also was quite "feminine." The instructor of the class, Ms. Washington, also inspired Shaquita by the amount of knowledge she had on the subject. Soon Shaquita began attending the class regularly and asked Ms. Washington for additional reading material. She began looking at herself differently, quit the gang, and established a fairly good relationship with her younger siblings, whom she proceeded to teach about their "roots."

In our expanded vision of Gestalt therapy with African-American adolescents, it is imperative that the clinician thinks beyond the traditional platforms of individual and family psychotherapy. For both Malik and Shaquita, the development of self was inseparable from the deepening of their connections to religious and historical ground. If Gestalt therapy is to fulfill its potential for impacting these youth, it must translate its theoretical emphasis on field and ground into practical strategies for creating contextual support for the development of self.

Another important and well-recognized form of contextual support for adolescent development is mentoring. Basically, mentoring is a concept where one or more individuals act as counselors, guides, tutors, or coaches to one or more additional individuals (Tukufu, 1997). Although clinicians already assume a counselor role, mentoring may mean moving beyond the scheduled therapy time.

Consider the case of Dr. Gallo, a psychotherapist with a large, African-American adolescent client pool. Being White, Dr. Gallo was deficient in the area of African-American culture and history and decided he needed to branch out, particularly when he found that some of the traditional psychotherapeutic practices had little effect on a great many of his clients. He decided to attend a local professional meeting to discuss and possibly network with other therapists who had a number of African-American clients. He soon helped form a diverse (White, African-American, and Latino) group of clinicians who began to meet and plan activities for interacting with their clients in order to (1) serve as mentors and/or (2) recruit mentors for their clients. Shortly after networking with this therapist group, Dr. Gallo discovered that his attendance at a Kwanzaa program, together with his clients, assisted him in more effectively working with his clients. Even more importantly, his clients' self perceptions changed dramatically as a result of attending Kwanzaa and the mentoring opportunities provided by the program.

Rites of Passage as a Contextual Intervention. In addition to the other helping sources, a significant contribution for healthy adolescent development is that of Rites of Passage. African-American centered rites of passage processes usually cite books by Nathan and Julia Hare (1985), focusing on males, Mary Lewis (1988), focusing on females, and Paul Hill, Jr. (1992), focusing on both males and females. Shared by groups throughout the world, Rites of Passage were designed to regenerate the community. Experienced during puberty, they prepare males and females to enter manhood and womanhood. Insofar as it relates to adolescents, the overall goal of Rites of Passage is to provide opportunities for African-Americans and to prepare them--spiritually, physically, socially, emotionally, intellectually, and culturally--for the challenges of development. Thus, the following components are found in most Rites of Passage experiences (Tukufu, 1997):

Foundations of African Spirituality and World View;
Bonding and Team Building;
African and African-American Culture and History;
Mental/Emotional Development;
Physical Development;
Discipline and Responsibility;
Community Service;
Initiation.

Thus, the Rites of Passage experiences include aspects of the helping sources we have previously discussed, namely, religious belief, positive, mental attitude, knowledge of African and African-American culture and history, and mentoring.

The Rites of Passage process can function as a contextual therapeutic intervention by directly supporting the emergence of a grounded sense of self in adolescence. A case example will be instructive. Mpatanishi, a former participant of a Rite of Passage process in his younger years, moved from a large metropolitan area to a medium-sized city. He began working for a local community organization. In this city there were a number of low-income housing apartments, like the Knot Hill "projects," which many people had written off because of drugs, gambling, and overall crime waves in these areas. The adolescents from this area were enrolled in mental health facilities and/or had various counselors in nearby community centers. Nonetheless, a general belief was "stay away from Knot Hill because the children there are impossible and won't amount to much anyway." Mpatanishi did not believe what he heard. He arranged to be introduced to some of the indigenous leaders in Knot Hill. He began working first with male adolescents and the following year with females. He taught them African and African-American culture and history, began mentoring them in groups, and taught African dance. Soon the community began to notice the changes in their environment, such as the lower crime rate. Therapists and counselors began to notice a change in their clients, such as consistent attendance and involvement in their growth process. Programs such as those started by Mpatanishi in his community are in high demand. Clinicians would be well served to investigate the Rites of Passage process in their area, and to consider this process not simply as an adjunct to psychotherapy, but as an important intervention in its own right. As a contextual support to the development of the adolescent self, Rites of Passage provides fertile ground from which to draw. Therapists' participation in the program allows them to engage more fully in the development of the adolescent self as a new gestalt. Programs such as the Rites of Passage incorporate the larger field and include racial identity. Thus, the adolescent is able to claim the capacity to organize personal experience into meaningful and contextually supported patterns and wholes. Coupled with individual therapy as a means to create a feedback loop for the integration of self and racial identity, Rites of Passage affords the adolescent the most fruitful of possible growth mechanisms.

Conclusion

Attending has been described as the backbone of Gestalt therapy. It requires the therapist to organize the self in relationship to the environment and pull out what is figural. The meaning of any figure can never be found in the figure alone, but rather with and in relationship to the field. McConville (1995) has offered a Gestalt field model of adolescent development and psychotherapy that goes beyond traditional intrapsychic and family therapy models. His work supports the idea that therapeutic interventions must address the larger field of adolescent development, but falls short of spelling out the concrete therapeutic praxis of such an approach. In this chapter, we have extended the Gestalt model by encouraged therapists working with African-American adolescents to enlarge the therapeutic field to include racial identity as a critical component of self-development. We have invited them to extend their therapeutic practice to include other processes such as religious services, Kwanzaa, culture and history lessons, and the Rites of Passage as supplemental healing tools.

The challenge in the African-American developmental process is that adolescents must be both confluent with what it means to be "Black," while differentiating the self that is so heavily embedded in Blackness without losing the racial self. Therapists, particularly Gestalt therapists, function to develop or restore a person's sense of choice. From this perspective, we have no choice but to incorporate racial identity when working with African-American adolescents. As visitors to their world, we must remain cognizant that almost daily, they are faced with choices that must be examined at the boundary of self and culture for them to remain alive and whole. What an awesome task for the therapist to remain in that awareness. Yet, how better supported we are in this work when we have that awareness and utilize the healing tools that are already there in the cultural ground.

References

Erikson, E. (1968). *Identity: Youth and crises*. New York, NY: Norton.

Gibbs, J. (1989). Black adolescents and youth: An update on an endangered species. In R. Jones, (Ed.), *Black Adolescents* (pp. 3-27). Berkeley, CA: Cobb & Henry.

Hare, N., & Hare, J. (1985). *Bringing the black boy to manhood*. San Francisco, CA: Black Think Tank.

Hendin, H. (1969). *Black suicide.* New York, NY: Basic Books.

Hill, P. (1992). *Coming of age: African american male rites-of-passage.* Chicago: IL: African American Images.

Lewis, M.C. (1988). *Herstory: Black female rites of passage.* Chicago, IL: African American Images.

Marcia, J. (1966). Development and validation of ego identity states. *Journal of Personality & Social Psychology, 3*(5), 551-558.

Marcia, J. (1980). *Identity in adolescence.* In J. Adelson, (Ed.), Handbook of Adolescent Psychology (pp. 159-187). New York, NY: John Wiley.

McConville, M. (1995). *Adolescence: Psychotherapy and the emergent self.* San Francisco, CA: Jossey-Bass, Inc.

National Institute of Drug Abuse (1995). National Institute of Drug Abuse (NIDA), Division of Epidemiology and Prevention Research. Washington, DC: CSR, Inc.

Thornton, W., James, J., & Doerner, W. (1982). *Delinquency and justice.* Glenview, IL: Scott, Foresman and Co.

Tukufu, D. (1997). *A Guide toward the successful development of african-american males.* Richmond Heights, OH: The Tukufu Group.

3

Late Adolescence:
A Gestalt Model of Development,
Crisis, and Brief Psychotherapy

Robert Ferguson and Charlie O'Neill

Introduction

Every period of human development has its own form of crisis. Every stage of life provides situations in which previously successful ways of making meaning are strained or seem inadequate. Every person encounters critical moments when some necessary adjustment seems just out of reach. Such emergencies, depending on how much reorganization is called for, tend to create emotional instability, confusion, and anxiety. In Gestalt terms a person in developmental crisis is experiencing a new level of challenge in the ongoing process of forming and destructuring phenomenological figures, and the sense of lost meaning may be so distressing that the person feels as if the very ground has shifted.

Adolescence is fraught with developmental crises as young people navigate the often difficult transition from childhood's dependence on adults to a greater reliance on their own resources, as well as increased need for support from and interactions with their peers. Late adolescence--the years between 18 and 22--is in some ways a distinct stage of development. Some psychological separation from the family of origin has already been initiated; earlier achievements toward a general sense of autonomy and competence continue to expand. Others may view people in late adolescence as capable of managing many adult responsibilities, such as handling one's own money, living separately, and so on. The dominant tasks of late adolescence, initiated much earlier in life, are to consolidate a sense of personal

72

identity and to gain an increased capacity for intimate relationships (Erikson, 1968). Major career and lifestyle decisions are often made in late adolescence. In a college or university setting there is an additional pressure to develop a more complex process for construing events--ways of thinking that evolve from dualistic to relativistic (Perry, 1970). Certainly the college environment also creates academic achievement related stress.

These life upheavals offer ample reasons for many late adolescents to choose traditional, long-term, individual therapy. Yet therapists who work with late adolescent clients, either in college counseling centers, community mental health centers, private practice or other settings, are under pressure to keep therapy brief. The expectations of HMOs, the limitations of the academic calendar, the increase in students seeking services, as well as a professional culture evolving toward more of a problem-solving model all contribute to such pressure. But perhaps the most influential factors contributing to the need for brief therapy with late adolescent clients are their own desires and expectations.

At the counseling center where we practice, clients are asked at intake how many sessions they anticipate needing to deal with their problems. By far the most frequently endorsed category is "two to five" sessions. The average number of personal counseling sessions actually used ranges between four and six, despite there being no fee for service. This is generally consistent with other counseling centers as indicated in the literature (Slavin, 1987; Webb & Widseth, 1988; May, 1988; Hersh, 1988). At least at university clinics, late adolescent clients are choosing not to stay long in therapy.

The brief therapy literature offers some expectations and guidelines related to effective therapy in such limited time frames. Definitions of brief therapy vary, and expectations about what can be accomplished correlate with the length of the therapy. For our purposes we define brief therapy as ten or fewer sessions. Hersh (1988) offers a breakdown of time-limited therapies by number of sessions and by what therapists can expect to accomplish. He defines five or fewer sessions as *crisis counseling*, and advocates a focus on symptom relief and immediate crisis resolution. Ten sessions or less is considered as *ultra-brief therapy*, and has as its focus new learning such as cognitive restructuring or helping a client get another perspective on present events (including normalization of present concerns as appropriate developmental tasks). His view of *brief therapy* (15 to 30 sessions) emphasizes the opportunity to provide new learning which considers the present situation, historical material, and the therapist-client relationship, *within a focused framework.*

In like fashion, Budman and Gurman (1988) say therapists practicing brief therapy must radically alter their expectations about what therapy is and what it can do. These include changes:

1. From seeking changes in basic character structure... to an emphasis on pragmatism, parsimony, and the least radical interventions.

2. From a belief that without therapeutic intervention significant psychological change is unlikely in everyday life... to adoption of a developmental perspective that sees significant psychological change as inevitable.

3. From a view of presenting problems as reflective of more basic pathology... to an emphasis on client's strengths and resources and a view that presenting problems are to be taken seriously for what they are.

4. From wanting to "be there" as clients make significant change... to accepting that many changes will occur "after therapy" and will not be observable to the therapist.

5. From the perspective of therapy as an indefinite process designed to give the client all the time needed... to a recognition of the benefits of establishing a definite length for therapy.

6. From the ideal that therapy is the most important part of the client's life... to an increased value on being in the world, and an emphasis on interactions with significant others, in therapy and in less contrived settings, as a major component of change.

In the Gestalt therapy literature, Harman (1995) and Polster (1990) both stress that the approach has always had the potential to be brief. Harman (1995) notes that Gestalt therapy often has been practiced as a form of brief therapy by (a) emphasizing a highly focused thematic contract between therapist and client in each meeting, (b) examining and experiencing the figure-formation to figure-completion cycle as it relates to the thematic need or desire,[1] and (c) focusing on "undoing" interruptions in that cycle as they manifest themselves in the therapy encounter. These three facets can be aimed at a specific problem--or some aspect of a problem--that has been mutually chosen as the focus of a given session. The client is likely to achieve a sense of closure and new learning *in each session or couple of sessions*; the relatively self-contained quality of each piece of work offers frequent points of evaluation regarding whether or not to continue therapy.

Polster (1990) credits Gestalt therapy's emphasis on heightening the here-and-now focus within the therapy relationship ("tight therapeutic sequences") as an important contribution to brief therapy. He attributes quicker progress in therapy to (a) the client learning that trusting the process of staying present-centered will in itself foster change, and (b) meta-awareness--the notion that change is further facilitated by knowing *how* one knows and organizes oneself. We acknowledge that turning up the rheostat of present centered awareness definitely has the potential for making change happen quickly and thereby reduce the length of therapy. But, as we will argue throughout this chapter, late adolescent clients are often not capable or willing to accept this kind of intensity.

Other writers have also questioned the efficacy of such an intense style of therapy being applied to all clients. Yontef (1993, p. 8), for example, analyzed the history of Gestalt therapy and described two overall trends in how the method has been applied. He criticizes the first trend, the highly figure-focused form of therapy described above, as too technique-centered and catharsis-oriented (especially as made famous by the workshop demonstrations of Frederick Perls) and believes that at its worst it is theatrical and manipulating. He argues for the second main trend in Gestalt therapy, a dialogical method emphasizing a genuine person-to-person involvement between therapist and client, a procedure less likely to fit into a brief model. Wheeler (1991) likewise calls for a longer course of therapy, one apparently more similar to Yontef's (1993) dialogic process. Wheeler emphasizes greater exploration of the client's "structured ground" (i.e., historical background, interpersonal style, and general pattern of organizing self-in-environment), as well as the relationship of the unique figures emerging from such a complex configuration of life experiences and phenomenological structures.

Either mode of Gestalt therapy--the figure-focused or the dialogic examination of a person's structured ground--is likely to assist some late adolescent clients. But both approaches also have significant limitations; many clients are likely to drop out of therapy in response to either one. The figure-focused method tends to bring clients immediately to their impasse, their inner conflict. This can lead to a break-through if they can understand the purpose of such emotional discomfort, if they can tolerate the anxiety that often comes with such inner-focusing, and if they can support such a process. But it is just as likely to feel overwhelming to them. The more grounded, dialogical approach is very personal and thus scary and intimate, especially for people struggling to control intimacy with adults, with authority figures, or with members of the therapist's gender, ethnic group, or sexual orientation.

Compared to their older counterparts, late adolescent clients allow the Gestalt influenced therapist a narrower range of possibilities. While referring specifically to adolescents of pre-college age, the following description is often very relevant to the use of a Gestalt approach in a university counseling center:

> I found most of my adolescent clients skittish and anxious when I engaged them in the manner that had become familiar to me with adult clients: concentrating on immediate here-and-now experience, heightening awareness (often of bodily states and other quite private aspects of experience), at times proposing relational experiments and fantasy explorations that from time to time only increased my adolescent's clients' sense of emergency. (McConville, 1995, p. xx).

In the chapter that follows, we will address the fit between late adolescent development and brief approaches to treatment, and show how Gestalt theory, particularly when appropriating the insights of other schools of thought, contributes to an effective, developmentally based model of brief psychotherapy. Specifically, we will address the following three questions:

What do late adolescent clients bring, in terms of their developmental tasks, crises, and perspectives, to the therapeutic encounter that is likely to make it brief?

What does the Gestalt approach contribute that is likely to make the therapeutic encounter with a late adolescent client more effective?

What insights can Gestalt therapy utilize from other therapies in order to be more effective with late adolescent clients?

Developmental Tasks Characteristic of Late Adolescence

Late adolescence is for most young people the successful culmination of developmental tasks begun earlier in the teen years. Based on published developmental theories and our own experience from the perspective

of Gestalt therapists, we identify five main dimensions of growth and crisis related to late adolescence:
1. How one (re)*organizes immediate awareness;*
2. How one (re)*organizes peers relationships;*
3. How one (re)*organizes relationships with authority;*
4. How one (re)*organizes self;*
5. How one *organizes the reorganizing process itself.*

The Process of Reorganizing Immediate Awareness

McConville (1995) describes stages of adolescent development in terms of preferred focus of attention, from the strong external focus of early adolescence, to the middle adolescent emphasis on "interiority," and ultimately to the late adolescent style encompassing both. The *early* adolescent focus on external awareness through experimentation with interpersonal boundaries serves the purposes of building one's own experience base for knowing the world, for learning to set and hold boundaries, and to establish oneself as a person set apart from one's family.

In contrast to the external focus of early adolescence, according to McConville, *middle* adolescence is a time when awareness drifts inward, heightening attention to the inner world of emotion, reflection and fantasy. Preoccupied with inner life-by definition self-conscious-the person in middle adolescence frequently experiences the elevated anxiety that comes with increased awareness of personal responsibility for feelings and reactions. The *late* adolescent, in turn, is often immersed in the work of integrating the relationship between the interior and exterior worlds.

The sorting out of this relationship involves the gradual discovery that these two worlds mutually influence each other-that what is observed in one world has an impact on experiences in the other world. Failure or delay in this integration compels a person to stay focused on one of these two domains at the expense of adequately knowing the other. McConville (1995) defines healthy adult functioning as having "worked out" this relationship:

> In well-functioning adult personalities, we look for
> the capacity to move fluidly between the figural expe-
> rience of self and the figural experience of the other.
> Adolescents who are struggling with maturational
> issues display many of the same characteristics of dis-
> turbed adults, becoming stuck in the figure-ground
> organization of their experience around one boundary

or the other (p.12-13).

Crises involving the organization of immediate awareness include such things as: (a) inadequate sensitivity or over-sensitivity to interpersonal cues, leading to social rejection by peers and (b) an other-focused person (i.e., one who tends to focus on the external world at the expense of knowing his or her internal experience) experiencing increased requests by a romantic partner to be more intimate, to disclose more information about his or her inner world.

The Process of Reorganizing Peer Relationships

The late adolescent task of reorganizing peer relationships involves expanding and deepening interpersonal connections with friends and romantic partners, and is predicated on the successful integration of the interior and exterior worlds as discussed above. Key to improved peer relationships is a move toward a more mutual exchange and reciprocal influence while still preserving and developing a secure sense of one's self and a respectful sense of other. This means going beyond "hanging out" to being more intimate, and developing the ability to achieve a sense of mutual support for difficult feelings and problems. In the area of romance there is the shift away from mutually dependent relationships to an interdependent alliance between partners. Learning not to overtax the other in terms of needs and wants and relying instead on a social network for some needs is an important accomplishment. Peer relationships remain the main laboratory for these tasks and the main source of support, guidance, and need gratification (Grayson, 1989). All this happens in the context of a society that promotes individualism, materialism, depersonalized sexuality, homophobia, and racial tension. If one is a member of an outgroup for whom support for this process is minimal or absent (e.g., lesbian, gay, bisexual) one is very likely to have a more difficult time achieving more intimate peer relationships. Related developmental crises may be activated:
- when an experiment with a new level of intimacy is
  not supported;
- when intimacy is punished;
- when experiencing rejection, especially as part of a
  pattern of rejections.

The late adolescent in crisis is struggling with questions about intimacy such as, "Am I doing it wrong?" or "Will I ever get it right?" or "How much should I share about myself?"

The Process of Reorganizing Relationships with Authority

The process of reorganizing one's relationship with authority is not new to late adolescence. There has been a lifelong involvement in this task (highlighted during the toddler period and early adolescence), but it takes on new importance in late adolescence. This is especially true for those who have physically removed themselves from daily contact with the family of origin, or the larger community of origin.[2] New symbols of authority and dependence abound, and individuals have to strike a new balance between dependence and autonomy in their basic orientation to those who supply support and guidance, and who are perceived as also having an interest in limiting freedom and experimentation. The process involves learning new competencies, new ways to juggle self-support, peer-support, and adult support, as one moves toward being one's own personal authority. Successful individuation involves less reacting against authority out of a counter-dependent stance than it does the formulation of a personal code of conduct. This process has to be negotiated gradually. It is likely to be characterized by some degree of ambivalence under the best conditions. It is further complicated by its interactive nature. As one separates from parental authorities, these figures react to that separation, and the person reacts to those reactions, and so on. If a parent or other significant authority reacts with hostility or an expressed fear of abandonment, the adolescent may lack the support needed to engage in the task of achieving a more adult relationship with authority (Grayson, 1989).

Any life event that requires asking for help from an older adult or other authority figure may precipitate a developmental crisis. To ask late adolescent clients to assume a dependent role, albeit temporarily, and share personal information about themselves, especially their innermost thought and feelings, is both very inviting and scary. Seeking therapy is often an attempt to attain help and support for resolving a developmental crisis, as well as being a crisis in and of itself.

It is commonplace to hear older adults remark with frustration that it is impossible to tell an 18-year-old anything of a cautionary or limiting nature. Even older, more experienced peers echo these sentiments and simply say that their younger peers will have to find out for themselves. Many students cannot wait to remove themselves from the residence halls and its parent-like restrictions. Holidays and summers often precipitate crises within families as the late adolescent person returns home having proudly determined many of her or his own limits, only to find the parents eager to reassert their prerogative to impose restrictions.

Most late adolescents need only moderate support to navigate these developmental crises related to responding to authority. A more difficult and distressing version of crises related to this task might take one of the following forms:

- Extreme difficulty with autonomy, manifested in a *high dependence* on authority figures (confluence with authority);
- Extreme *dysfunctional variations of independence*, in the forms of egotism (narcissistic preoccupation and entitlement), self-contained rigidity (controlling oneself and one's world to maintain independence), or counterdependence through rebellious behavior;
- Cycling back and forth between high dependence and reactionary anti-dependence, coping with the inner conflict by resorting to passive-aggressive behaviors.

The late adolescent in crisis is struggling with questions about authority such as "Can I be my own person?" or "Will I be a successful adult?" or "Can I trust my own judgment?" or "Will people respect me?"

The Process of Reorganizing Self

From a Gestalt therapy perspective, all five of these developmental tasks involve a reorganization of self. While we ultimately define the self as a holistic entity, we find it helpful to conceptualize it as having two interrelated functions: process and structure. As a process it is the immediate, in-the-moment subject of consciousness, actively organizing an encounter as it happens. Self-as-process is that which directly experiences phenomena from the inner and outer worlds and makes them available to the other dimension, self-as-structure. As such, this process aspect of self is an evolving, changing gestalt-a complex, flexible configuration through which an individual is negotiating and re-negotiating how things appear to consciousness. Self-as-structure is the enduring product of that act. The structural self exists as a relatively cohesive, stable pattern of values, biases, memories, cultural habits, and so on. While the emphasis here is on the psychological notion of self, neither dimension exists only as a concept. The self is holistic and embodied (Kepner, 1987), and is inclusive of anatomy and neurology. It exists in a larger interpersonal field from which it cannot be absolutely separated. The self might be thought of as both the musician and instrument of awareness, and completely interdependent with an orchestra of other conscious beings.

Table 1 further explores and clarifies the complementary differences between these two phenomenological views of self.

While this relationship between the different functions of the self is important in any clinical consideration, we believe it is especially so when working with a population that by developmental design is in a heightened state of trying to balance their needs to affect change and make sense of themselves. Negotiating this balance between growth and stable structure, between experiencing and integrating, is at the heart of the late adolescent's life task.

This juggling task is illustrated further by the tension between component gestalts coexisting within the self-as-structure. McConville (1995) describes this tension by discussing the relationship between a child-self

---

Table 1
Complementary Functions of Self

Self-As-Process		*Self-As-Structure*	
1.	The subject of consciousness in process.	1.	The subject of consciousness is organized as structure.
2.	The "now" self; figure-oriented; experimental.	2.	The organized sum of all previous experiences available for the creation of the meaning and continuity; a structured ground that influences self-as-process.
3.	The subject is experiencing *what* is.	3.	The subject is focused on what is familiar.
4.	The subject is focused on the boundary or frontier of its experience as a conscious being.	4.	The subject is synthesizing *what is new* with *what is familiar* and creating enduring patterns.
5.	The subject has the sense of being influenced by what is happening.	5.	The subject is experienced as an enduring, cohesive "I."

---

gestalt and the emerging structure of an adolescent-self gestalt. He theorizes that the child's organization of self remains intact as a continued presence in adolescence, and remains confluent with values and standards introjected from the family of origin. It continues to provide structure for the adolescent's experience, and is often felt to be in opposition to the tentative adolescent self. But as it comes under the growing influence of the adolescent self, the self-as-process takes in and organizes phenomena through more reflective and critical processes than it did under the exclusive sway of the childhood self structure. These two alternate configurations-the child-self dedicated to preserving the status quo and the adolescent-self aligned with breaking out of the status quo-can create divergent meanings when applied to the same experience. It is analogous to having two distinct methodologies or conceptual structures for processing the same data base, leading to different assumptions, evaluations, and conclusions about identical facts. It could even be thought of as a kind of multicultural experience: the family culture often clashes with the peer culture as each asserts its respective meaning and values.

> As adolescence gets under way, the individual begins to feel the differentiating internal tension, not just of fragmentary polarities, but also of significantly different paradigms for organizing the entire field of self experiences. Another way of describing this state of affairs is to say that the intrapsychic life of the adolescent comes under the organizational sway of an *overarching developmental polarity* made up of opposing paradigms for knowing the self and the surrounding world (McConville, 1995, p. 80; original emphasis).

Adolescents often experience conflict as they utilize one paradigm to the temporary exclusion of the other, then react in the opposite direction. If this inner conflict becomes too intense, it may take the form of interpersonal friction, as the person becomes fixed on one paradigm and projects the other onto the interpersonal world. Successful resolution of this developmental tension is most likely, according to McConville (1995), when there is a dialogue between the child/family oriented self and the emerging adolescent configuration.

> In the simplest and most straightforward case, development proceeds as a sort of dialogue between these alternative possibilities. For most teenagers, there is

an evolving interplay between the introjected organization of childhood and family and the budding,
authentic, experimental self of adolescence. Each
pole of this emerging duality informs and tempers the
other, and their interplay is readily apparent. The individual is able to identify with, own, and feel responsible for the contact style, affective tones, and cognitive
states that belong to each pole. Each serves to limit
and challenge the other, which promotes contact
between the two and ultimately, their growth and
mutual accommodation (p. 81)

An integrated self emerges from the tension between the child and
adolescent self-gestalts. This developing configuration observes and
processes the internal relationship until an awareness of self emerges that
knows and recognizes the "rightness" of each perspective. The child-self
speaks to security and conservation, to preserving relationships with others,
especially with significant adults. The adolescent-self speaks to risk-taking
and experimentation, to a self-agenda that might alter or damage relationships with significant adults. This emerging self, that will become the adult
self, incorporates the viewpoints of both the child and adolescent selves,
assuming a field perspective regarding experience, realizing that self and
other mutually influence each other, and recognizing the interdependence of
self-interest and other interest. McConville (1995) states:

By the latter part of the teen years, this ambivalence
bears fruit. The adolescent's independence and world-
liness become grounded in a realistic sense of limits,
tradition, and responsibility. His feelings of attachment, obligation, and moral constraint become
exposed to the light of empirical reexamination. And
while the polarity of old childhood experience versus
current experience will continue throughout life, the
framework of a self that can accommodate both will
be established, with any luck, by the end of adolescence, approximately between the seventeenth and the
twenty-second year (p. 83).

This structural synthesis expands the limits of self-as-process, giving several benefits to the subject of consciousness: increased flexibility
regarding figure formation and figure completion,[3] new stability to allow
for being influenced without losing self definition, and new freedom to go

beyond transference and to experience *what is* in a fresh context. The late adolescent is liberated to experiment with finding the right balance between dependence and independence, safety and risk, self-interest and other interest. Finding such balance requires experimentation, and can be unstable and inconsistent by older adult standards.[4] There is strong pressure, both internal and external, to make decisions based on a stable, consistent, and purposeful sense of self in the areas of career, sexual identity, racial identity, moral decision making, and preferences in friends (Chickering, et al., 1981). Any situation (including being in therapy) that risks undoing this new, vulnerable, and tentative reconfiguration of self is approached with caution. Any situation that demands too rapid or radical a reconfiguration of the uncertain adult self-structure, or that disturbs this new, precarious balance, is experienced as a crisis. The following examples are adapted from Grayson (1989):

- acknowledging chronic dissatisfaction with choices;
- recognizing an inability or reluctance to make key decisions;
- preoccupation with and holding onto childhood fantasies or those from early adolescence;
- realizing that goals introjected from parents are unrealistic or not integral to self;
- realizing that submersion in a cause or activity is at the expense of a well integrated sense of self.

In short, the late adolescent is struggling with questions such as "Who am I really?" or "How do I want to fit in?" or "With whom do I belong?" Implicit in all these struggles is the question of how much to let in, how much to allow self-as-process to be open to novel experience, or to be limited by self-as-structure with its emphasis on integrating information into a cohesive and continuous sense of identity.

The Process of Reorganizing the Organizing Process

As progress is made regarding the tasks described above, the late adolescent continues to build an "observing ego," an ability to participate and also observe and reflect on that participation. Meta-awareness involves the ability to follow shifts in conscious focus, from the external focus to the internal, and then back to the outside--from thoughts to feelings and back, etc. The process of meta-awareness increases one's ability to know the process through which one comes to know something, and to be aware of how one organizes one's awareness.

Consciously organizing and reorganizing one's ongoing observations of self gives a person the ability to see patterns of behavior as a manifestation of a larger gestalt, as being related to one's basic organizing principles, such as beliefs, rules, and styles of resistance to awareness. It promotes the understanding that reality is an interactive process and contextual in nature, that things and experiences do not simply exist in some objective way but rather are affected by one's participation. At some point for many late adolescents there is an epistemological paradigm shift as they begin to realize that meaning is created and not merely given.

Many new influences encourage such a shift, especially in college. Exposure to different lifestyles and values, along with the continued presentation of divergent theories for explaining the same experiences (whether in the physical or social sciences or the arts and humanities) can produce inner tension and possibly a reorganization crisis. Taking in and sorting out these new experiences involves an increased ability to tolerate anxiety and ambiguity, and a gradual acceptance of a more relativistic way of thinking about experience. This task of gaining insight into one's organizing process is more likely to reach crisis level when it interacts with certain life events. A crisis can be stimulated by events that call upon the individual to reconfigure a previous understanding of family or other aspects of one's history. Uninvited experiences that contradict long-standing beliefs--about what one can control, about how relationships work, about personal safety--can also precipitate a crisis. Some specific examples are:

- intrusive memories of traumatic childhood experiences;
- coming to a fuller realization of the dysfunctional conditions within one's family;
- an encounter with prejudice and/or violence that makes more evident the extent of bigotry in society;
- an unexpected reaction that is dissonant with one's self image (e.g. sexist or racist thought)
- a friend dies unexpectedly;
- a partner is unfaithful;
- a person is a victim of acquaintance rape;
- inability to meet the academic requirements for a long-held career aspiration.

A self-initiated change in behavior can also activate a developmental crisis by influencing the person's understanding of how he or she organizes perceptions and relationships, thus opening up unforeseen interperson-

al possibilities and subsequent new awareness. Examples would be:
- trying for the first time to go without a steady boyfriend or girlfriend;
- attempting to make friends outside of one's high school crowd;
- reducing the quantity and/or frequency of alcohol or drug use;
- trying to be more assertive;
- intentionally listening to previously ignored supportive or critical statements from others;
- experimenting with less initiating and pursuit in one's relationships.

These growth initiatives tend to shake up the status quo. While it is is liberating to open up new perspectives on one's own self process, it is also terrifying because it leads to identity destabilization and reconfiguration. Maintaining some ego-observation perspective in the ensuing organizational crisis is often difficult. Late adolescent individuals obviously vary in their capability and willingness to do this.

It is important to remember that these tasks are not mapped neatly, in stepwise fashion, but vary by culture and subculture, as well as by individual development. Resolving such conflicts can be immensely difficult and painful for the late adolescent client, and typically requires much trial and error--and involves much frustration. It is this frustration that often brings them to therapy, and frustration that leads them to drop out prematurely. They feel frustrated about not being more in control of the many changes, and frustrated about not fully understanding what is going on. But they can become equally frustrated at not being offered immediate answers, or when they feel that therapy simply creates more "stuff" with which they have to deal. Progress toward meta-awareness is likely to look more cyclical than linear as such conscious efforts come and go.

Need for a Brief Therapy Format

Late adolescent clients seldom think of therapy as a protracted process partly because crisis experiences often pass quickly. So much is going on that an adjustment tends to be made quickly so that order can be restored. They tend to see problems discretely and frequently miss the bigger picture of self-defeating patterns over several problem areas. Given their limited life experience, they probably have not seen these problem areas emerge again and again to defeat self-efforts to change, as have many adults. They are often experiencing rapid life change that contributes to an expectation that change *should* be rapid, especially if someone has gone to all the trouble to seek help from an "expert." They often minimize the severity of their problems or see them as transitory or environmentally determined, as opposed to the therapist's view of something more severe and related to other life challenges.

At our counseling center, for example, it is not unusual for late adolescent clients to indicate on a problem checklist that they have been suicidal within the previous week or month. When asked to rank their three most important problem areas, however, suicidal ideation frequently does not make it to the top three. The extent to which late adolescents are looking or want to look at their life problems through a contextual lens varies widely and thus has a profound impact on the duration and methods of therapy.

Other aspects of late adolescence work against a long-term approach. As discussed above, the person's self-boundaries are often tentative. There is a sort of narcissistic vulnerability that comes from an immature measure of self-support and definition. Clients can easily feel misunderstood and injured, and are likely to leave therapy when they do.

There is ambivalence about interacting with a caring adult, especially from a vulnerable emotional state in which the desire for a more protective, dependent relationship might be more prominent. Most clients are ambivalent about what they want from the therapist, often requesting to be told what to do but also wanting to find a way to figure it out themselves. There is frequently a fear of an older adult taking over and the opposite fear that not enough will be done.

Ambivalence about cross-cultural or cross-orientation therapy is common for many late adolescent clients. It may be like asking for help from someone who symbolizes an oppressor, a rejecter, a stigmatizer. Many minority students come from a culture in which seeking help refers to instrumental assistance, not an emphasis on expressiveness and phenomenological exploration. Likewise, persons oppressed on the basis of gender, sexual orientation, disability, or history of abuse may bring an expectation of being wounded or exploited, and often set narrow limits on contact possibilities with a therapist.

There are cognitive factors as well. Late adolescent clients vary in their ability to think relativistically. They often come to therapy with mostly dualistic thinking styles, framing problems and possible solutions in an either/or fashion. Even though they find this restrictive, it also feels "right" in that this is how life seems to be. They often find relativistic responses in therapy to be irrelevant or overly complicated, or interpret them as some form of equivocating or avoidance. For example, a late adolescent client might demand to know the therapist's beliefs about whether "shacking"[5] is right or wrong. The therapist is likely to be met with frustration if she attempts to get the client to state his own belief, or if she responds that she does not think there is a simple answer to the question. Late adolescent clients often struggle in their efforts to understand various behaviors in terms of moral categories.

Interrelated with a dualistic cognitive style is an either/or style of relating to others, manifesting as the polarity of confluence/withdrawal, making many late adolescent clients difficult to engage interpersonally, especially in only a few sessions. They have a smaller data base than older clients, so even "insightful" persons may not see how much of their immediate problem is part of a larger pattern in which they play an active part. They want to believe the problem is only the situation, rather than anything about themselves they might have to change. Because of this narrow perspective, college age adolescents tend to stop therapy when the immediately stressful situation stops hurting so much.

Sex role socialization is a factor as well. Late adolescent men are likely to be more invested in introjected forms of masculinity. Since one must be willing, to some degree, to enter an intimate relationship in therapy, men who are invested in the traditionally masculine, individualistic, problem-solving perspective may be less likely to seek such help, or to make full use of it. Two-thirds of our clientele seeking personal counseling are women. It is simply counter-cultural for many young men to ask for help.

To balance this picture, it is important to remember that there are several developmental characteristics that facilitate effective change and growth in a brief therapy format with late adolescent clients. For instance, they are often less established in some defensive style. Psychological exploration is a big part of the lifestyle of this period of life so therapeutic-type behaviors are occurring naturally a lot of the time. In college, students are often immersed in a potentially supportive social environment that provides ample opportunities for experimentation and obtaining support and feedback. Radical withdrawal into oneself is likely to be noticed, a condition that provides a kind of safety net if therapy becomes scary or overwhelming. College students tent to be bright, eager to learn, and psychologically minded. They have their basic material needs met and so can afford to focus more energy on emotional needs. Finally, late adolescent clients usually expect and want something to happen quickly, which can shape what actually happens.

Contact Reconsidered

Our work with late adolescent clients in developmental crisis has led us to closely examine and clarify one of the basic constructs in Gestalt therapy. We will articulate a heuristic model of contact that considers *forms*, *functions*, and *probable feedback*, as well as the notion of a *spectrum of intersubjective exchange*. We will argue that such a multifaceted view of contact helps build a theory about the development of human contact, and provides a framework to support an empathic understanding of dynamics that are frequently seen as pathological. It also serves to widen the theoretical lens through which clinicians guided by phenomenology select and critique various therapeutic interventions. We believe that a more complex and flexible theory of contact is necessary to fully appreciate the perspective and common needs of late adolescent clients in developmental crisis.

Contact is about relationship (Yontef, 1993, p. 299). The concept of contact is grounded in the notion that no person or thing exists outside of relationships with other persons and things-there is always context. It furthermore involves two dimensions of relationship, reflected in the different emphases of Frederick Perls and Paul Goodman (Clarkson & MacKewn, 1993; Wheeler, 1991). Perls focused more on the individual organizing relationships within the phenomenological field based on a figural or dominant need, or "figure formation against a ground or context" (Perls, Hefferline & Goodman, 1994, p.231). He highlighted the importance of "aggressive"[6] energy directed toward the external world to satisfy one's needs. Borrowing a concept from biology, Perls often referred to the importance of "assimilation," the need for an organism to digest and destructure sustenance from the environment. Despite his references about the importance of attending to what is novel, his conceptualization of contact displayed a bias toward favoring what is familiar to the self-to making things conform to an established process.[7] In contrast, Goodman's interest was more about *creative adjustment* as he viewed contact as how people create conditions for an intersubjective exchange (Stoehr, 1994). Contact, in Goodman's thinking, involves both innovation and compromise. The subject attends to what is novel and looks for possibilities for exchange that are likely to involve adjusting one's psychological and interpersonal processes. Creative adjustment is a shift in emphasis from acting *upon* the environment to working *with* it. Participants in contact transform some aspect of themselves and their relationship *to make use of what is available in the interpersonal world.* "Having it my way" is superseded by the importance of respecting ongoing relationships.

While contact has always been a model to help understand individual and interpersonal processes, Yontef (1993) observed that the latter was largely eclipsed by the popular Perlsian emphasis on the former (p. 111). Yontef also criticized the historical interpretation of "self support," claiming it overvalued self-sufficiency and obscured the importance of interdependence and cooperation (1993, p. 112). At its most simplistic, contact has been misinterpreted as something dichotomous (a person is either in contact or "resisting" it) and selfish (if the individual meets his or her needs, contact has been full and successful).

Wheeler (1991) alludes succinctly to both the individual and contextual dimensions in his comprehensive definition of contact as "the organization of the subject in the field" (p.119). Put another way, contact is comprised of two interconnected tasks on the part of conscious beings: (a) each subject's organizing of phenomena and (b) the intersubjective exchange of phenomena, as they are organized, between two or more conscious beings. The individual subject of consciousness is always organizing, but never outside the context of a field, a completely interdependent web of relationships. This two dimensional quality of contact creates an ever present tension between an individualistic focus and a contextual or field focus. Likewise, there is always an attempt to balance the innovation that comes with attending to what is novel with the safety that comes with attending to what is familiar.

Forms, Functions, and Feedback

We believe that all human interaction is functional. It is always purposeful in some immediate sense as well as in some long term, adaptive, relational context. Wheeler (1991) speaks to this when he conceptualizes the traditional Gestalt therapy notion of resistance, or "contact disturbances" as *"functions of the contact"* When considering the subjective organizing aspect of contact, the terms "interruptions" and "disturbances" are misnomers; nobody can stop organizing reality; nobody can stop having contact. When contact is thought of as an exchange, so called interruptions to organismic need satisfaction can have the positive use of limiting an interaction in favor of respecting each other, and of meeting the long-term need of living well *with* the environment. As such it puts the emphasis not only on meeting goals but also on sensitivity to context, and to the mutual satisfaction, preservation, and development of interdependent relationships over time.

According to Wheeler (1991), the Cleveland School was the first to reframe "the resistances to contact" (projection, deflection, introjection, etc.) as potentially having positive functions *if done with awareness and to meet certain goals*. But he points out that such a reinterpretation ultimately clings to the idea that resistances interfere with or dilute some ideal contact experience: they are still considered something in the way. He asserts instead that the so-called interruptions *are contact*; they are means of organizing the meeting with the environment and are always present. According to Wheeler, the resistances are regularly utilized *forms of contact*, as we prefer to call them, employed with or without awareness to organize interpersonal encounters according to the developmental tasks, personal goals, and capacities of the person. We would add, from a field theory perspective, that forms of contact can also be appreciated insofar as they facilitate the goals and developmental needs of a relationship. In short, evaluation of forms must be contextual and phenomenological.

Wheeler takes his perspective a step further by postulating a constant bipolar relationship between various forms of contact. Confluence, for example, is in a polar relationship with differentiation. Wheeler sees both as necessary for contact. To avoid confluence is to separate, to create boundaries that differentiate self from others. To de-emphasize separation and self-definition involves some degree of confluence. Contact, especially over time, is both. It involves being connected and maintaining boundaries. Both are necessary, with the likelihood of one being more prominent at any given moment. The two sides of this polarity can be regarded as opposites for their apparent lack of congruency, or as complements in that together they comprise a whole. All forms of contact *and their polar complements* play a part in any person-to-person exchange, with some more noticeable than others, and some more directly related to the goals of the specific encounter. The appearance and experience of any level of intersubjective exchange is based on the "mix" of contact forms. This understanding of contact moves from a prescriptive notion of some tainted ideal that needs to be reestablished if interrupted or disturbed, to something more human and descriptive, an almost inevitable meeting in need of regulation according to form, degree of awareness and mutuality, and shared purpose. The "contact resistances" are no longer seen only as the brakes; they are the brakes *and the steering mech-*

anism. They provide maneuverability, and each vehicle has a unique "feel" and style. Although they sometimes need fine tuning and even outright repairs in order to achieve maximum efficacy, they are not necessarily something to be fixed in order to restore functioning. In short, *these forms of contact,* previously thought of as resistances, interruptions, or disturbances, are central to contact; *they make the exchange possible; they are the contact.* The question, consequently, is not whether some "resistance" is being employed, but rather *how.* What combination of forms is in use, and how flexibly can the person and the relationship switch to a different form as context and need changes? "Is this form of contact (or combination of forms) working for each of us in the context of this relationship and the developmental tasks in focus?"

We suggest two additions to Wheeler's reconsideration of the resistances: the notions of functions and feedback. First, we propose that forms of contact can be analyzed according to their function. What is the purpose of a certain form of contact? Why would someone behave in such a way? What is a person's motive or intention for, say, deflecting, or introjecting? More specifically, what function is served at each point on the continuum bridging the various forms in bipolar relationship (e.g., confluence vs. separation)?

We hypothesize that contact functions can be reduced to two primary factors: (1) the Field Orientation Factor and (2) the Interpersonal Influence Risk Factor.

The *Field Orientation Factor* is a way of thinking about behavior as it varies along a continuum between the two poles comprised of an individualistic focus and a contextualistic focus. This factor refers to whether a person at any moment, or in general style, tends to focus on the figure of *self* or the figure of *other* or *context.* "Individualistic" is not meant in any pejorative sense. We simply refer to the experience of feeling a clear primacy in awareness of self-interest over other-interest. For example, a person might be irritated when interrupted during a favorite TV show, or distracted from a conversation because of hunger pangs. Conversely, "contextualistic" refers to a dominant focus on the other, the context. It comes at some expense to awareness of self-interest. Moving back and forth between the two poles of focus allows a person to navigate the competing interests that occur when self-interest and other-interest are notably different.

The *Interpersonal Influence Risk Factor* refers to a person's modulation of openness to being influenced in an encounter with another human being. Although there is potential benefit, the integrity of the self is put at risk when one allows for something new to happen, and this risk is often accompanied by discomfort. As in economics, stability must be balanced with the possibility for growth. This factor thus refers to the function of contact boundary permeability or, in the words of Polster & Polster (1973), "the I-boundaries." The I-boundaries are the parameters of permissibility for expression, exposure, body contact and spacing, personal values and behaviors, and familiarity. People vary in the flexibility of their I-boundaries and in their degree of attraction to and tolerance for operating at their personal frontier of comfort and perceived safety. Adopting a play-it-safe strategy keeps a person well within their I-boundaries and gives a feeling of safety and control in a situation. Adopting a risk-taking strategy leads to an increased probability of being influenced, for better or for worse, by another person, and also increases the likelihood of discomfort.

We further contend that the function served by any given form can be reversed as context is altered. For example, a person utilizing a form of contact weighted more toward confluence than its polar complement, separation, is probably emphasizing a contextualistic strategy over an individualistic one. Such a person is trying to preserve some human connection at some expense to the experience of a differentiated self. Conversely, separating from someone--clarifying self-boundaries--is most easily thought of as emphasizing an individualistic strategy, preserving the psychological status quo. But these functional polarities can be reversed. The same form of contact can serve the polar opposite function in a different context. A person can, for instance, emphasize separation in service of creative adjustment by responding to a demand by someone else for distance. The same could be said for an emphasis on destructuring over introjection; a parent, friend, or therapist could encourage a person to develop a stronger identity or an increased use of critical thinking. If the person responds as requested, he or she is actually alternating between an individualistic and contextualistic focus. In the same way, a person who usually accommodates others psychologically by almost constantly expanding the boundaries of the self to make way for the needs of a relationship will, in fact, be expanding self-boundaries in a different way by setting limits on a specific encounter. At the macro-analysis level, then, with its consideration of culture and probability, one can assume with a limited degree of accuracy that a certain form is associated with a certain function. But, at the micro-analysis level, wherein specific encounters are in effect building blocks for an ongoing social system, the relationship between form and function depends on context. In short, *no human behavior, relationship dynamic or "resistance" can be understood without knowledge of context.*

Our second addition to Wheeler's reconsideration of the resistances, as mentioned above, is this: forms of contact are associated with a probability related to positive or negative interpersonal feedback, again *according to context.* Forms of contact vary in how people are likely to interpret and respond to them. The demands of a specific situation, certain relationships, or various cultures and subcultures determine whether a form of contact "fits."

Tables 2 and 3 graphically illustrate the ideas of contact forms, functions, and feedback. Forms most likely related to the Field Orientation Factor are graphically illustrated in Table 2. If a person experiences the need to be more individualistic in focus, the forms of contact used are likely to be those listed on the right side of the table (e.g., separation over confluence, destructuring over introjection, etc.). Forms most likely related to the Interpersonal Influence Risk Factor are shown in Table 3. Someone needing to be less influenced by another person is likely to be utilizing those forms listed on the left side of the table (e.g., deflection over openness to discomfort, proflection over being straightforward, etc.). Table 3 also borrows from other theories concepts that might be considered forms of contact.[8] Finally, Tables 2 and 3 also depict our notion of probable feedback. In Table 2, for instance, the use of confluence can be interpreted negatively in a social setting that disparages the need for contextualism. Confluence is likely to be depreciated as a weakness (e.g., "He can't stand up for himself.") In a different arena, one that values some submersion of individualism for the good of the group, confluence would receive positive feedback (e.g., "She's a real team player"). Similarly, the more extreme and frequent a manifestation of any form or function of contact, the more likely it is to be considered inappropriate or pathological across contexts; extreme individualism as a constant personality style is likely to be seen as narcissism--constant, extreme contextualism as undifferentiated, "co-dependent," or "wishy-washy." Even at the extremes, however, social context never becomes irrelevant.

In brief therapy, positive and negative versions of each form of contact are seen as dynamics to be understood in a contextual and developmental light, and as behaviors to highlight and affirm for the function they serve, rather than something to frustrate. The focus becomes the meaning or function of the resistance behavior, and the guiding principle is that all forms of behavior evolve out of some fit with the environment and hence have a use in some context. Each form can be acknowledged for its utility in some context, and at appropriate moments also acknowledged for its anachronistic quality in other contexts. Such illumination heightens the late adolescent client's awareness of the function of each form--how and when it might be useful, how and when it is not likely to be useful. Emphasizing affirmation and context also assists in establishing a creative alliance with the client and

Table 2
The Field Orientation Factor:
Related Forms of Contact,
Complementary Poles, and
Probable Feedback

Weighted toward *CONTEXTUALISM*	⟨◻ Field Orientation Factor ↱⟩	*Weighted toward* *INDIVIDUALISM*
(-) No identity; hyper-dependent **Confluence** (+) Team player; part of something bigger	*Polarity*	(-) Us/Them; alienation; untrusting **Separation** (+) Can resist influence
(-) Gullible; uncritical follower **Introjection** (+) Quick learner; effectively uses role models	*Polarity*	(-) Hyper-analytical **Destructuring** (+) Critical thinker
(-) Blaming; not owning **Projection** (Other focused) (+) Bridging/empathizing	*Polarity*	(-) Shame; abasement **Self-focus** (+) Introspective; knows self
(-) Deferent; exploited **Yielding** (Unconditionally favorable) (+) Altruistic	*Polarity*	(-) Selfish; "Me first" **Egotism** (Conditionally favorable) (+) Confident; good negotiator
(-) Dependent **Other-reliant** (+) Trusting; able to rely on others	*Polarity*	(-) Self-contained; isolated **Retroflection** (i.e., self-reliant) (+) Self-supportive

reduces the probability of being perceived as a critical authority figure.

This revised perspective on contact, with its emphasis on *how* the person is organizing contact rather than *if* the person is in contact, makes Gestalt therapy more compatible with other interpersonal therapies. Many interpersonal theorists (e.g., Kiesler, Millon, & Berne) have talked about organized patterns of interpersonal initiatives across contexts, analogous to the Gestalt notion of a rigid contact style. A patterned initiative elicits a predictable response from another person. The familiarity of the elicited response has value to the initiator, sometimes at the expense of other functional considerations.

This framework also offers a structure for examining various elicited responses. Working with couples offers examples, as it is not uncommon

Table 3
The Interpersonal Risk Factor:
Related Forms of Contact,
Complementary Poles, and
Probable Feedback

Weighted toward SAFETY (decreased probability of being influenced by others)	Interpersonal Influence ⟨⎯ Risk Factor ⎯⟩	Weighted toward RISK (increased probability of being influenced by others)
(-) Inhibited **Retroflection** (i.e., holding back) (+) Respectful of others	Polarity	(-) Impulsive **Active/Moving Toward** (+) Spontaneous
(-) Flitting; impressionistic **Deflection** (+) Able to shift focus or direction	Polarity	(-) Bias toward negative experiences **Open to Discomfort** (+) High tolerance for negative feelings
(-) Hidden agenda; indirect **Proflection**[i] (+) Bridging/empathizing	Polarity	(-) Aggressive **Straightforward** (+) Assertive
	Concepts From Other Theories	
(-) Emotionally stuck; unfinished business **Transference** (+) Over-learned response; predictable; reliable	Polarity	(-) No consideration of context **Here & Now Orientation** (+) Fresh; childlikewonder
(-) Entitlement; grandiosity **Needing Only Affirmation**[ii] (+) Able to gain needed support	Polarity	(-) Bias for criticism **Openness to Disaffirmation** (+) Seeks constructive feedback
(-) One-down/one-up relating **Setting Up Idealized Relationships**[iii] (+) Able to make use of mentors	Polarity	(-) Unable to look up to others; no heroes **Setting Up Real Relationships** (+) Recognizes inherent human equality
(-) Us vs. Them **Assuming Identical Outlooks**[iv] (+) Feeling a part of something bigger	Polarity	(-) Feeling alone; hurt; misunderstood **Acceptance of Different Perspectives** (+) Tolerance; appreciation

(-) = Increased probability of negative feedback.
(+) = Increased probability of positive feedback.

for one member of a relationship to specialize around some polar functions while the other member compensates by emphasizing the opposite functions. One partner may be a specialist in spontaneity, while the other partner forms a counterbalance with a more retroflective style characterized by inhibition or caution. One partner's naive or impressionistic initiatives might

96

elicit overly analytic responses from the other. Members of such couples are attracted to each other for complementarity, but often pay for the attraction with divisive rifts and sterile functioning as one pole is left undeveloped in both partners. Using this lens with individual clients can be diagnostic of developmental strengths, challenges or deficits. For example, egotistic initiatives on the part of a client, especially in extreme, increase the probability of evoking a yielding reaction from a therapist. Conversely, the deferent client invites a leading response.

Time limitations inherent in brief therapy often call upon therapists to emphasize a sense of safety, and to "go with" clients' strengths. Providing the complementary response to an observed form of contact serves the purposes of establishing a medium of exchange familiar to the client and building a therapeutic alliance (see Kiesler, 1988). This may be true in all therapy but is more critical in short-term therapy. Inevitably some particular elicited response will be contrary to the therapist's preferred style, (e.g., asking more questions, filling in the silences, following content, etc.). The therapist is ideally well aware of his or her change in style, and understands these atypical interactions in the light of well-considered models of development and therapy so he or she can remain self-supportive as well as attendant to the client's needs. This awareness is accompanied by the conscious bracketing of non-complementary responses such as frustration, boredom, anger, or even the strong urge to directly describe the here-and-now process in the exchange. The therapist's expression of any of these may be appropriate once the relationship is firmly underway, but initially there is an emphasis on how the patterned initiative is a strength for the client in certain contexts. The therapist can inquire about how a patterned exchange works in the client's social network, first by looking at benefits and then gently probing for the disadvantages. Gradually the work might evolve toward highlighting the client's ambivalence about the behavior pattern and its often negative consequences. More extensive therapy would probably address the pattern as a problem in and of itself, gradually moving toward a focus on the pattern as it expresses itself in the therapy relationship. But in the first few sessions--which may be all there is--the emphasis is on how this familiar pattern can help with the immediate problem.

An example would be the very deflective client who moves frequently from story to story. The therapist's initially elicited response might be fascination or a sense of being overwhelmed by the breadth of the material. The therapist can appreciate the strength and potentially positive aspects of using this contact function while assessing for how aware the client is about what she or he is doing. Clients with greater awareness of the patterned use of any particular form of contact invite feedback and exploration about what it means at that moment and in other situations. Other clients indicate less awareness of the process by focusing on how the nature of events prompted some presentational style. In brief therapy the therapist is likely to make a conscious choice of taking on the complementary contact function, in this case by directly helping the client focus. Over some time, if provided, this complementary exchange might be explored in terms of outside relationships and in the therapeutic relationship itself. If time and motivation allows, the client might develop or reclaim an ability to shuttle between deflecting and focusing.

There is variance, however, in what late adolescent persons need from therapists, across sessions and across clients, and there is no all-purpose formula to guide therapists through every decision about whether or not to offer the form of contact a specific client is attempting to elicit. There are clients, for instance, who are quite aware they have drawn others into an intrapsychic split: they see that their social world is split similarly, with different people allied with one or the other sides of the split. Such clients often state clearly that they want an objective voice--someone who will not be drawn into the split only to perpetuate it. Other clients fail to see any connection between their experience of the inner world and their organization of the interpersonal world.

Contact is ultimately a juggling act. It involves the selection and emphasis of various forms, some emphasis of one function over another, and a regulation of awareness, as a person attempts to optimize how reality is constructed for the mutual satisfaction of self and others. In clinical terms this interpretation of contact forces a reconsideration of the theoretical belief that no matter what the client's goals are, the therapist's goals are always to increase awareness and facilitate contact. It also challenges the idea that "disturbances" in contact need to be processed for therapy to be effective. At least with late adolescent clients, the more appropriate therapeutic goal is to determine whether a client's style is the right mix for the context and for his or her purposes in the moment and in the context of the current developmental crisis. In other words, *the client is always in contact with the therapist*, and employs some mix of contact forms she or he knows best, for the purpose of meeting certain goals within the contingencies of the therapeutic experience as perceived. Adolescent clients, much more so than adults, are still experimenting with the "mix" of these forms of contact.

A late adolescent client, for example, may be choosing or reflexively using a mainly "introjected" form of contact with the therapist, but adopt a more critical or "chewing" approach on some particular issue. The sudden and occasional reversal of polarity may be functional in light of needing to exploit the therapist's perceived expertise on the one hand, while also needing to draw self-boundaries on the other. The ability to reverse polarity may even be a subtly acknowledged goal of therapy in and of itself, as the transferential tendency toward compliance with caring parental figures continues to be useful, although to an increasingly limited degree, and the client uses the therapeutic relationship to test a new balance between dependence and self-reliance. The so-called "resistance," in other words, actually facilitates some level of exchange based on the clients developmental goals (Wheeler, 1991). This, however, can lead to difficulty--especially in brief therapy--if the therapist and client have different goals, especially if the therapist assumes that introjecting is necessarily unhealthy, or that all introjects should be frustrated or challenged.[9] In a longer course of therapy, acknowledging such differences might be therapeutic as perceptions of the relationship are exchanged for the purpose of finding some common ground on goals and how to collaboratively organize the encounter. But that in itself is an intersubjective exchange built upon a longer relationship history, a more stable and structured ground. Introducing such a level of overt phenomenological exchange during the time frame typified by brief therapy for developmental crisis is quite possibly outside the therapeutic window of many late adolescent clients.

It is crucial for therapists to remember that the form of contact a late adolescent client brings to each momentary encounter makes sense given the structured ground; i.e., the organization of prior life experiences and where that person is developmentally. This structured ground is in turn constantly being modified or reorganized (depending on the level of restructuring needed) with new information derived from each new moment of exchange.

Because late adolescent clients are limited in the number and variety of prior experiences compared to adult clients, and because they are often invested in a vast reorganization of the meaning of those experiences, they typically and understandably practice a "resistance" to full expressive and collaborative therapy.

A Spectrum of Intersubjective Exchange

The common thread tying together contact forms, functions, and feedback is the significance they have in modulating the intersubjective exchange. The potential exchange of subjective experience and reciprocal influence is also based on the combined support resources of both parties and the purpose of the encounter. Table 4 represents the notion of contact as a range of availability for intersubjective exchange, a felt experience of reciprocal influence between two conscious beings. We organize this spectrum of exchange into three continuous areas: diminished, modulated, and full. The left extreme of the spectrum represents the least measure of intersubjective exchange wherein conservation, self-protection and preservation of the status quo are emphasized over novel existential experiences and availability for immediate reciprocal influence. The result is a diminished opportunity for nourishment of self and others, as well as decreased probability of conflict resolution. Further to the right on the continuum growth through exchange is emphasized. The points along the spectrum do not represent traits or permanent conditions. This is the range of contact in which most people up-and-down regulate on a moment-to-moment basis with some stylistic preferences noticeable over time.

In a diminished state the intersubjective exchange may be so because of a person's underdeveloped abilities, or the exchange is down-regulated to the extreme as a reaction to massive threat or absence of support. The extreme avoidance of any subject-to-subject exchange might be based on choice and awareness or reactive style. If manifested as a pervasive style, interpersonal differences are likely to be so threatening that exchange has to be severely limited for any relationship to happen at all. There is neither a desire to process the lack of exchange nor an openness to experiment. A person in this state believes there is more to lose than to gain. This state is frequently experienced by people with personality disorders, as well as persons undergoing traumatic stress. It is very functional in certain contexts, severely limiting in others.

At modulated levels of intersubjective exchange, many forms of contact are utilized functionally, with or without awareness. In interactions represented by the left portion of this middle area, forms of contact might be obvious, especially if they are stylistic or utilized in the context of severe stress. Awareness has a cost; there is limited willingness to look at these functional dynamics and what they mean in terms of organizing and limiting the exchange. Outside the therapy room, a person engaging in this modulated range of exchange might be able to meet a need from another, but the person on the other side of the interaction, if open to and seeking a more full interchange of subjective experience, may experience an unsatisfying struggle. In clinical terms, the client might organize the therapist as an object in service of emotional and developmental needs, and invite the therapist to enter into an encounter through a very narrow opening. This notion is similar to the Self Psychology concept of selfobject, in which only very specific aspects and behaviors on the part of the therapist are likely to create opportunities for what might eventually evolve into a fuller form of

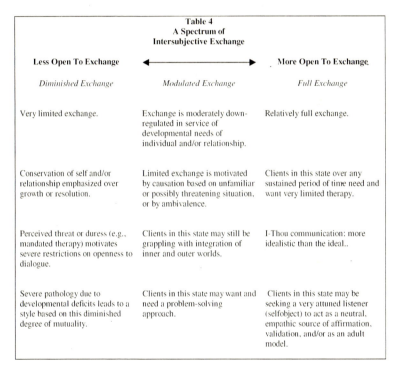

Table 4 **A Spectrum of** **Intersubjective Exchange**		
Less Open To Exchange ⟵————————⟶		**More Open To Exchange**
Diminished Exchange	*Modulated Exchange*	*Full Exchange*
Very limited exchange.	Exchange is moderately down-regulated in service of developmental needs of individual and/or relationship.	Relatively full exchange.
Conservation of self and/or relationship emphasized over growth or resolution.	Limited exchange is motivated by causation based on unfamiliar or possibly threatening situation, or by ambivalence.	Clients in this state over any sustained period of time need and want very limited therapy.
Perceived threat or duress (e.g., mandated therapy) motivates severe restrictions on openness to dialogue.	Clients in this state may still be grappling with integration of inner and outer worlds.	I-Thou communication; more idealistic than the ideal..
Severe pathology due to developmental deficits leads to a style based on this diminished degree of mutuality.	Clients in this state may want and need a problem-solving approach.	Clients in this state may be seeking a very attuned listener (selfobject) to act as a neutral, empathic source of affirmation, validation, and/or as an adult model.

exchange (Lynch, 1991). If the therapist is indeed willing to bracket off the expression of many of his or her reactions and provide an opportunity for a restricted but nonetheless supportive exchange, the client can take something from the interaction. The therapeutic encounter, though restricted in this sense, is an investment in the developmental progress of the client, and in future interactions that are likely to be more reciprocal.

Moving to the right within the area of modulated exchange, both sides of an interaction are more likely to experience a reciprocal exchange of needs being met, but not necessarily equally. If two people cannot find a

similar "place" on the spectrum where they can meet, one or both will probably experience a noticeable and unresolved level of frustration and dissatisfaction. One person is sustained in some need, the other's needs are largely deferred, but not at the level of exploitation. Differences are somewhat
threatening but navigable.

Moving still further right into the area labeled "full exchange," the
various forms of contact are employed more consciously, and function in the
service of expectations and purposes. There is heightened curiosity about
intrapsychic and interpersonal processes and thus more willingness to experiment in the moment. As two or more participants in an interaction approach
a relatively full level of intersubjective exchange, their inner lives become
more available and influential to each other; all sides of an encounter experience gaining something. All sides are very aware of and have a context for
stimuli on either side of the phenomenological boundary. There is a mutual
sense of worth, in tender intimacy, passionate discourse, and in conflict, all
parties are respected, respectful, and open to influence by the other.

In the context of therapy we consider the full exchange as idealis-
tic, as opposed to ideal. Much of human interaction, including therapy, takes
place somewhere in the modulated range of exchange. A relatively full
exchange, or what in traditional Gestalt therapy terms would be called "full
contact," is not necessarily better as it depends on the situation. The capacity or option for such dialogical encounters is, however, a mark of successful development in late adolescence and adulthood. But if there is an ideal
level of exchange between late adolescent client and older therapist, it is the
level at which the adolescent is accepting of his or her degree of awareness,
thus experiencing a sense of choice and responsibility, and the level at which
she or he is most likely to effectively "mine the resources of the adult world"
(McConville, 1995) so as to be able to relate more effectively to others outside of therapy. What we are describing as "full intersubjective exchange"
happens on a very limited basis between therapist and late adolescent client-
-especially in brief therapy--as people in this age group modulate the degree
of exchange according to pressing developmental, cultural, and self-organizing needs. In theory, bracketing off part of one's experience, or at least the
expression thereof, is certainly not antithetical to Gestalt therapy. In practice
and in temperament, however, seeking such a full person-to-person
exchange may be a strong preference for most Gestalt-influenced therapists.
Many who are attracted to Gestalt and other humanistic approaches are so
oriented because of the opportunities for the dialogical encounter associated
with contemporary existential therapy. But for the many reasons discussed

above, such an encounter is not always what one gets with adolescent clients. Expecting to achieve a mutually expressive, full intersubjective exchange is not realistic, and can have a prescriptive quality to it. We find Yontef's (1993) statement about humanistic tyranny relevant to all therapy, but perhaps especially so when working with adolescents: "when (a therapist) demands a mutuality that is so complete as to eliminate a differentiation of roles between the professional therapist and the patient, this does violence to the allowing aspect of I and Thou" (Yontef, 1993, p. 225; parenthetical clarification added).

Two Levels of Therapy

Many late adolescent clients come to therapy hoping and expecting the problem is not connected to other aspects of their lives and thus can be handled simply and quickly. They come interested in symptom relief, and by older adult standards are overly focused on a specific manifestation of some pattern; they often fail to appreciate the structured ground from which figures emanate and are given meaning. They also have a fairly simple cause and effect process for thinking about their problems, especially in crisis mode where interpretations tend to be developmentally regressive. Previous attempts to solve a problem may have been unsatisfactory as context and style of relating were left unexamined; the problem with a girlfriend was not seen as connected to the problem with a roommate or parent--or therapist.

The "big picture" can provide both support and frustration for the client. Missing the larger developmental context often leads the late adolescent client to minimize the significance of a problem. Conversely, it can create or magnify fears of pathology or inadequacy. Clients frequently apologize for their problems and believe (with prejudice to self) that their peers and certainly older adults are coping more readily with some stated concern. But examining the larger developmental context comes with a cost; it involves more self-disclosure, more time, energy, and responsibility. It may indicate the problem is wider in scope that previously thought, and that a more difficult response is needed for adequate resolution. Seeing life in more relativistic terms often requires major reorganization, and has implications for other issues, both academic and personal. All of this can feel overwhelming.

On the other hand, discovering patterns is precisely what draws some clients to therapy in the first place. Given enough failed relationships or another long enough string of painful events and many late adolescents will eventually look (or accept an invitation to look) at their own ways of construing reality and relating to others as tentative explanations for their suffering. They might overstate or understate such hypotheses, but at least they consider them. They may find a broader understanding comforting for its elucidation on why previous attempts at resolution were not successful. And an interpersonal focus will feel supportive for some clients in that the presenting problem can be addressed in the safety of the therapeutic relationship. Others will appreciate the practicality of having the immediate data of the therapist-client relationship available for study and experimentation. Anchoring an interpersonal issue in a developmental context will seem totally relevant to some clients who are eager to reorganize their relationships towards a more satisfying balance of intimacy and independence.

But many late adolescent clients simply do not have the data base, as it were, or enough perspective about existing data, to lead them to such "natural" hypotheses. Perhaps more importantly, many do not have enough experience with success in one or more of life's domains to have the basic sense of self-worth required to face such potentially painful thoughts. They may cling tenaciously to a narrower perspective on their problems, placing corresponding limitations on therapists' options. Clients who do not see problems as related to interpersonal style are obviously unlikely to see the potential benefit of an interpersonal focus in therapy. Group therapy also seems less relevant to them, unless it involves structured groups dealing with a single topic. An interpersonal focus in individual or group therapy is experienced as too intense and anxiety provoking for some late adolescent clients, especially if the interpersonal system being analyzed is the therapist-client relationship itself.

But the fact is that most adolescent clients do not fit neatly into either of the two categories described above. While some are motivated toward exploring a developmental and interpersonal perspective, and some are adamantly against it, most are ambivalent. They want a limited amount of help from the adult world in their attempt to solve "the problem," but are willing, at certain moments or in some sessions, to entertain the notion that they are actively organizing the phenomenological and interpersonal worlds and have more choice and power than originally conceived. We therefore conceptualize two levels of therapy for late adolescent clients. The first level of therapy addresses the demands of the presenting problem; the second level, if needed and allowed, explores the bigger and more complex picture.

Podolonick, et al. (1979), describing his psychoanalytic "Time Specified Therapy," advocates a ten-session model with late adolescents.

The approach consists of two assessment interviews followed by eight treatment sessions in which the therapist and client work on two interrelated goals, one concrete and the other more abstract. Goal One is based on the assessment of the presenting problem and aims at symptom reduction or problem resolution. This goal works with what is immediately available in awareness concerning specific behaviors and conscious feelings. Goal Two is an attempt, in psychodynamic language, to stimulate the development of ego functions. It is focused on process and developmental themes and includes conscious and unconscious issues within which the presenting problem is embedded. Goal Two is directly stated to the client in the form of an interpretation about what is going on developmentally, and aims to foster the client's awareness of the connection between the presenting problem and current developmental demands. Goal Two also involves creating an appreciation of the analytical, perspective-taking approach for exploring and understanding one's underlying dynamics. Podolonick does not see this second goal as being resolved in such a brief therapy format. The aims of Time Specified Therapy are to achieve goal one and introduce the perspective of looking at problems more deeply, examining current dynamics as a method of understanding unconscious motivation. Extensive work on Goal Two was seen as beyond the scope of brief therapy, and in fact as a life-long task.

While a pre-determined number of sessions is likely to be useful with some clients, especially a therapy-wise and therapy-desirous population, it is generally not flexible enough for the varying needs of most of the late adolescent client we see, most of whom have very high ambivalence about seeking professional help. For the many reasons discussed above, we believe only a limited number of our clients would agree to such a structure. We also take issue with the emphasis placed on the therapist uncovering the underlying dynamics that contribute to the presenting problem, rather than having the therapist offer tentative interpretations and attempting to foster more of a client discovery process concerning developmental context. Nonetheless, we find it quite useful to organize our brief therapy interventions within a two-level intervention model. Each level is subdivided according to two broad categories of interventions: Developmental Phenomenological Reflecting (D/P-R) and Developmental Phenomenological Experimenting (D/P-E). Table 5 summarizes levels or therapy and categories of interventions.

As in the Time Specified Therapy, we advocate focusing attention on the presenting problem and as opportunity allows introducing the possibility of exploring the relationship between the presenting problem and its developmental and interpersonal context. In Gestalt terms we suggest alternating attention between Level One, focusing on the figure, and Level Two, subtly but honestly shifting focus to developmental ground and the more complex relationship between various figures. The goal of Level One is the destructuring of a well-formed, phenomenological figure manifested behaviorally as a reduction in some symptom of distress or the amelioration of a problematic situation.

Level One asks questions such as:
- What is the problem/symptom as the client currently sees it?
- What thoughts and feelings are the client aware of?
- What developmental task is the client most focused on?
- How has the client tried to solve the problem or reduce the symptom?

The goals of Level Two are to promote a broader understanding of self from a field theory or interpersonal perspective, to encourage an appreciation for the influence of family of origin on phenomenological and interpersonal style, and to facilitate a deeper level of creative adjustment that will enable the client to become more flexible and adept at meeting a wide range of psychological and developmental needs from his or her world of relationships. Level Two asks questions such as:
- What is the bigger picture, the larger gestalt? What are the general organizing principles employed by

Table 5 Levels of Therapy and Categories of Interventions		
	LEVEL ONE	**LEVEL TWO**
DEVELOPMENTAL/ PHENOMENOLOGICAL REFLECTING (D/P-R)	Empathy Highlighting awareness of presenting problem and the developmental task to which it is related	Grounding in historical developmental context Facilitating awareness of dilemmas and splits Here-and-now interpersonal reflections Promoting a field perspective
DEVELOPMENTAL/ PHENOMENOLOGICAL EXPERIMENTING (D/P-E)	Problem-solving experiments (e.g., brainstorming, role-playing, "what if" fantasies, etc.) Behavioral experiments outside of therapy with results evaluated and explored in next session	Integrating splits Here-and-now interpersonal experiments Experiment with client-therapist relationship

this individual?

- How is the presenting figure shaped or sustained by historical developmental context?

- How is current distress created or maintained by the relationship between the child self gestalt and the family of origin?

- How can the child self and the emerging adult self integrate their apparently competing efforts in such a way as to eliminate the need for the presenting problem?

- How do the dynamics of the therapist-client relationship manifest the intrapsychic and interpersonal struggles which brought the client to therapy, and how can the therapeutic relationship allow for a relatively safe exploration of and experimentation with new dynamics that can be eventually applied outside of therapy?

And while the language is likely to be different, these questions are asked directly to the client. While many late adolescent clients do not start therapy with a well-developed notion of a larger configuration, many are amenable, depending on several variables including the art and perceived caring of the therapist, to begin considering such a perspective. They are likely to do this by permitting digressions, as it were--side trips that consider the larger meaning of the current problem--but returning from such deliberation until psychological and interpersonal resources can support another visit. Influenced by Podolonick, et al.'s (1979) model, we do not see Level Two as something to be completed in brief therapy. While it does have immediate utilitarian value in that many clients are relieved or motivated by a deeper and more contextual understanding of their difficulties, it ultimately remains an introduction for many if not most adolescent clients.

Level One includes some interventions commonly associated with Gestalt therapy as well as those comparable with other traditional therapies such as client-centered and cognitive-behavioral. The therapist demonstrates empathy and other Developmental/Phenomenological Reflections (D/P-R1) that highlight awareness of the presenting problem and its immediate structure (e.g., "So you're angry at your roommate, and she's dating your friend, Tom, and you feel guilty whenever you talk to him--its hard to sort out these different relationships, isn't it?"). Level One also includes Developmental/Phenomenological Experimenting (D/P-E) aimed at addressing the immediate problem within the limited context of the contemporary factors that sustain it (e.g., "Imagine telling Tom that your feelings about your roommate have nothing to do with your friendship with him.") Furthermore, we allow for the importance of methods that call upon the therapist to act as a source of expertise and encouragement--the therapist-as-coach (e.g., mentoring, teaching, consulting, advising, reassuring)--and at times to suggest specific response-oriented behavior strategies. Such methods can serve as both reflections and experiments. As reflections they indicate to the client that he or she is being understood in a request for immediate, tangible help. Coaching, if properly timed, is an investment in a subsequently more collaborative relationship. It also functions as experimenting if the therapist calls his or her plays, so to speak, in a spirit of throwing out a possibility that may or may not work, and remembers to always inquire as to the effect of such suggestions (and their attempted implementation) on the client. At some point the client comes to realize that along with encouragement there is a question implicit in the suggestion, and that he or she alone can find a suitable answer.

We believe that as long as this aspect of coaching is kept in mind, any technique or approach promoting developmental progress, regardless of the theory with which it is originally associated, is compatible with a Gestalt therapy framework. Techniques (such as behavior analysis and consultation, hypnosis, relaxation training, etc.) can help a client to achieve a tangible sense of relief from a figural problem or symptom while still being integrated into an existential framework. Such techniques may in fact be the medium through which some late adolescent clients initiate a meaningful connection and exchange with others, including a therapist. Level One, in short, is the gateway to a potential connection that is necessary if Level Two is to be an option.

As McConville (1995) has noted the ability in younger adolescents to make use of the resources of the adult world is often one of the successful *process* outcomes of therapy. The therapist who focuses too much on helping to build a fishing pole when the client is focused on simply catching a fish is likely to become frustrated, or feel like an inept salesperson. Many brief therapy clients return for additional therapy at a later date because they felt taken seriously in their first encounter. To ignore this investment potential can be quite costly to the therapeutic relationship. Consider the following fantasy dialogue:

> *Client:* I'm hungry. Got a fish I could eat right now?
> *Therapist:* Sure, but if you were to discover how to

use a fishing pole, think of how many fish you coul-
get on your own. You'd never go hungry again.
Client: (I guess this person didn't hear me. I'll try
again.) I'm hungry. I mean really hungry. Got a fish I
could eat right now?
Therapist: (I guess this person didn't hear me. He
doesn't understand that the locus of change is within.
I'll try again.) Consider the incredible possibilities of
having your very own fishing pole, maybe even one
you designed yourself. Think of the human potential!
I can help you get that, if you give me some time.
Client: (Either this person doesn't have a fish or he's
messing with me. How clear can I make it?)

After a few more rounds of this the late adolescent client will probably leave
therapy prematurely. "Oh well," thinks the therapist, "That young person
just wasn't ready to change."

Some of these proposals may seem incompatible with one of the
guiding principles of Gestalt therapy. The Gestalt approach has always valued the creation of a client-discovery environment, as opposed to supplying
solutions and formulas, or "uncovering" the client's unconscious feelings
and thoughts. There is an emphasis on not providing "the answer," the "correct" interpretation. But a client-discovery environment presupposes that a
collaborative relationship has been achieved. For many late adolescent
clients this acceptance of a collaborative process is eventually attained,
assuming they stick around, but it is resisted for understandable reasons
related to normal development discussed above. The typical brevity of the
therapeutic relationship intensifies the need for flexibility and a fundamental commitment to honoring the client's world and a willingness to meet in
a relationship that fits the client's current developmental needs. Such a commitment may come at the expense of some therapists' preferred methods of
a dialogical exchange and an interest in creative therapeutic experiments.

In short, we think it is possible (and sometimes necessary) to hand out fish
while intermittently alluding to the life-long developmental goal of constructing and reconstructing a functional, flexible, strong fishing pole. Level
One interventions, both reflecting and experimenting, are the foundation
upon which Level Two interventions are based. Put another way, the therapist practicing brief therapy influenced by Gestalt thinking and methods can
employ very focused problem solving methods, some associated with
Gestalt therapy and some apparently contrary to it. Whatever the method,

the posture is *"Hello, I understand that you're out on a limb here, that coming to me is in and of itself a developmental dilemma. I'll meet you here and point to some other places we may or may not choose to go today, or maybe tomorrow."*

The first intent of Level Two interventions is to support the client in developing a broader understanding of the problem, hopefully to assuage anxious and shameful feelings related to a particular response or lack of response. If this is all that is achieved beyond the Level One focus, therapy is likely to be significantly helpful to the client, even if the problem eventually reemerges in a different form at a later date. Learning is cumulative and the seed of a more comprehensive grasp on the problem will eventually sprout in due time if conditions are right. Another intention for Level Two interventions is to stir up interest in still further exploration of the client's phenomenological and interpersonal process beyond the resolution of the immediate problem but always keeping the Level One goal in sight for the sake of the client's satisfaction and sense of being taken seriously. In those cases in which Level Two interventions lead to a rapid redefinition of the problem and a commitment to a wider exploration of the structured ground, the therapist proceeds accordingly.

Level Two includes narrative exploration of the historical developmental context, which we refer to as groundwork. It goes beyond the quick references to developmental tasks characteristic of Level One, and involves exploration of present developmental themes and problems *over a number of situations*. Level Two D/P-R's involve the therapist explicitly making sense of the Level One problem in such a context ("Your descriptions of your father's angry outbursts help me understand why you got so anxious when the coach criticized you.") Level Two D/P-R's may also include facilitating awareness of dilemmas and splits. Facilitating dilemmas is an idea borrowed from McConville (1995) to promote the awareness of internal conflicts. Such heightened awareness contributes to an assessment of the presenting problem and offers the client a glimpse of the complexity of one's inner life and how it influences human relationships and related difficulties; (e.g., "Yes, you would like to be different in this situation, I can really hear that, and I guess I'm wondering if any part of you is okay with things as they are now. Do you think you get anything positive at all with the present situation?") McConville (1995) suggests and illustrates several other ways of trying to get the client interested in the unaware and projected part of the inner self, such as role playing and fantasy musings about successful resolution which we consider being Developmental/Phenomenological-

Experimenting. Other Level Two Reflections might involve the here-and-now interpersonal focus by simply pointing out that the client had a similar reaction or adopted a similar stance with the therapist as in the problem situation, and wondering aloud about the parallel experience. A favorable response by the client might lead to Level Two Experimenting, such as inviting the client to "try on" different responses to the therapist--behaviors the client wishes to implement regarding the presenting problem--for example being assertive or critical or complementary. Other Level Two Experimenting could include facilitating the client toward owning the projected sides of a dilemma, doing polarity integration work, and/or exploring how one acts out the dilemma in the interpersonal arena. A Level Two Reflection that attempts to promote a field compatible perspective on the presenting problem may simply involve the therapist alluding to instances wherein the client and some peer or older adult apparently held divergent perspectives on some phenomenon. A related Level Two Experiment might be to gently challenge the client's presuming to know about the thoughts or intentions of someone else, and asking him or her to consider an alternative hypothesis as well as the implications it would bring.

Needless to say both Level One and Level Two interventions, and both Reflecting and Experimenting, need to be graded according to the strength of the therapist-client bond and the capacity and interests of the client. Higher graded interventions tend to highlight differences of perspective between the client and the therapist and may be threatening to many late adolescent clients, especially early in the relationship. Many late adolescent clients react with defensiveness to feedback that sheds light on what is outside their present awareness. Such feedback, however well intended by a therapist, is often not accepted as new and relevant information but rather as some basic threat implying they are missing something important. There is a fragility in the late adolescent perspective on self. People in this age group are often defensively invested in the idea that a given perspective be "right," rather than appreciating the potential valuable of a point of view simply because it is different. There is often the expectation that the therapeutic encounter will be a one-up/one-down relationship. Some clients therefore adopt a controlling stance, offering few if any opportunities to be influenced by a therapist. Others are very compliant, wanting to be told what to do and how to do it. Either extreme may be jettisoned outside the therapist's office. There is often a lack of internal and environmental support for exploration of different vantage points--or even for different vantage points within the self, the inner conflicts. There is frequently a dualistic tendency toward establishing rightness and utility, rather than an interest in and tolerance for exploration of various ways of organizing phenomena that can lead to more lasting effectiveness in some area. It is crucial for the therapist to attend to all of these possibilities early and gently. With additional developmental progress, and in part because of a supportive therapeutic field, a stronger sense of self can evolve along with a more balanced perspective between control and compliance; between being committed to a perspective and yet remaining open to other influences. Much of this is related to the potentially intimate nature of therapy and the client's lack of confidence and familiarity relating to an older adult in such a way. This produces a strong reluctance to disclose and explore information about areas where late adolescent clients may be judged to be lacking by an adult.

Compared to older clients, there is often less of a need to experience and experiment. The late adolescent college student is probably experimenting on a daily basis in one or more areas of development. University life is extremely social and experiments with altering consciousness, exploring intimacy and sexuality, and being influenced by authority figures are common. College students often need someone to help them consolidate and make sense of such experiences rather than be encouraged to experiment further. Many clients indicate that their friends are not much help with the integration of new information because the friends themselves are also in flux and have the same need. Clients therefore often express a desire for an "objective" advisor to help them make meaning of life experiences. They are seeking someone who will not "take sides" with one side of the polarity between child and adolescent selves. This necessitates the therapist dealing with counter-transference feelings and avoiding identification with either a rebel or a parental perspective. It sometimes requires playing the devil's advocate role for the sake of exploration rather than persuasion.

Using a sports metaphor, one could look at late adolescent clients as having tried a bad play, and are conferring with the coach for instruction--an experience that can feel like support and punishment. The players want to get quickly back into the game to redeem themselves in their own eyes and in those of their friends in the stands. They want to prove they can do it right, that the bad play was a momentary lapse, and not a large deficiency. When players get hurt, they want to "play through the pain," hoping it is not a major injury. There is strong desire not to let the pain change how the game is played--not to attend to the pain as a message of limitation or guidance requiring some major adjustment. The coach is heady and strategic, focused on the big picture; the players are afraid to get too self-conscious, and thus off their game. The coach has a role to play, but the game is much more important than the practices, the strategy sessions, and the review.

Finding a Figure

Working with late adolescent clients in developmental crisis necessitates finding both a focus and a context, and helping the person connect the two. It is linking the content of their problems to some vernacular expression of developmental tasks; a process that produces a lot of "Yeah, that's right." This makes sense to clients and calms their fears of abnormality. Receiving this developmental vantage point also allows a client some breathing room, some distancing from the urgency of the immediate problem.

When the content touches on more than one task we try to direct our comments to the task that seems to evoke most energy from the client. In this section we will provide examples of relating content to each of the five tasks.

1. Reorganizing immediate awareness

Late adolescent clients tend to experience a high level of anxiety around a moment-to-moment focus on current awareness. To discover how one is organizing the awareness process during the immediate act of being aware can be intense and difficult. Focusing on content as a way of introducing this concern is certainly less threatening to most clients than a more here-and-now approach to heightening awareness. Example: "Your story suggests that you get stuck on what you are feeling or what some other person is feeling; you can't seem to go back and forth. Finding a way to have both available to you is very important and something you seem to be working on." The therapist might then ask a question about how this happens in other situations, "When is it better and when is it worse?" After assessing along these lines, the therapist might invite the client to practice in the session, and/or select a safe peer to experiment with outside of therapy. A Level Two probe related to this example would be: "I can see how this makes sense from what you have said before, how you had long periods in your life where you felt you mostly focused on the other person and then on yourself, and now you see you need to do both." A deeper Level Two intervention would be: "The way you responded in that situation reminds me of your descriptions of your mother--you said she tended to be either really focused on you or really absorbed with her own feelings."

2. Reorganizing peer relationships

Peer relationships are still maximally important to the late adolescent. It is important to assess for the importance of various peer relationships, as well as recent changes in peer relationships. Example: "You seem to be valuing your new friends more and feel you have more in common with them, that they know you better than your friends back home. It is hard to break out of old roles with old friends?" A Level Two probe might be to focus on the ambivalence about giving up some of those friends or those old roles. Particularly important is having them know and keep track of who is being supportive and affirming and what they do to elicit those responses or deny themselves those responses. Who they choose to be close to and how well they use peers for support can certainly be grounded in the family of origin context.

3. Reorganizing authority

Shifting the authority from parents to self and at the same time learning to respect and be critical of other authority figures is a challenge for adolescents. Connecting interrelated tasks can be very helpful. Example: "You know you have to make this career decision but you know you haven't made many decisions for yourself before, so you don't feel very confident." A Level Two probe might involve looking at the split: "You seem to go back and forth between wanting to make this decision yourself and wanting your parents or these career tests to make it for you. That must be frustrating." A more intense intervention would be to suggest that the client is also hoping the therapist will make the decision.

4. Reorganizing self

Loss and trauma are often what reorganize self. It is certainly not uncommon to hear about a history of abuse, deaths of significant others, or the loss of an important romantic relationship, to name a few. A Level One reflection might point out how a loss is contributing to current distress. Example: "You've really been dealing with a lot of sadness and regret. I wonder if that is related to the disagreements with your girlfriend." A Level Two reflection might point out a wider scope of reorganization. Example:

"You seem to be saying you've become much more critical of yourself since you broke up with her. You must be in a lot of pain."

5. Reorganizing the organizing process itself

One immediate aspect of reorganizing the organizing process is found in answers to the question "Why now?" Budman and Gurman (1988) use the question to begin the process of focusing the goals of therapy and listening for what shift in perspective is already happening. They point out that the client's issues have been around for a while but something related to how the problem is interpreted, or about how seeking help is evaluated, has shifted, and finding out about that shift leads to an energized focus for therapy. They advocate framing the answer to "Why now?" in terms of a very specific developmental and generally interpersonal event. Example:

Therapist: I wonder what event led you to come here today instead of a few months ago. It sounds like you were unhappy in your relationship then too.

Client: I just thought I should talk to somebody about this.

Therapist: What specifically was going through your mind when you picked up the phone to make the appointment? Who or what were you thinking about?

Client: Oh, that. Well, I had another fight with my girlfriend the night before. And then that morning I just couldn't stop thinking about some of the stupid things I had said to her, just to hurt her. The fact is I've been a real jerk with several different women that I've dated.

Therapist: It sounds like how you thought about that fight was different, that you felt bad about what you said in the fight.

Client: Yeah. I know it's me, I get so jealous of her past boyfriends. I know she was pretty close to some of them and even had sex with some of them. I just start thinking that she would rather be with them. Then I throw it in her face, you know, her being sexual with somebody else before me and all that. I even called her a slut the other day. Really, she doesn't give me any reason not to trust her.

Therapist: I hear you thinking more about you and what you are thinking and feeling in this relationship. It sounds like you're struggling with how to be intimate with her when you know she has cared about other people before you. It's like you get scared and then you try to push her away.

Client: Yeah. I've never admitted that before. But it's true.

Therapist: So now you're also looking at yourself in a different way, and allowing yourself to feel things that you used to somehow keep out of your mind.

Client: Yeah. Because I don't want to lose her.

Therapist: I know you said your previous relationships usually didn't last very long. Do you think this scared feeling, this insecurity, happened in those relationships?

As illustrated here, the connecting conceptualization should be linked to the client's focus, should be very conscious on the part of the therapist, and should be shared with the client in consumer-friendly or "experience-near" language. In addition to the larger tasks of re-organizing self and intimate relationships with peers, this client is offering a specific interpersonal focus. He is describing an unresolved conflict with a specific peer with whom he is attempting unsuccessfully to have a more intimate relationship. Both things are evident: a reorganizing about his contribution to the interpersonal problem and the momentum for coming to therapy. The young woman he is dating is very figural in his mind and is important enough to him that he took the rather risky step of asking for help. This leads to the possibility of incorporating his girlfriend into the therapy or of at least keeping her and their system in focus as he explores the larger issue of his relationship with women and with himself. Her reactions will influence how he feels about therapeutic experiments and the changes he attempts to make in the relationship.

Assessment Consideration
1. Degree of distress

Some degree of distress is always what brings people to therapy. Distress is very analogous to the relationship between anxiety and motivation. A certain amount of anxiety is motivational; if it gets too high it becomes debilitating. When distress gets too high the client wants crisis management, not therapy. Late adolescent clients are especially focused on something happening right away. We distinguish crisis counseling from brief therapy, but acknowledge there is a gray area. So the first assessment issue addresses the question of how much distress the client is experiencing. Clearly with more distress, the client is seeking immediate relief and is pulling for some real structure and directiveness from the therapist. Working in a college setting frequently calls upon the therapist to enter into the client's construed notion of crisis and provide the more directive responses, knowing full well that many clients will disappear as soon as the distress level drops. But even in one session crisis counseling it is imperative to meet the late adolescent client in his or her reality. Many times these clients return later with less distress and higher motivation for therapy. Other clients come with little or no stress, accompanying someone else as a system participant, or coming because someone else has asked or demanded that they seek help. These clients often lack sufficient personal distress to be interested in therapy.

2. Level of developmental maturity

Getting to Level Two work in a brief format requires a certain level of maturity or having acquired certain psychological capacities. This can be broken down into self-support, psychological mindedness, and relativistic thinking. Relevant assessment questions include: Can the person find sufficient support to tolerate the anxiety and discomfort that accompanies increased awareness? Does the person have a support network in place or has that system been taxed to its limit (and may have referred the person for help)? Is the person already overtaxed with demands for time and energy? How compartmentalized are problematic situations or events? Is the person looking for patterns and looking for the bigger picture? How much is the person trying to deal with the problem but limit its scope? Can the person appreciate the gray area in each of life's many decisions and issues?

3. Level of awareness

Level of awareness is another important area of assessment. Generally the more aware a client is already, the more and sooner they can tolerate intensity in therapy, which makes for more productivity in a brief format. How much can they tolerate an inner focus and maintain that focus in a relationship context? Do they have a balance between inner and outer focus? In general, the less the late adolescent's willingness and capacity to tolerate an inner focus, the shorter their stay in any kind of therapy. The therapist might be willing and able to help the client increase tolerance for awareness, but this is unlikely to be identified or accepted as a goal of a late adolescent client. Similarly, being able to shuttle fluidly between and inner and outer focus may be readily identified as a problem but the client may not be willing to work on or practice that in here-and-now due to self-consciousness.

4. What are the person's expectations about length of therapy?

Our center's intake form asks how many sessions the client expects to need. Clients often comment during the first interview, "I didn't really know what to put, so I just guessed." This "guess" is not assumed to be a contract or even an accurate assessment, but it does offer some insight into how a client begins to organize the therapeutic encounter. When an 18-year-old circles that they expect one or two sessions to meet their needs, it suggests that they have a very limited interest--if any--in the big picture, as it were. In contrast, when a late adolescent client indicates they want the maximum number of sessions (fifteen per year at our center), it raises other possibilities. Perhaps it is a mature or therapy-wise client who is ready to work on a perceived pattern of problematic behaviors or interpersonal interactions. Or perhaps it is someone who is confluent in their relationship to authority figures. All of this is hypothesis, of course, but offers the therapist some idea of how brief the therapy might be, and how narrow the goals need to be.

Concluding Remarks

As therapists working with late adolescent clients, we struggle to preserve a coherent approach to counseling while looking for ways to meet young people across a gulf of divergent developmental needs and experiences. To accomplish this, we have had to reorganize some of our beliefs and expectations about effective therapy, and enter into dialogue, as it were, with other theories. This process has led us to a more flexible interpretation of the concept of "contact," and to sometimes accept as a form of contact the need of many late adolescents to seek from a therapist what self-psychologists call mirroring, rather than a more personal relationship. We have also challenged ourselves to alternate our focus between levels of therapy, and to remain patient and empathic when a client's "big gestalt" was clearly the only thing that mattered to the young person sitting across the room.

We see these and other adjustments as emanating from the dialogic heritage of Gestalt Therapy theory, which values meeting people where they are, and deeply respects how human beings configure their worlds.

References

Budman, S., & Gurman, A. (1988). *Theory and practice of brief therapy.* New York, NY: Guilford Press.

Chickering, A., & Associates. (1981). *The modern american college: Responding to the new realities of diverse students and a changing society.* San Francisco, CA: Jossey-Bass.

Clarkson, P. & Mackewn, J. (1993). *Fritz Perls.* Thousand Oaks, CA: Sage.

Crocker, S. (1981). Proflection. *The Gestalt Journal, 4*(2), 13-34.

Erikson, E. (1968). *Identity: Youth and crisis.* New York: W.W. Norton.

Grayson, P. (1989). The college psychotherapy client: An overview. In P.A. Grayson & K. Cauley (Eds.). *College Psychotherapy* (pp. 8-28). New York, NY: Guilford.

Harman, R. (1995). Gestalt therapy as brief therapy. *The Gestalt Journal, 18*(2), 77-87.

Hersh, J. (1988). A commentary on brief therapy. *Journal of College Student Psychotherapy, 3*(1), 55-59.

Kepner, J. (1987). *Body process: A gestalt approach to working with the bod in psychotherapy.* New York, NY: Gardner Press.

Kiesler, D. (1988). *Therapeutic metacommunication.* Palo Alto, CA: Consulting Psychologists Press.

Lynch, V. (1991). Understanding self psychology. In H. Jackson (Ed.), *Using Self Psychology in Psychotherapy* (pp. 15-26). Northvale, NJ: Jason Aronson.

Marcia, J. (1966). Development and validation of ego identity status. *Journal of Personality and Social Psychology, 3*, 551-558.

May, R. (1988). Brief psychotherapy with college students. *Journal of College Student Psychotherapy, 3*(1), 17-39.

McConville, M. (1995). *Adolescence: Psychotherapy and the emergent self.* San Francisco, CA: Jossey-Bass.

Perls, F. (1969). *Gestalt therapy verbatim.* Moab, UT: Real People Press.

Perls, F., Hefferline, R., & Goodman, P. (1994). *Gestalt therapy: Excitement and growth in the human personality.* Highland, NY: Gestalt Journal Press.

Perry, W. (1970). *Forms of intellectual and ethical development in the college years: A scheme.* New York, NY: Holt, Rinehart & Winston.

Podolnick, E., Pass, H., & Bybee, D. (1979). A psychodynamic approach to brief therapy. *Journal of American College Health Association, 28,* 109-113.

Polster, E. (1990). Tight therapeutic sequences. In B.J. Zeig and S. Gilligan (Eds.), *Brief therapy: Myths, methods, and metaphors* (pp. 378-389). New York: Brunner/Mazel.

Polster, E., & Polster, M. (1973). *Gestalt therapy integrated.* New York, NY: Random House.

Slavin, J. (1987). Readiness of psychotherapy in late adolescence. Presented at the Fall Conference of the Philadelphia Society for Psychoanalytic Psychology, Philadelphia, PA, September, 19th. Cited in R. Webb & J. Widseth (1988), Facilitating students' going into and stepping back from their inner worlds. *Journal of College Student Psychotherapy, 3*(1), 5-17.

Stoehr, T. (1994). *Here, now, next: Paul Goodman and the origins of gestalt therapy.* San Francisco, CA: Jossey-Bass.

Webb, R., & Widseth, J. (1988). Facilitating students' going into and stepping back from their inner worlds. *Journal of College Student Psychotherapy, 3*(1), 5-17.

Wheeler, G. (1991). *Gestalt reconsidered: A new approach to contact and resistance.* New York, NY: Gardner Press.

Yontef, G. (1993). *Awareness, dialogue, & process: Essays on gestalt therapy.* Highland, NY: The Gestalt Journal Press.

Footnotes

1 The figure-formation to figure-completion cycle consists of identification of desire or need (the figural experience), motivation arousal to try to attain the desire or need, identification of the object of the desire or need, directed action toward that object, and the exchange with the object to attain the desire or need. For the purposes of therapy, the object of desire or need is most often a significant person in the client's life.

2 From the field theory perspective, this is inaccurately referred to as "being on one's own."

3 See Footnote 1.

4 When viewed in this light, Erikson's theory of identity development, especially as expanded by Marcia (1966) could be seen as a theory about the acquisition of an integrated sense of self that incorporates childhood and adolescent identity. *Identity foreclosure* could be viewed as the process of elevating one self paradigm and suppressing the other as a way to deal with the ongoing tension of separate agenda. *Identity diffusion* would refer to getting lost or overwhelmed by the whole process, not feeling comfortable with a foreclosure choice and not being able to create a synthesis.

5 a.k.a. pre-marital sexual relations.

6 Perls valued behaviors that were "aggressive" in the phenomenological sense rather than the frequent connotation of aggression as violent or abusive.

7 As we see it, this way of relating decreases the probability of a mutually satisfying exchange. This is most graphically portrayed in the "Gestalt prayer" (see Perls, 1969, p. 4).

8 Concepts from psychodynamic and self psychology were chosen for their influence on our understanding of what form the therapeutic exchange might take.

9 Ironic examples of introjection, indeed.

Footnotes from Table 3

i The concept of proflection as a resistance or "contact boundary disturbance" was introduced by Sylvia Crocker who defined it as the unawares attempt, typically through modeling, to induce another to provide something (such as caretaking or reassurance) that the self is reasonably capable of providing for its self (Crocker, 1981).

ii In Self Psychology, the person would be thought of as seeking "*mirroring.*"

iii In Self Psychology, the person would be thought of as "idealizing."

iv In Self Psychology, the person would be thought of as seeking "twinship." To seeking mirroring, to idealize, or to seek twinship is done in the interest of safety. It limits the encounter so that any influence must happen within narrow, predetermined criteria. Little is risked, nothing novel is likely to happen. The probability for creative adjustment is minimal. In extreme form, it is indicative of narcissism, wherein a person is in effect trying to completely control and encounter according to his or her need for protecting a very fragile self structure.

4

The Self in the Eye of the Father: A Gestalt Perspective on Fathering the Male Adolescent[1]

Gordon Wheeler

Jerry and Miguel

Jerry and Miguel sat slumped in opposite chairs in my office, four arms locked tightly--and separately--across two male chests, staring at each other across a father-son divide, each of them closer to tears than they cared to show or maybe even knew.

"It's hopeless," said Jerry, tightening his jaw to keep his voice from trembling. "He won't listen no matter what I say. I'm just his father, so of course I don't know anything."

"You're right about one thing," Miguel almost spat back. "It's hopeless all right. And I'm not the one who won't listen. He is. He isn't even interested in what I have to say. He doesn't even care."

For a moment I thought Miguel was going to add something different, something softer, as his eye lingered on his father's cheek muscle, which was twitching visibly. Then his gaze shifted to Jerry's clinched fist, and the moment was gone.

Gene and Kevin

"But *Kevin*," Gene, Kevin's father, threw up his hands in exasperation, "*I did* take you out. You and I went to my office and played with the computers *all Saturday morning*. The whole morning. How can you say I never took you anyplace all weekend."

Kevin, 14, both hulkingly large and somehow babyish at the same time, said nothing, continuing to play with the marble-shoot game in the corner. His mouth was shut in a grim line, jaw tight, but around the eyes he looked close to tears. It was the same story every week--or rather every other week, after the weekends Kevin spent with his father and his father's "new family," as Kevin put it--meaning the family he didn't feel part of. Kevin felt bitter, left out, neglected, which he expressed by being both sullen and (as his stepmother felt it) vaguely menacing around the house. Gene felt over-worked and unappreciated, which he expressed by fussing mildly and then trying to figure out a way to do more.

Bill and Todd

Thirteen-year-old Todd's cerebral palsy was almost imperceptible, especially when he was sitting down. A mischievous boy with soft, intelligent eyes, Todd stared at his dad with a frozen look now, across a seemingly unbridgeable divide. Bill, his father, athletic and youthful under his banker's uniform, looked away. "I can't reach him," Bill gestured hopelessly. "I try to talk to him, but it doesn't go anywhere, it's like he's avoiding me. I hate to say it, but we just don't connect. I love him, but it's his mother who knows how to talk to him. Maybe it's because--because I'm just not good at it. I don't know, at work I'm good with people, but at home..."
"Because I'm different," Todd finished for him.
"No, no, that's not it," Bill flushed, "you're not different."
"Yes I am," said Todd quietly. "Different than you."
Both males cast a helpless look now in the direction of Terry's mother who obligingly steps in and takes over.

Fathers and Sons: The Background of Cultural Expectations

Why are painful father/son scenes like these so familiar in child and family therapy offices, and in our families and lives? Why are father-son relationships notoriously difficult, especially in adolescence, and so often characterized by tension and at times even an undertone of violence, as in the first of these snapshots--or worse than an undertone? What is it about sons, about fathers, and about development that makes us less than surprised by awkward, even anguished exchanges of this type? "It's developmental," we're likely to say, at least as long as the veiled threats stay veiled. "Let a few years pass," we may add with a shrug, "it's a male thing." These are the justifications we often hear and may use ourselves for a kind of resignation we feel or see around us about male-male relationships in general, and perhaps father-son issues in particular. But why? Is this "nature?" and if so, what assumptions, what presumed facts about "human nature" (and about gender) account for it? Or is it "nurture" which is to say socialization and culture? And either way, what if anything should we try to do about it?

According to much prevailing tradition and gender mythology in our culture, all this is just the way it has to be. The role of the father, in the view of social theorists of our own century from Freud (1933/1999) to Parsons (1993) (and much social philosophy and religious tradition for centuries before that), is to represent the *authority of the culture*, and to carry or impose that authority onto sons, however painful or conflictual that process may be--indeed, must be, at least to some degree (and of course on daughters as well, perhaps more indirectly, in a way more obviously mediated by the mother). This is the tradition we have come to call patriarchy, and if the order of nature is for one patriarchal authoritarian generation to be succeeded by another, we can hardly expect that process to anything much besides conflictual and problematic.

The role of the son, in this model, is a delicate mix of a certain amount of resistance and rebellion against paternal authority, together with an ultimate acquiescence as the son gets in line to be the authority figure himself for the next generation himself. As Mark Twain put it (1901/1988, p. xx) in capturing this developmental dynamic more gently, "When I was a boy of fourteen my father was so ignorant I could hardly stand to have the old man around. But when I got to be 21, I was astonished at how much he had learned in seven years" (Letter to E. Dimmitt, 1901). Twain's classic novels of adolescent boyhood are noted of course for fathers who range from totally absent to murderously abusive.

By their resistance and rebellion, in this mythology, the sons carve out their own identity, which remains weak and incomplete (read "feminine") if they *don't* engage in a defining battle with their father, who is himself by definition bent on domination. Freud took this cultural theme and gave it a scientific gloss with his theory of the Oedipal complex, on which development and maturity entirely depend in his system, at least for males. Curiously enough, in the process he completely reversed the original Greek story, which was actually one of infanticide and child abuse--and not of the son's supposed wish to murder the father, which Freud posited as the universal human legacy of the "primal horde" (1933/1999). In the original Greek version, it was Oedipus's father Laius (a kidnapper and molester of boys, who was himself destined to die at a son's hand for his crimes against children), who originally determined to murder his infant son Oedipus, not the other way around. The baby was saved from death-by-exposure by the traditional kindly shepherd, and then raised in a neighboring kingdom as the adoptive son and heir of the royal house. In adolescence, Prince Oedipus learns from a prophet that he is destined to kill his own father--by which he understands his adoptive father, the local king, who apparently has shown him nothing but kindness. In horror he flees his adoptive home, giving up the throne in his determination *not* to harm the only loving father he has ever known. But of course as fate would have it, he encounters his biological father King Laius on the road, the older man attacks him in a right-of-way dispute, and Oedipus ends by killing him in self-defense. Thus Freud can well say that the battle between the two is somehow fated, but he transfers all the homicidal intent from the abusive father, where it belonged, to the abused son, whose only desire, it would seem, was not to do it (apparently Freud made this reversal unconsciously; certainly he was exposed to the original version in the course of his own adolescence. See Gay (1998), for Freud's classical gymnasium education).

What we can take as clinically and developmentally valid out of this confused tale is the idea that if the father is domineering and abusive, the son/victim will mysteriously repeat that pattern in some way--a process which Freud variously described as internalization of the paternal superego, or "identification with the aggressor" (see A. Freud, 1937/1984), and Perls characterized developmentally as "introjection" (Perls, 1947). Certainly we internalize what we live with by processes which are perhaps better described by cognitive schema theory than by drive models such as Freud's or Perls's (see Fodor, 1996). Thus the culure and its values, including the terms of male identity, will be carried forward pretty much unchanged. The "warrior" or domesticated outlaw remains, in this view and in much of our culture today, the cultural developmental ideal for males despite some decades of critique and deconstruction. And surely if one partially-domesticated outlaw (which is to say, male person) confronts another younger one (even less completely domesticated), well, we'll be surprised and in a way disappointed if sparks don't fly. The question of whether all this is nature or nurture, however, remains.

What is certain is that this is a set of myths and underlying assumptions about development and gender with deep cultural roots in our Western tradition; roots and myths which Freud codified and scientized and may have overstated, but did not invent. In the Greek pantheon, for instance, the adolescent Zeus leads a palace revolution against his own infanticidal father,

Cronos, who had earlier done much the same thing to his (also infanticidal) father, Uranus. Zeus wins and proceeds to rule over Olympus but, of course, never securely and always in fear of another rebellion by his own brothers or sons.

On the Judeo-Christian side, the other great mythic source of our culture, the definition of Judaic tradition begins with the legendary revolt of the youth, Abram, against his father, who traffics in false idols. Abram smashes the idols, taunts his father with their (and his) impotence, and leaves home forever to follow a new god. He receives in the process a new name, Abraham, as a reward and a sign indicating that individual identity is crystallized for the male youth by the act of rebellion and the cutting of all childhood ties. And then, of course, Abraham fulfills the other side of this tricky cultural recipe. Having defined himself through rebellion, he promptly submits to a new male authority, Yahweh, who then helps him forestall a similar rebellion by his own son by staging a terrifying ritual scene of child sacrifice. The boy, Isaac, is actually bound and laid on a sacrificial fire, at which point Yahweh and Abraham stop short of the final blow, commuting the sentence, as it were, to the ritual scarring of the son's penis (a gesture which Freud takes, not unreasonably, as a sign of submission to patriarchal authority and a reminder of castration threat (Freud, 1933/1999). No mention is made in the story of what relations were between Abraham and his son after that point, but we do know that when Isaac himself is old and blind, his own sons are such strangers to him that he can't distinguish one from the other, and can easily be fooled into thinking his smooth-skinned son Jacob (with a goatskin draped over his arm) is really his hairy favorite, Esau. And so the tradition is passed on.

This is a sobering legacy for fathers, sons, and those of us who work with them. It means our own quest as fathers and as professionals or family/community members interested in supporting a different kind of fathering and father/son relationship is going to be an uphill one in some senses, going at times against powerful prevailing norms and beliefs in the culture at large.

The Context of Individualism in Developmental Thinking

In our view, these norms and beliefs are part of a larger cultural legacy, which, as a set of developmental assumptions and cultural/clinical practices, we call the *paradigm of individualism* (Wheeler, 1995; Wheeler & Jones, 1996). Briefly, this is the basic assumption set, deeply rooted in

Western tradition, that what is significant about a person, ultimately, is his individuality (or possibly hers, but less so--the tradition is heavily gender-typed). What is unique, separate and different about him, in this view, is more important and finally more real, than what is universal, communal, and shared. The individual, in this paradigm, developmentally as well as in adulthood, *precedes* relationship and context, and exists in some meaningful way apart from our connectedness with others. To be sure, childhood is characterized by intense connectedness and dependency, but this is an unnatural condition, one that violates the individual's nature (at least in the male case), and is to be thrown off in adolescence as soon as is physically possible. This means, since separateness and differentiation are our basic nature, that the proper course and healthy progress of development through childhood and adolescence is always in the direction of increasing emotional/relational separateness, the breaking of childhood ties, and individual independence in a hyper-autonomous, emotionally isolated sense--as opposed to more elaborated interdependence and richer interpersonal connections. (For further discussion of these points and their implications for developmental self and clinical models; see Chapter One in Volume One of this two-volume series; also Silverstein & Rashbaum, 1994).

Plainly this kind of self- and developmental paradigm has powerful implications for our notions and finally our experience of adult males, fathers and the fathering role in general, and the fathering of boys, especially adolescent boys, in particular. In this model, adolescence is the make-it-or-break-it time for the self-consolidation and masculine identity of the growing boy--developmental tasks which are seen as involving his full and final break with dependent (again, read "feminine") ties of the past. To Freud (19333/1999), by far the greater danger to the boy's development was never too harsh or authoritarian a paternal experience, but always the opposite, too soft and loving a father (again, read "weak" and "effeminate"). Indeed, you could hardly be too harsh as a father from Freud's point of view, because greater authoritarianism just gives the boy more provocation for the necessary battle, while at the same time insuring his necessary defeat, submission, and identification with the hyper-autonomous, emotionally cut off, and authoritarian male role. No pitched battle occurs and so no healthy independent son ready to cut dangerous ties to infantile passivity and assume his proper patriarchal role in society results. (For an alternative self-paradigm and gender model based on the Gestalt perspective, see again Wheeler, 1998; Wheeler & Jones, 1996).

And thus our lack of surprise, tending ultimately to a kind of resignation, about the kind of emotional pain, disappointment, and distance (or worse) that we find so often between fathers and sons in vignettes like the ones above, in our offices, and in our lives. Dan Jones and I (see Wheeler & Jones, 1996) have taken a different view, based upon the Gestalt model and our years of working with men and boys in general and fathers in particular--and upon our own raising two and four sons respectively, to the best of our abilities. We present below a model of fathering which looks beyond this Father = Authoritianism legacy to a richer elaboration of the possible modes of fathering attitudes and behaviors. It looks to the potential for nurturant or detrimental effects of each mode--on the son, the relationship, and the ongoing personal growth and lifelong development of the father as well--which we see (in contrast to this sad legacy) as directly dependent on the creation of a fuller range of satisfying nurturant relationships on the part of the male adult himself.[2]

The Fathering Relationship

In our work over the years with men, we and our groups, working together, have distinguished four basic clusters or modes for the enactment of the fathering relationship and the male caretaking processes we call *fathering*. Particularly as applied to the father-son relationship, these four modes in the order given below have *decreasing levels of support in the culture* and correspondingly increasing levels of uncertainty, risk, and shame on both sides. That is, these problematic dynamics for all the modes, in various ways, correspond to increasing dissonance with traditional male roles and images of masc....ity in the culture as we go down the list. As we examine the modes in turn we will begin to see how and where these mythic strains and legacies of our cultural assumptions play out in real life relationships, particularly those of fathers and their adolescent sons.

The four modes we have used together with our groups to organize fathering attitudes and behaviors are: (1) teaching-providing-directing-taking charge; (2) nurturing-caretaking-listening-accepting; (3) joining-sharing-playing-enjoying; and (4) depending-needing-asking-receiving. Again, these are listed in descending order of social comfort and support for the particular mode; from the most socially comfortable and expected (the one that "raises the fewest eyebrows," as one of our participants put it) to the least expected (the one "I just never think of" in the words of another group member). And, by the same token, they are given in ascending order of dissonance or contradiction with traditional masculine images and role behavior.

That is, the first mode is the most socially expected and supported and, at the same time, the least discrepant with traditional male role norms, which is another way of saying the same thing. The second is socially supported to a considerable degree if not necessarily expected of a male caretaker, and only discrepant with male role norms if it seems "excessive," as our groups put it--or if the first mode isn't there to "back it up"--and so on down the list. The modes are not completely mutually exclusive--one trait or gesture might have aspects that belong to more than one category, but we do believe they are fairly exhaustive. That is, they are meant to be inclusive enough so that any transaction between father and son can be helpfully mapped somewhere in these categories.

But first a word about the limitations of categories as a way of organizing and talking about complex behavior and experience. Certainly any sorting into categories is a grid or map we impose on the data, which are our own experiences, for the purposes of clarifying and discussing those experiences and comparing/contrasting them with each other, both within one person's experiences and across the thoughts and feelings and beliefs of more than one person. In our belief, and in the perspective of the Gestalt model, categories and maps of this kind are never purely or uniquely given in the data themselves as the older individualistic/positivist world-views would have it. Rather, a map distinguishes salient features of a terrain to facilitate navigation, where "salient" always depends, as the Gestaltist, Kurt Lewin, pointed out, on the subjective point of view and the needs/interests of the particular observer at a particular time. This is the *phenomenological constructivism* that makes up the real heart of the Gestalt model as we see it. That is, we construct a model to orient us to particular features of the terrain out of our own purposes and interest. Our interest here is in this dimension of *field conditions of social-support/personal-comfort* which we see as the ground, often unexamined, of the figures of interaction between father and son (or non-support/personal-discomfort, which in a Gestalt perspective is the organizing affect of *shame*; see discussion in Wheeler & Jones, 1996). These social conditions of support/non-support, we believe, constrain and shape fathering behavior, as they do all behavior. Therefore, to make a change, to enlarge our comfortable repetoire as male caretakers, and partic- ularly with adolescent sons, who are at a time of maximum sensitivity to social support and climate issues, we had better pay attention to the organ- izing and constructing of new supports. This will back up new behaviors and experiences for father and son alike, if we are to see lasting change (which can be a problematic enterprise, to the extent that the notion of support itself is dissonant with traditional male role values). This too is the essence of a Gestalt intervention based of a field definition of self which we will discuss after we have discussed the four modes or categories.

With these Gestalt caveats and guideposts in mind, let us now turn to the modes themselves.

The Modes of Fathering

To begin with, when we say "modes of fathering" here, we will be talking in the first instance about gestures and attitudes between a father and his literal son, step-son, foster-son, son of his primary couple partner, and so forth, but also and equally importantly about all the other male-male care-taking relations we include under "fathering," more broadly conceived. This includes at least a man's relations with his students and trainees, employees and supervisees, junior colleagues, patients or clients, even at times peers and older men--in short, any man or boy who may be in a relation of being taken care of, depending on, or needing something from him. These relationships and moments, we submit, are particularly charged in our culture because of the contradictions already discussed between dependency/state of need and the traditional images of manhood as competent and autonomous. Such relationships and transactions may be evaluated at any moment or over time along an axis which we will call affirming/nurturing-to-disaffirming/shaming *from the point of view of the son or recipient* (and certainly a given exchange could be both, in different ways). We say this in this way because much of the learning from the "modes of fathering" model, we believe, lies in increased awareness for the father of the discrepancy between the *intent of the father* and the *experience of the son*. And characteristically, we find (in ourselves as in our participants and clients) we often may tend as men to load all of our fathering impulses and intent onto the first most role-congruent mode; hoping or taking it for granted (against our own misgivings and experience) that somehow, later if not now, our nurturant intent will come through to our sons, and the whole experience will be affirming and supportive, rather than diminishing and shaming for them. As we turn now to the first mode, we will examine how it is that this mode constriction can happen so easily, and what the relational consequences can be for both father and son.

1. Mode One: Teaching-providing-directing-taking charge

Fathering the Male Adolescent

This is the cluster of attitudes and behaviors that are most readily associated with "fathering" in the culture in general and in a long tradition of sociological ideology on the subject. (Again, see Parsons for the dominant voice in American academic sociology in the period of around 1940-1970). To Parsons, the mother's role is to induct the child into the family and the world of relationships while the father teaches the child the culture at large. The accent again is on the male child here, because presumably all the girl needs to know of the culture, really, is the fact of those roles themselves.

In other words, teaching skills and beliefs and values, teaching and enforcing behavioral standards and role expectations, discipline, and so forth are the direct, hands-on aspect of fathering in this mode--backed up by the provider role which, like the discipline role and the skills-in-the-world role, remains primarily the father's expected responsibility, in our experience, despite some decades of softening of absolute gender role boundaries. Both parents (if there are two) typically work outside the home today but, if the family doesn't have enough money, our participants and our own experience as men tell us, it is still the father who is likely to be in a state of inadequacy and shame about it in his own eyes, and the eyes of the world.

Plainly, this fathering mode expresses or hopes to represent a position of power, competence, and efficacy in the world (and thus presumably in the family). This is what makes it so consonant with traditional masculine role identity which aspires to (or falls painfully short of) those same traits and dimensions. And just as plainly, in our experience, these are good and valued things that are widely or nearly universally desirable for fathers, both from a societal point of view and from the point of view of individual men themselves, and their sons as well. At the same time, the mode can be problematic in several different ways.

First is the burden on the father, in a difficult and competitive world, of bearing the load for these responsibilities alone or primarily, without the support either of a full partner for these crucial parts of parenting, or of a society which is constructed to support families and children (or women or men) with conditions fostering full human growth and expression. Many, many men feel terribly alone with the burden and failure risk associated with the provider role, and the disciplinarian role as well, and feel, as we reported our participants feeling above, that the shame of failure for either of these tasks falls overwhelmingly on them.

(We say this knowing well that many women are fulfilling these aspects of parenting/providing today without the full support of absent fathers, as well as that a small but growing number of men are acting as sole

131

parents. Without making any excuse for absentee fathers, we would point out that as long as the felt burden of shame for inadequacy in this mode falls disproportionately onto the male provider, then that fact will tend to exacerbate the problem, in a vicious circle of failure-shame-flight-more sense of failure and inadequacy-more shame-more absence. Some men will find the support to overcome cultural male shaming for low socio-economic status or professional success and manage to hang in responsibly; but many others will not).

A second problem with this mode is the looming menace of the dark side of all these same traits. Providing can veer off into owning, as in "I supported you all these years, so you have to go into law/medicine/family business," and so forth. Or the owning may take much more subtle forms as when the son is not allowed to think for himself and construct his own system of beliefs, values, politics, and ways of living. (And here a father's rejection of a son's sexual orientation could be an example of this kind of possessiveness, the underlying statement being that the son's inner experience actually belongs to the father). In the same way authoritative can become authoritarian, directing and guiding can become controlling and curtailing, taking charge can mean taking over. In all these cases we would want to look into the father's sense of self and self-cohesiveness with particular emphasis on shame issues. This is because of the way shame is *not* supported as an experience for men; to feel shame is itself weak and shameful, and therefore something to be hidden. And shame feelings, when they are denied, have a way of coming out in compensatory and counter-shaming gestures, so that the father's shame may be felt in and by the son, who feels constantly belittled and diminished, like Miguel in the opening vignette above. (Indeed, all three of these fathers and all three of these sons turned out to be experiencing significant shame, both in their lives and right in the moment, in their relationship to each other).

And finally, a third way that the teaching/providing mode can be problematic in father/son relations is the one already mentioned in the previous section. This mode, because it is so socially supported and holds natural expectations upon a father and thus making it congruent with "normal" masculine role demands and expectations, may come to "carry the freight" for all the other modes, all the other caring impulses and gestures that a father may feel for a son or a son may need from a father. In this kind of case, all the longing, all the contact hunger, all the nurturant urges of the father are subsumed and "coded" into being a good provider with the hope and even the belief, oftentimes, that the gesture and the love behind it will be decoded by the son in the way that was intended. The trouble, of course, is that the son's experience may be overwhelmingly one of absence, not of caring; particularly when the genuine caring intent is accompanied and underlayed with a deep relational awkwardness and intimacy phobia, which the son of course also picks up. This kind of distant relationship isn't pictured directly in the opening vignettes to this essay, but often shows up in later life and in our groups. As one participant put it, "My father was always working. He wasn't abusive, he wasn't dictatorial, I guess he did discipline me a little at times, but he wasn't harsh about it--more awkward I guess, and a little grim. He was a dad, and you didn't expect anything much from dads. I guessed he loved me. I guess I had some idea that was why he was always away, always at a meeting, always working. It was like he had more important things to do--it wasn't like we were poor or something like that, he didn't have two jobs, just one job all the time. Bottom line is, I never knew him, and then he died. And he never knew me. That's it."

"That's it." And with these words we could almost wish--indeed this son did wish--for some of the more hard-edged aspects of this first mode, which might have included some good (or bad) head-to-head battles with the energy and intimacy of real struggle between two men feeling their own strength and that of the other. Certainly we hold no brief against this kind of contact which, at its best, is full of respect, love, and passionate investment. Aggression and resistance are healthy, growthful parts of a full relationship and a full self *when they are experienced in a context of basic belonging and affirming.* Our brief is only against the idea that aggressive/assertive contact means the breaking of ties, that the breaking of ties is the only or best route to self-definition for an adolescent male, that a take-no-prisoners battle between father and son is both salutary and inevitable, and most of all against the idea *that the other modes of contact, which are less directive, authoritative/authoritarian, and "powerful" in some traditional sense, hold the son back from maturity and true individuation* (which we would define as wholeness, not separateness or hyper-autonomy). On the contrary, we hold up these other three modes, increasingly as we go down the list, as the shadow sides of fathering; sides which are often felt by their absence and need to be enlivened and lived out in a fully contactful relationship between father and son which, by definition, means one that is growthful for both parties.

2. Mode Two: Nurturing-caretaking-listening-accepting

"You don't listen to me," was the complaint at one moment or another of all three of the boys shown in the opening clinical snapshots, and surely the most frequent reproach from an adolescent to a parent (and perhaps vice versa), ranking right above the one that often follows it, "You just don't care." And the truth is, often as fathers (and as men) we don't listen. Or, perhaps better, we don't give signs of listening, and may not even know how.

This is not because men in general, or fathers in particular, don't care, have no feelings, are "not relational" (whatever that means) nor is it in our view because fathers and their adolescent sons are mutual natural enemies, as the stories of Abraham and Isaac; Uranus, Cronus and Zeus; Laius and Oedipus (in Freud's version), and so many others in our cultural tradition would have us believe. Rather, our sometime difficulty of "just listening," as we know from our groups' reports and from our own personal experience as fathers, is something that follows directly from the first mode above: *the social/cultural demand that men in general and fathers in particular solve everything, know everything, fix everything, provide and pay for everything, and generally stand at every moment in a state of readiness to prevent some disaster from occurring, to the son and family, and to the self.*

In our experience, clinically and personally, many men in this culture (including many high-functioning and outwardly "successful" men) report a sense of always "living against failure," a feeling of self and self-worth that is always contingent on solving the next possibly insurmountable problem. *In short, the feeling we have come to recognize as a gnawing sense of impending, menacing shame.* So pronounced is this kind of experience, and so endemic in the culture as we know it, that it has led us to conclude that the normative process of male socialization in this culture, and the normative subjective experience of self, is not essentially different from the processes and the personality/contact style we recognize as chronic post traumatic stress (Wheeler & Jones, 1996; also Lee and Wheeler, 1996). This we see this as following directly from the terms of the *ideology of individualism* in its extreme form in late capitalist society in the West particularly as applied to the socialization of men (cf. Wheeler, 1998).

In practice, as many of our participants and others report, this leads to the familiar male sequence in which "You've got a problem" equals "I'm responsible for solving it." If I don't solve it, then I am menaced with (or confirmed in) a state of inadequacy and shame against which I can defend by moving directly into activity and solution or, failing that, by blaming and shaming behaviors of my own with the aim of demonstrating that the inadequacy here is in the other person (in this case the son) and not in myself. If I feel powerful enough and competent enough in the world in the area of the problem of the moment, then I move toward the former (I'll pay the bill, speak to the teacher, straighten out the bully, buy a bigger house, fix the broken item, call the doctor, etc.). If not, then I may well move toward the latter--or worse.In extreme shame states, into verbal or physical abuse, substance abuse and addiction, outright abandonment, and so on. Again, in our view the extremely high rates of these behaviors among men are directly related to the heavy shaming and threat of shaming which is culturally normative in their upbringing, reinforced by social policy and social conditions in the culture at large, and passed on in part by process dynamics such as the one described here. Either way, the feelings and the experience of the son have been left far, far behind, oftentimes from the first word or look of distress, which may have triggered the familiar male hyper-autonomy/hyper-responsibility/risk-of-failure-and-shame sequence in the father.

Meanwhile, the adolescent boy, even in the most progressive and nurturant of environments, is not free of these cultural programs and messages either. As Gestalt writer, Allan Singer, points out so simply and incisively in writing of gay male couples, *wherever two males are relating and interacting intimately, we have to remember first of all that both of them are bringing their own history of male socialization,* which inevitably includes at least some prohibitions against dependency, longing, and need, all of which are tinged or more than tinged with shame. Singer was speaking of couple's therapy, but the same point applies here. (As often, the non-sexual process dynamics and social experience which are "in the face" of a gay man in the culture may stand as well for more hidden, out-of-touch dynamics for all men; cf. Wheeler & Jones, 1996). Thus, we may well have in the interaction an adolescent who is himself already hesitant about presenting a problem or an experience in feeling terms in the first place met with a father who immediately reacts by changing the subject of moving from the experience to the advisable solution, to the son's mistake, and so on, or worse. This is a dynamic and a problem much discussed and much lamented in the popular literature on couples (see e.g., Gray, 1994). The difference here, with a father and an adolescent son, is that both members of the dyad may be suffering from it.

In each of the brief excerpts from clinical scenes recounted at the outset of this article, the father involved was shaky in one way or another on the listening-receiving-nurturing mode. To sense just how deficient--and how much emotionally cut-off we experience as normal for males in the culture--just imagine Jerry, the father in the first vignette, turning and saying to his son, Miguel, "Son, I realize I haven't really been listening and hearing you. Sure, I have my values and my standards and concerns and my point of view, and I want you to hear them and work out a way to respect them, but I haven't heard yours. I know it's a different world out there now for young people from what I knew when I was your age--that's what worries me. I need to know what it's like for you, out there and at home with me. So tell me, I'm listening." And, since all the fathering modes are really part of a whole of relating, imagine if Jerry were to go on, drawing now on what we call mode four--depending/needing--which will be discussed in its own section below: "And to tell you the truth, a lot of times I don't know myself what kind of stand I should be taking here as a father. I want to help you and make your life better--not harder or worse. But I can't do that by myself. To work this thing out, I'll need your help."

Jerry was a "working-class" man, high school dropout (with a G.E.D.) who repaired cars for a living. He'd done his share of "drinking and helling around," as he put it, perhaps in emulation of his own absent father, who had left the family, as Jerry told it bitterly, to devote himself full-time to those activities. "But we didn't have drugs back then," he explained. "It's not sex and beer I'm worried about--it's the drugs. Those things can kill you, and they're everywhere." And lest class prejudices kick in here on our part, let us add right away that later on in individual parent counseling Jerry was perfectly able to say basically all these things, to the therapist at first, that we were wishing him to say to his son. The deficiency in mode two, that is, was not purely "in Jerry" as we are accustomed to thinking about that kind of problem under an individualist model. Rather, it was "in the whole field," which is to say, very much related to the absence of a listener for this kind of voice in Jerry's personal history, and in his world now.

Eventually he said this to Miguel too in the therapy office and not long after that Miguel was working Saturdays with Jerry at the garage, doing real work for good money, something his father had long yearned for; a yearning he had expressed mostly in the bafflingly encoded form of putting down his son's mechanical abilities, which had never been much developed up to now. In terms of our model, that interaction of working together held a set of fathering gestures that comprised and integrated modes one, three, and four, at least (and probably two as well). That is, it involved teaching/guiding/training (mode one), companioning-joining-sharing (mode three), and depending-needing (mode four: where Jerry really needed the help) as well as some ongoing dose of mode two, we can imagine, listening-receiving, without which teaching easily degenerates into power struggles and one-up/one-down control.

Jerry was a dad whose life so far had been focused on mastering and living out mode one: the role of the provider, trainer, and disciplinarian. In this he was forging a path that had not been blazed for him by his own abandoning father. He worked hard and had quit his daily drinking years ago--though he "cut loose with the boys" once in awhile, he recounted, usually at and after some sporting event. Miguel had long refused to join in on these occasions finding his father and his drunken friends "weird" and "embarrassing." Underneath this criticism and shaming, to be sure, lay Miguel's own longing for his dad and his secret fear that Jerry would end up repeating his father's disappearance into alcohol and absence. On Jerry's side the therapist wondered about the possible connection between his hurt at Miguel's rebuff over going to the games, the consequent extra charge of difficult feelings that these events took on, and Jerry's always getting, as he said, "pissed" on these occasions; (an interesting double word in male parlance, since it can mean both drunk and angry--either of which, we believe, may often be among other things a cover for hurt and shame). As we discussed before, Jerry was not a non-nurturant father, like his own father--quite the opposite. It was just that he expressed all of his nurturant fathering through mode one--providing and being a consistent, non-violent authority. Given the cultural messages he had grown up with about fathering and about masculinity--and in the absence of any countervailing or role-expanding personal experience from his own father or other important male caretakers--he just didn't know any other way.

3. Mode Three: Joining-companioning-enjoying-playing

This mode was the great strength of Gene, the father in our second vignette. For years after the marital separation, beginning when his son was only two, he had taken Kevin with him one day a week to his work as a computer programmer where the toddler had played busily on the computers almost before he could walk and talk. As with many software companies, the atmosphere was relaxed, hours were highly individualized, and Kevin was tolerated as a sort of mascot around the office. Once the little boy reached kindergarten his dad continued this tradition one afternoon a week after school, ending up with pizza and the video arcade where the two of them sometimes played for hours on separate consoles; (they didn't play with or against each other, because Gene played hard, and Kevin became upset when he lost). And then every other Saturday Kevin spent the day and night at his dad's small studio apartment in a distant suburb which was equipped with all the latest in home video games.

By the standards of many divorced fathers and their sons, this was a lot of time together, a lot of attention, and a lot of contact--most of it to be sure in the form of the kind of "parallel play" afforded by video games without much range of interaction and exchange. And yet Kevin was far from happy with his dad or with his life. An immature, physically awkward boy, he was teased and picked on at school, often involved in fights, and because of his large size, able to do some real damage. By the age of 14 he had already sent several of his attackers to the emergency room, one with a broken bone. He was extremely bright but failing eighth grade. All this baffled his father who blamed the mother for "coddling the boy" and advised his son impatiently to "Just keep your head down and stay out of trouble."

What was missing here, in our view, was above all the listening part of mode two and the needing, self-revealing part of mode four. Gene joined and companioned Kevin a great deal on the level of activities anyway and yet Kevin didn't feel given to, nourished, filled up from all the time his dad spent with him. After four hours alone together on a Saturday morning, he felt as empty and lonely as he had before. Why? We believe this was because in a real sense, for all the time they spent doing things, Kevin and his dad never got to know each other. They knew next to nothing about each other's inner lives, thoughts, feelings, dreams, and correspondingly little about their own. This just wasn't a kind of conversation they had with each other or, to a great extent, with anybody (except for certain feelings, mostly of injury and despair, which Kevin could share with his mom--who was not so much "coddling" him, as Gene put it, as she was welcoming him into her own depression and stance of general resentment against the world).

We've already observed that each of the modes can have its negative or destructive side. For mode four (the father being in a state of needing something, and depending on the son), plainly a case in point would be the father who presents himself as helpless, overwhelmed, and maybe addicted so that the son becomes the parent and stabilizer both in order to have a relationship at all and sometimes in the service of holding the family together. This extreme was very far from Kevin and Gene's situation. The truth was, Gene had little idea of Kevin's life and experience (mode two: listening). For instance, his struggles at a large urban junior high school, utterly different from Gene's own early adolescence as an "accepted misfit," as he put it, in a small town. Nor did he give Kevin any inkling of all the pressure he was under himself, at work and at home, or how much the hours he spent with Kevin cost him, both on the job (where he now had to make up the Thursday afternoons he was still spending with Kevin, in and out of the office) and with his wife as well (who was left alone with an infant and a toddler, Kevin's new half-brother and -sister, most of the day Saturday while Gene and Kevin were off together). Unlike Miguel, Gene had had a model of a traditional, reliable, good provider and active teacher for a father--but one who had also been, in Gene's experience, controlling, authoritarian, rigid, emotionally remote, and encapsulated behind his own importance and considerable professional success. But like Miguel, Gene was fathering as hard as he could using the only mode or channel he felt he knew and could believe in, which he derived more from his relationship with his older brothers, who had "saved my life," than from his remote and "important" dad. To Gene this meant having Kevin "tag along" and including him in games as his own older brothers had done with him to his eternal gratitude. That he was also repeating a pattern of emotional distance he learned from his father, was something that had never occurred to Gene, who knew his own feelings only pretty generally, and didn't share most of them with anyone.

Once this did occur to Gene, it wasn't all that easy to do anything to change it. If he turned and asked Kevin, somewhat awkwardly, what he was feeling, the reply was likely to be an injured and surly, "Well, what do you *think*?" Gene had no idea--nor, for that matter, did Kevin beyond a general sense of deprivation and injury, which he was reluctant to spell out "Because you'd just talk me out of it." (This was another pattern Gene had picked up from his own father who was "never wrong" about anything, including other people's thoughts and feelings!) What did work better was for Gene to begin to tell Kevin something about his world, how overwhelmed he felt at times by the pressures of a demanding job, a bad local economy, supporting two households, two babies and a wife with her own pressures and problems. Kevin's eyes widened as he put down the marble shoot game and listened. "Not that I mind paying for you," Gene hastened to add, then blurting suddenly, "I just wish you lived with us all the time!"

"You *do*?" Kevin was amazed. Not once in twelve years had Gene spoken to Kevin of his pain at being separated from his son and how he tried to make it up to the boy (and to himself) with a near-frantic level of activity. Indeed he hardly knew he felt it himself, or felt it so strongly, until he found himself unexpectedly fighting tears. Instead, he had concentrated all his energy, which was considerable, *on doing and doing with*--modes one

139

and three in our model--leaving out the "being" modes, two and four, which were more unknown to Gene, and more charged with feelings of dependency, loss, failure, longing, sadness, grief and shame (and anger, which he held in with the support of a rigid jaw and painful neck, so as not to be "angry and explosive, just like my father.") The paradoxical result of all this activity and all this holding back, as often when men are restricted to purely role-congruent behavior, was that the father felt completely drained while the son felt undernourished and alone.

Kevin's reaction to all this--in best male style and family tradition--was to throw himself straight into the problem, firing off suggestions for how he could help his dad, which it was by no means easy at first to get Gene to listen to and accept. He didn't need to spend Thursday afternoons with his dad anymore, Kevin said, if those work hours were difficult. An after-work evening would be just as good, and he would do his homework in the afternoon on that day since his mom wouldn't let him be out after six or seven unless his homework was done (quite reasonably, except that he wasn't doing the homework anyway--for reasons directly related, as we saw it, to his relationship with his father). As for weekends, they could take Kevin's baby brother with them, just as Gene's brothers had hauled him around, and Gene had Kevin at that age. Or they could do projects together on the house when Kevin was there on Saturdays so that his dad would be under less pressure, not more. Once Kevin felt needed, instead of like a duty or a chore to his dad--an idea that was sadly reinforced by his mother, in one of those lingering aftereffects of a painful divorce, transferred now onto the child--he began to be "less of a nudge" (in his own words) and to have more room for and relationship with his baby siblings. This in turn improved his relationship with his stepmother as the two of them began to see each other less in terms of competition for Kevin's dad. Fighting began to decrease in school and, in the therapy office, Kevin was even able to tell his mom to "Get off my dad's back--he's dealing with a lot of stuff, and doing the best he can."

Kevin was feeling better about himself, about his father, and about his world--a change which was very much related, we believe, to his dad's sharing more and more, over time, and within appropriate boundaries of his own world, his own needs, frustrations and pressures, and, most of all, his own need and longing for his son. On the other hand, these changes were gradual and needed the support of regular father-son sessions every month, without which Gene in particular was prone to slip back into privacy and tense silence, substituting activity for the dialogue that nourished and relaxed them both. There was no way beyond urging for the therapist to push Gene all the way into the individual therapy he could so well have used; but he couldn't slack off on the monthly joint sessions, because the minute he did, Kevin would be back in trouble at school again, in one of those rare perfect correlations, one-to-one, between rise of therapy and fall of symptom, or vice versa. Thus the therapist could put it to Gene, teasingly, in straight efficiency terms: an hour a month in the clinic or an hour a week or more at school after being called into the principal's office after one of Kevin's fights. And thus Kevin too encoded his longing and his need for real dialogue with his dad into the mode one track--action over words and feelings--a message which his father, with some help, was fortunately able to decode.

4. Mode Four: Depending-needing-asking-receiving

As we've already had occasion to remark, the modes are really all of a piece and distinguished here for diagnostic and discussion purposes. Thus the sections above have already led us into discussion of mode four: the importance of the father's needs for the son, and of finding ways to express and communicate those needs appropriately, affirming the son's strength and importance without burdening him with responsibility for the father's life and well-being. This is not an easy thing for many men to do at all, especially with another male and, perhaps least of all, with a young son whom our cultural mythology depicts as locked in a competitive struggle with his father. Of all the modes, this is the one that most contradicts traditional male and father role expectations, which is to say the one most easily potentially charged with discomfort and shame for many men.

And yet we want to insist that this aspect of male caretaking of sons is essential, and that without it both the father and the son are held back in their full growth and humanity. This is not to say there is no other way to grow fully; certainly boys without fathers and boys with destructive fathers can still heal and grow in other relationships. This aspect of the mode is illustrated by Kevin and Gene's case, both of them males with a constricted language for inner experience and correspondingly limited knowledge of self and other. For Kevin, for all his emotional vulnerability (he was known as "cry-monster" among his assailants at school, for his tears and his large size), there was a way in which he had been so preoccupied with his own problems and injuries that he didn't quite take in the reality and inner state of other people. This is the self-organizational pattern known traditionally as narcissism, but more important to us than the label is the inner experience, and the intra- and interpersonal processes involved. Caught between a mother who tended to see the world and her inner life in the single lens of injurious deprivation, and a father who was warm but presented no inkling of his own inner experience, Kevin had a sharply diminished sense of what complexly articulated and richly nuanced inner experience was all about--in himself and in others. He couldn't tell you in much detail about his own feelings, fears, dreams--and for the most part he seemed to treat others (his mother in a way excepted) as if they simply didn't have these things, or weren't significantly motivated by them.

Now in an individualist model--one that pictures "self" as somehow developing prior to and apart from relationship--this inner blankness would be something to work on in individual therapy while "relational issues" would be the focus of family or dyadic work such as that with his father. But clinicians and others who work with young people know from experience, no matter what our received theories say, that this is a false dichotomy, and that the children and adolescents (and adults) who are limited in one of these areas are limited in the other. With a Gestalt developmental model, we are perhaps in a better position to see how this has to be the case and how working on either pole of self-experience (the private/inner side, or the relational/ "other" side) will necessarily impact both these experiential domains (see discussion in Wheeler, 1998).

To Kevin it was a revelation--and none too soon at fourteen--to begin to see his dad not just in terms of someone who satisfied or frustrated Kevin's needs, but also as a person in his own right, with his own problems, pressures, desires, worries, dreams and so on; all related to yet separate from his son. Certainly Kevin's or anyone's sense of his own needs is important too, and not to be lost sight of but, in fact, Kevin had little clear sense of what his own needs and desires were in any positive sense. (He was more aware of what he didn't want, didn't like, didn't need, than what he did). Again, in our view, these two things go together, and even children and others who seem "self-centered," as Kevin did, and apparently think of little else but their own desires, actually turn out in most cases to have little clear knowledge of those desires or of their own inner landscape in general. And that clear inner knowing, the Gestalt model insists, that articulation of the features of one's own individual inner landscape, does not arise spontaneously in the course of child development, nor is it something the child or adolescent gains mostly by private introspection alone. Rather, we develop it through *intersubjective dialogue*; organically and informally in the "good enough" developmental case. This kind of contact consists of (a) the repeated presentation of themselves, by the parents and other caretakers, as "subjects"--which is to say, people with an inner life and landscape of their own, who make that inner realm known to the growing child, and show by example how they use it to orient and integrate their world--and (b) the repeated and basically consistent treatment of the child as a subject in this sense in his/her own right. This is how we learn to experience and organize ourselves as subjective agents: *by being treated that way, by people who present themselves that way*. And this is how we become *intersubjective beings*, which is to say fully human subjects and agents, dealing in life with other subjective agents, and not as objects bouncing off other objects, in the way of the impulse-disordered child or the "narcissistic" adult. (Again, for further discussion of these and related topics from the point of view of a Gestalt developmental model, see Wheeler, 1998, the first chapter in volume one of this set).

Like any other mode or transaction between father and son (or any two people), as we have said, this can clearly reach extremes and lead to abuse. As we discussed in the previous section, if a father (or a mother) presents as dysfunctional and dependent on the child for basic equilibrium and self-organization, then the child will likely make the *creative adjustment* (the Gestalt term for the best adaptation or self-organization in terms of the real problem that feels available and achievable to the person at the time) of becoming "parentified," "codependent," "a little adult." All of these terms for a kind of self-organization which pays overwhelmingly more attention to the needs and inner state of the other person than to the self, often knowing that person better than he/she knows him/herself (for want of this same intersubjective history discussed above). At the same time, people who work with children and adolescents recognize that the "parentified" child is often in a better position than the "underbonded" or disorganized child to recover from developmental stress and deficit and grow toward a fuller range of human experience. This is not just because the "oversocialized" child (to use Perls's term [1947]) is less likely to be a behavior problem at home or in school but for deeper reasons of self-organizing process. Again, this is clear in a Gestalt perspective: our fundamental life challenge is always to "organize the field of experience" to find and construct some livable, meaningful relation between the inner world of needs, feelings, beliefs and desire, and the outer world of resources, conditions, and other people. The child who has reached the age of 10 or 12 or 14 with highly developed self-organizational skills and processes in place, but mostly or entirely focused on other peoples' needs exclusively, is often better off, diagnostically and prognosti-

143

cally, than the child without those well-developed processes. To be sure, the "adultified" child has to learn how to attend to and articulate her/his own inner world (through the intersubjective attention and reception of another important person, which was missing before); but the underlying processes for doing that--scanning, holding and remembering, planning, relating action to goal, organizing all this coherently over time, and the like--are already largely in place.

The other danger, and one that is less appreciated in our individualist tradition, is for the child to have no window at all into the inner world of his or her caretakers (and by extension other people), whether because they place a value on protecting her/him from adult problems (perhaps in reaction to the other extreme in their own childhood), or because the adults simply don't have that self-knowledge themselves and don't know how to get it and use it. Something like this is the case of many fathers and sons in this culture, and it was the case in its own particular way of Gene and Kevin. As this began to change for Kevin--with the support of his own therapy--his life with his peers at school continued to change as well, moving beyond just not fighting now to actually having friends, for the first time ever (it's hard to maintain any successful peer relations at all without some intersubjective skills, imagining the state of the other person, knowing and remembering their desires and dislikes, negotiating, and so on). As his school principal put it, he "settled down," which we understand as an everyday way of saying that he began to operate in his life like a person with thoughts, feelings and goals organically connected to his actions, reactions, plans, and behavior in general--instead of like an unpredictable volcano in the school, not knowing himself when he would erupt or why. In other words, he grew as a young man, through his father's opening up to him, which drew him into opening and exploring (and creating) a richer inner life of his own, a process that organized and "held" his feelings, thoughts, goals and behavior as an integrated whole that made sense to him and worked for him in the world in a new way. Something similar happened to Kevin's father, who saw his marriage improve as he began to transfer some of these new self-revelation skills to that area, saying, for example, that he was too tired or stressed or worried to take on some new house project by himself rather than just tensing up, bearing it, redoubling his efforts, and then sooner or later exploding ("Just like my father"). This was by no means a quick fix and there were still more difficulties and setbacks along the way. But through it all, father and son managed with support to be in dialogue with each other, in a process of growth and self-expansion that ended by being as beneficial for the father as it was crucial for the son.

A different picture of mode four problems emerges from the case of Todd and his father Bill, whom we left in a tense standoff at the end of the third of the opening vignettes. Like Gene (and Jerry), Bill was a man who was deeply committed to his family and his son, a man of great warmth and depth of feeling--and perhaps somewhat more able than the other two fathers to give voice to inner feelings and experience (though again, we are cautious about locating a deficit of that kind purely in the individual, when oftentimes the "missing" capacity begins to emerge as soon as there is a receptive *listener* for the man's inner experience). And yet he felt blocked at taking up any kind of relationship with his son. "It's the sports thing," he explained to the therapist when Todd wasn't there. "I don't know, I never thought of athletics as my whole life, but I guess it is a pretty big part of it. Or was," he added. "I don't do any of that anymore, because I figure it will make Todd feel bad. You know, because of the CP--he isn't any good at team sports. I work out, but I do it downtown, from my office, you know, so it's not in his face." "CP" meaning of course cerebral palsy, which made Todd's left wrist droop just a bit, and gave him a slight drag on the left side at some moments when he walked, but otherwise was barely noticeable.

"And the thing is, somehow we don't have anything else to do together. I mean, he doesn't do video games either, he's just not coordinated that way. I know I dreamed of having a son I could teach things to, football and baseball and hockey and everything I always loved as a kid--still do love. I was on teams till a few years ago, when I thought it was starting to bother Todd. And we can't do any of that. It's okay, I got over that a long time ago. But the thing is, it doesn't leave us anything to share. I try to talk to him, but I feel like he's just tolerating me, because *I'm* not good at *that*. Especially when we can't talk about sports! I ask him what he did at school, he says "The usual, Dad," and that's it. He's thirteen years old, and I swear he's patronizing me. He does that--he manages people. Because he can see right into people, he knows what they're thinking and feeling, when I have no idea. His sisters, for instance--I can be fussing at one of them about something, and she's fussing back, and he cuts right in with what everybody is really thinking. It's almost uncanny sometimes..."

Bill trailed off in hopeless silence, a man who loved his son so much he deprived himself of the athletics he loved, for fear that it might be making the boy feel bad about himself--yet felt he had "no relationship" with the boy. Not that they had ever talked about it! To the question of how he knew this was how Todd felt, Bill answered that he "just guessed"--a response which would have been hilarious if it hadn't been so sad, given that he had just finished saying he had "no idea" what other people were thinking and feeling most of the time. And yet this too is something we have often observed in fathers: the less adept a man feels at negotiating the whole terrain of feelings, the readier he may be to make unconfirmed guesses, right in the area where his guesses are the least reliable. Again, in our view *this is because not knowing how to express and negotiate this inner world and not knowing how to open up a dialogic inquiry in this area with another person* (especially a son) *are the same thing.* We think we know ourselves, but this private knowing is often really vague and sketchy, like a dream before we start to put it into words. We find out much more, about ourselves as well as the other person, in the inquiring intersubjective dialogue with others.

In Bill's case, parts of fathering modes one and three, teaching/directing and playing/joining, were pretty much blocked in his mind, at least on the athletic dimensions where he felt he had the most to offer. This left him, beyond the provider role itself, a choice of mode two, listening/nurturing, where he felt awkward and somehow incompetent--or mode four, depending/needing, which was "hopeless, you can't do that, he's just a boy." No wonder he felt blocked! And while theirs was in a way a special case because of Todd's slight physical limitations, we've seen the same pattern many times in other cases where a man, with the best intentions he can muster, stakes his whole hands-on fathering on a dream of passing on his own area of greatest strength and pleasure to a son--only to find that the boy is seemingly just not by nature inclined to that area. The area may be sports, or it may be books or music, or science or medicine, or business or politics--any area of passion and competence for the father in the absence of a full relational range drawing on all the modes in his interaction with the son.

And are these individual differences really just "nature?" This is hard to know for sure in an individual case, but what we do know is that a relationship which rests so heavily on performance (on both sides) quickly can become a vicious circle of competitiveness, inadequacy, and feelings of shame--leading to avoidance, which leads to more inadequacy, and so on. This was the case in a way with Jerry and Miguel whose "total lack" of mechanical ability turned out to have more to do with the distance between the boy and his father, and the father's difficulty in being attuned to his son in such a way that teaching or just being together didn't become a shaming experience. In Gene and Kevin's case, the "play as hard as you can" style Gene had learned from his brothers turned out to have quite a different meaning in a different context. Gene felt honored by his brothers' inclusion and enhanced as a person just for being associated with them. Kevin felt abandoned and then dutifully dragged along by Gene, and diminished by the distance between himself and his father.

With Todd and Bill, a further sad irony was that Todd was in many ways an outdoors person without Bill's even quite knowing it. He loved nature, hiking, water sports of all kinds, and longed to take up sailing and canoeing--especially whitewater canoeing, which he'd gotten a taste of at boy scout camp, and found thrilling. These were not the team sports Bill knew and loved. If anything, he felt awkward and a little at a loss in nature, alive to it but not sure how to take it all in, how to manage all that "being," without the structured "doing" of ball and team play. He was a good enough swimmer, but knew nothing of boats. And of course they had never talked about any of this.

When they did talk, with considerable directing and staging by the therapist, Bill was astonished to find that his son's feelings were not what he had assumed. Todd was shocked and almost angry (perhaps as a cover in part for feeling touched) to discover that his dad had given up the weekend sports he loved out of fear of hurting his son's feelings in some way. "That's you, Dad," Todd told him, in that slightly patronizing way Bill had remarked on. "You love all that stuff, teams and scoring and charging up and down the field. You should do it. I'm different. Not because I'm handicapped," Todd drew himself up straight in his chair, his tone a bit more openly defiant, "I don't think of myself as handicapped. You think that, but I don't. I just know I'm different. Different than you," he repeated firmly.

An awkward silence hung in the room, broken by Bill, leading as usual with an action plan. "What about lessons? I could arrange sailing lessons for you. I'd take you myself, but I really don't know much about it." Todd shrugged and looked away. "I already know how, I get lessons at camp. I can sail a sunfish now by myself. I passed my test. I just want to go sailing, that's all." More silence.

"Well," the therapist finally broke in, "since you already know something about it, why don't you both go, and you teach your dad? If you like it, once you've taught him everything you know, you could take some lessons together." Todd watched intently as a series of emotions played over Bill's face--surprise, puzzlement, doubt, something like total confusion. "Would you like that, son?" he finally managed to get out.

"I don't know, Dad," a little smile played around Todd's lips, and the habitual mischievousness was back in his eyes. "I don't know if you'd be good at it. It takes a lot of calmness. You're not a very calm person, you know." Bill flushed and looked in some desperation at the therapist, who shook his head just slightly, meaning to convey, "Don't do anything, just be with it right now."

"Let's give it a try," Bill finally let out a breath that sounded as if he had been holding if for a long time. When Todd still seemed to hold back, at last his father added the missing words: "I'd really like that, son. Let's do it." For all his remarkable poise and seeming self-assurance, Todd looked away and stiffened slightly, nodding without trusting his voice. Apparently Bill wasn't the only male in the family who had some difficulty staying with a strong feeling.

There were other areas where Todd could teach Bill a thing or two as well--and vice versa. When Bill was at a loss in the emerging dialogue between them and in the family, the therapist encouraged him to ask Todd directly for coaching and suggestions; both to move the exchange along and in order to recognize Todd's strength and expertise in reading others and knowing how to engage with them on a feeling level--things which Bill had long relied on Todd's mother to do for him, but in a more passive way, depending on her without learning much himself. Let us emphasize here, this was not a matter of being "pals"or of abdicating a role of parental authority. But authority not backed up by expertise is hollow, and "discipline" not exercised in a context of mutual respect for each other's strengths is diminishing to both parties, and ultimately self-defeating. As Bill was more open and more openly able to depend on his son for real needs, he became more, not less free in asserting his point of view, making demands for help with chores, and involving himself in decisions and limits about Todd's expanding adolescent range of behavior--things which he had previously left up to his wife, for lack of a direct relationship with his son. By the same token, with more real presence and respect from his father, Todd became more interested in the things his dad could teach him, including quite a bit about camping and rock climbing, as well as how to go about getting a job, managing money, and saving for a sailboat, all of them things Todd wanted and needed to learn. Eventually they bought a small sailboat together and did some racing, sometimes as a crew together, and sometimes against each other, mix and match with other father-son teams they came to know. Todd is in college out of state now, but Bill continues to sail, handing on to his daughters some of the skills and some of the calmness he learned from and with his son.

Conclusion

A breakthrough in therapy or in a relationship is only that--a breakup of an old block, an old rigidity in self-organization, making way for the construction of something new. The new construction process itself-- new integrated patterns of action, self-experience, relationship and meaning, which the Gestalt model takes as our basic nature and self-process--takes longer. In each of these cases, as in others, time and ongoing support were needed for making the kind of *continuing experiments in new contact patterns* by which we integrate new behavior and experience into our ongoing ground of feelings, beliefs, assumptions, social context, and other behavior; all those things that make up the coherent inner context for our "figures of action," and for our inner experience. This is the essence of the Gestalt model, this notion of the self as the constructor/integrator (or the constructing/integrating) of the "whole field," the inner world with its dynamic process structures (some of them outlined above) and the outer world of action, consequences, and above all other people with their own needs and desires--into coherent, livable, meaningful wholes of action and experience. At every moment, as the model has it and as we have seen in these snapshots, *the behavior that dominates will be the behavior that is supported*, both by that inner world of goals and feelings and beliefs, and/or by that outer world of the reception and expectations of others.

This, in turn, means that this notion of *support* becomes crucial to our developmental view, and to our work with children and adolescents, boys and girls (and their parents) alike. This is something we know intuitively from our work with kids, but which is itself supported and explained more clearly from a Gestalt perspective than from an individualistic one. *Over and over we see that the child or adolescent develops along the paths that are supported--both by inner capacities and creativity, and by outer receptivity in the social/relational field.* Expressed in this way, this may seem like a truism, but it is one that violates the basic terms of the traditional models of self (and of masculinity) handed down in our individualist cultural and clinical tradition. The Gestalt model, with its insistence that *the self can and must integrate and create itself out of the whole field*, outer *and* inner, is in a better position to show us how it is that the relational conditions of the child's environment are not just the environment of the self, but themselves become a part of the self, part of the stuff out of which the self weaves its own unique integration. And this then supports us to see where interventions in that outer relational world can influence and change the developing self-process, by changing that map of supports out of which the self-process steers and draws its essential nourishment.

But then this area--outer supports--is the very area that conflicts, for many men, with their internalized notions of the terms of masculinity and fatherhood themselves. "Support" is almost a phobic word to many men in this culture, heavily colored with notions of helplessness, "effeminacy," and shame, as opposed to "autonomy," which is typed as virile, masculine-- and safe. And the deconstruction of an old structure which is itself so deeply embedded in the cultural surround, the model tells us, will itself require extra measures of support. Oftentimes we find that the support most needed is the reception of that inner world of longings, hopes, disappointments, fears and dreams, by another person who knows how to decode coded messages of longing and shame--messages which became obscured (from the self as from others) by lack of receptive support in the person or father's own developmental history. In that way the more receptive modes of fathering, modes two and four, can serve to enhance, contextualize, and complete the more active, "doing" modes one and three. In the beginning this extra support may well need to come from a therapist, teacher, counselor or other interested adult, who translates the code and acts as a companion to father and son in the lonely-feeling journey toward more self-exposure, which goes along with more intimate reception of the other person. But as time goes on, fathers and sons can learn to provide this support for each other, then for others around them, and finally for themselves. In our view, there is no more urgent task in the general cultural change now in progress toward a different and more livable worldview and world, than the *deconstruction of the traditional western ideology of masculinity*, which we see as the linchpin of the broader ideology of competition and individualism that isolates us and threatens the globe. Our work helping fathers (and ourselves) along the journey to a different kind of care-taking and socialization for their male children, we see as one steppingstone in this long and important path. We wish you the reader, all the men and boys we and you work with, as well as ourselves and our sons, energy and support along the way.

References

Fodor, I. (1996). A woman and her body: Cycles of pride and shame. In R. Lee & G. Wheeler (Eds.), *The voice of shame: Silence and connection in psychotherapy* (pp. 229-265). San Francisco, CA:

Jossey-Bass.

Freud, A. (1937/1984). The ego and the mechanisms of defense. In *The writings of Anna Freud, volume 2*. New York, NY: International Universities Press.

Freud, S. (1933/1999). *The complete psychological works of Sigmund Freud (Standard Edition)*. New York, NY: Norton.

Gay, P. (1998). *Freud: A life for our time*. New York, NY: Norton.

Gray, J. (1994). *Men are from mars; Women are from venus*. New York, NY: Harper Collins.

Parsons, T. (1993). *Age and sex in the social structure of the United States*. Reprint Series in Social Science. New York, NY: Irvington. .

Perls, F. (1947). *Ego, hunger & aggression*. London: Allen & Unwin.

Real, T. (1997). *I don't want to talk about it: The secret legacy of depression in men*. New York, NY: Scribners.

Silverstein, O., & Rashbaum, R. (1994). *The courage to raise good men*. New York, NY: Viking.

Twain, M. (Clemmens, S.) (1901/1988). Letter to E. Dimmit. In *The works of Mark Twain*. Temecula, CA: Reprint Services.

Wheeler, G. (1995). The tasks of intimacy: Reflections on a gestalt approach to working with couples. In G. Wheeler & S. Backman (Eds.), *On intimate ground: Gestalt approaches to working with couples* (pp. 31-59). San Francisco, CA: Jossey-Bass.

Wheeler, G. (1998). Toward a gestalt developmental model. *British Gestalt Journal, 7* (2), 115-125.

Wheeler, G. (2000). *Beyond individualism: Toward a new understanding of self, relationship, and experience*. Hillsdale, NJ: GestaltPress/The Analytic Press.

Wheeler, G., & Jones, D. (1996). Finding our sons: A male-male gestalt. In R. Lee & G. Wheeler (Eds), *The voice of shame: Silence and connection in psychotherapy* (pp. 61-99). San Francisco, CA: Jossey-Bass.

Footnotes

1 The ideas of this essay in general, and the Modes of Fathering model in particular, grew out of work done collaboratively over a period of years with Daniel Jones, Ph.D.; see Wheeler & Jones (1996).

2 For more background outlining our Gestalt view of child, adolescent, and

lifelong development in general, we again recommend Volume One, Chapter One of this two-volume set (Wheeler, 1998), as well as Silverstein & Rashbaum's pathbreaking *The Courage to Raise Good Men* (1994), supplemented by Terrence Real's profound and sensitive treatment of male developmental issues, *I Don't Want to Talk About It* (1997), and our own discussion of developmental shame issues in male-male relationships, "Finding our Sons: A Male-Male Gestalt" (Wheeler & Jones, 1996).

5

A Field of Difference: A Gestalt Perspective on Learning Disabilities

Marlene Moss Blumenthal

Learning Disabilities and Education

The contemporary model of learning disabilities emerged during the 1950's when various theories about learning disorders appeared and effective educational interventions based on these theories were developed. The investigation of disorders of communication, perception and perceptual-motor abilities began to influence the movements toward special education. Early definitions assumed learning disabled children to have suffered some form of brain injury. More recent definitions require that there are significant gaps between measured ability and achievement. By 1969, when the Handicapped Elementary and Secondary Education Act amendments included a second section called the Children with Specific Learning Disabilities Act, educators began to assume the responsibility for providing treatment to most of the children with learning difficulties.

Current Federal law defines the learning disabled as "10 percent of the population that cannot read, write, perform math calculations or applications, comprehend language through listening or express orally at the level of their measured ability." The proposed guideline in Ohio, for example, (which is based on an interpretation of the Federal mandate) defines a specific learning disability as "a disorder in one or more of the basic psychological processes involved in understanding or in using language, spoken or written, which may manifest itself in an imperfect ability to listen, think, speak, read, write, spell, or to do mathematical calculations." The term includes such conditions as perceptual disabilities, brain injury, minimal brain dysfunction, dyslexia, and developmental aphasia.

Is this conceptualization adequate to the concrete tasks of assessing and helping learning disabled children? In essence, traditional thinking understands learning as a process that occurs within the child and disabilities as interruptions of these internal processes. In the language of Wheeler (1998), such conceptualizations are founded upon the self-in-isolation model of human psychological functioning, a model that has evolved from the body/mind and self/environment splits of Western philosophy. This view, which understands human beings fundamentally as isolated systems, underlies much of our contemporary understanding and treatment of learning disabilities. It is my intention in this chapter to challenge and widen this view, and to show, on the basis of Gestalt therapy theory, that these issues are better understood as belonging to the wider bio-psycho-social-cultural field.

The Field of Learning

From our earliest years, learning, like all meaning making, has to do with our relational world. "Intersubjective responsivity acts as a template to shape and create corresponding intrapsychic experiences in the child" (Stern, 1985, p. 108). In other words, from our first moments we begin to organize our sensory perceptions, begin to develop our self, structuring our ground in an interactive field. Our parents' or caretakers' desires, fears, prohibitions and fantasies begin to contour our experiential world. There is an interplay between our native capacity to interact with our environment (take in information and influence) and the interactive capacity of our early caretakers. Although Bowlby (1969) and Ainsworth (1969) initially viewed attachment as a specific developmental task of the early life phase, Stern (1985) suggests that this quality of relatedness or attachment continues to develop beyond the initial mother-infant bond, develops throughout childhood and applies to peers as well as to mother. Interpersonal relatedness, like learning, is an ongoing and dynamic life span issue.

Throughout our lives we continue our process of development and interpersonal relatedness by utilizing the nourishment from our interpersonal environment to fuel the process of growth. For Gestalt therapy theory, the most basic mode of human functioning is to engage in and maintain a "nourishing relationship with our environment" (Wheeler, 1991, p. 72). Psychological nourishment comes in many forms, verbal and nonverbal, but always through exchange with the environment.

In Gestalt therapy theory, this exchange takes place at the meeting place or boundary of our internal experience and the outer world, and this meeting place is referred to as the self. So when we speak of self, we are referring not only to internal experience, but to a co-created experience between person and environment. And this self, this dynamic co-creation, this "system of contacts in our present situation" (Latner, 1992), is the agent of change, the organ of growth, the integrator and organizer of experience. It is, in other words, the instrument of learning.

In Gestalt therapy theory, these processes of learning and growth are referred to as "contact...the awareness of, and behavior toward... assimilable novelty" (Perls, Hefferline, and Goodman, 1951, p. 230). Through contact, we make meaning, problem solve, follow rules, and make personal constructs by organizing perceptions in collaboration with others in our interpersonal world. "...What we are doing, all the time, is mapping the experiential field, 'inner' and 'outer' domains alike, into an organized, coherent, and meaningful whole that relates our figure of interest, to our ground of experience, expectation, hopes and plans, fears and beliefs and dreams" (Wheeler, 1997). How we organize our perceptions is influenced by meanings we have made before. Every moment-to-moment perceptual organization of experience is influenced with our subjective meaning of events based on expectations evolving from our structured ground of experience. Everything perceived in the field, both internal and external, is organized to satisfy a need. We negotiate perceived obstacles and resources to our goals, attempting to find the best possible resolution of the realms of inner world of needs and wants and the outer world of resources and demands (from Lewin, in Wheeler, 1991). The resulting perceptual organizations influence our problem solving behavior or action in the field. Again, this behavior or action in the field, this process of learning and growth, is considered our mode or style of contact. And this style of contact is multiply influenced. Inherent capacities for interacting and learning influence environmental response, which in turn affects the developing capacities for interaction and further learning.

School learning likewise involves dynamic interchange, or contact, at the boundary of individual and environment. Academic learning, solving math problems, negotiating peer interactions, are all instances of problems to be resolved. These are episodes of contact, the "fulcrum point of nourishment and change" (Wheeler, 1991, p. 60), requiring creative adjustment to novel circumstances.

When parents or teachers encounter a child whose capacities for interaction do not meet their expectations, there is potential for disconnec-

155

tion, for contact disturbances in the field. How parents or teachers adjust to their own disrupted expectations--how they interact, or make contact in the field with this child--has profound implications for that child's learning and development. One common way that contact is disrupted occurs when learning difficulties are identified and projectively located in the child, who is then forced to carry the full weight of the problem. But the act of identification and diagnosis is itself a contact process, and in this process it is too often the field conditions for learning that themselves become disabled. Whereas adults may conceptualize the learning disability as a content problem, it is often the process of disrupted contact that most impacts the child. Gestalt therapy theory has recently addressed the dynamics and process of such disrupted contact under the heading of shame.

Shame and Learning

Embedded within our culture are the values about how we learn and demonstrate our competence. Learning and academic competence are highly valued in our culture. When a divergent learning style emerges from our cultural ground, it becomes figural, standing out in its own creative and naked vulnerability. Adolescents with learning styles that diverge from the norm are, in a sense, members of a minority group. As members of a minority group, they are vulnerable to be targeted as different. And, being different can make one vulnerable to being discriminated against. The resulting experiences of negatively charged interactions, and the disruption of contact which so often ensues, leads to feelings of isolation and shame (Lee, 1995). Isolation and shame are the opposites of connection and support. Environmental support in the form of attention and appreciation for how one negotiates the world is extremely important for all of us, but it is essential during intensive periods of self reorganization. Adolescence is one of these times of reorganization. The experience of support leads to feelings of being connected to others. Connectedness in the experiential field is a condition for development of self and self process, and thus also for learning. A child or adolescent, if he or she has built a reservoir of supportive interactions, can be sustained by this nourishment during inevitable experiences of disconnection. Diminished nourishment inhibits growth. It also makes one vulnerable to and induces shame. Shame, that lack of fit between me and my environment, is experienced when the environment does not support an individual's way of being in the world. Shame producing organizations of experience are usually seeded in a nonverbal sense of being unworthy. So, if environmental supports are lacking, if a child or adolescent experiences a lack of fit within his environment, he becomes vulnerable to shame-based organizations.

Experiment

Most of us have experienced shame and support as well as isolation and connection in our learning histories. Our styles of learning have been shaped through various forms of support and non-support as we moved through our academic communities. I find it interesting to reflect upon my own experiences as a young learner in academic settings, and I invite you, the reader, to join me in your own reflection. What is it that others have valued about your learning style, your manner of expressing what you know? What was considered competent in your family of origin? What was valued or devalued? And how did you know what was valued or not? Was it made explicit or was it communicated in nonverbal ways? How well did your style fit within your family? How did your family's value system fit within the dominant culture? In your school setting, did you feel abled or disabled? How were you supported in the field? Can you identify areas where there was a lack of support--where you experienced shame? And how do you imagine these experiences are reflected in your interactive styles, your learning styles, today? Take a few minutes and reflect on these questions before reading on.

It is likely that each of us has, within our lifetime of interaction in the field, experienced a combination of support and nonsupport with respect to our learning style. I would like to offer several personal examples of shame inducing experiences that occurred in the social/psychological/cultural field of my own learning history. Early in my school career, I learned that my speed of processing was out of step with those around me. At home, my spontaneity was supported by my approving parents who valued my curiosity and academic achievement. They also, however, expected me to follow the rules and mind the teacher. In school, I learned to expect disapproval from my teacher if I spoke out "inappropriately" or acted spontaneously. So, I had introjected both parental and teacher values, and learned to expect shaming experiences if I did not interact as the social field demanded. This became an unverbalized dilemma for me, as my family field and my school environment began to elicit different perceptual organizations. In school I became quiet and verbally inexpressive. By the time I reached adolescence, I rarely responded in class. I had disconnected from

157

parts of my self-experience, inhibiting some of my natural and spontaneous ways of making contact in the social field, in order to satisfy my need for approval and to maintain social connection. I came to expect responses in the classroom that would call attention to my having lost my place or having failed to listen to directions, and this supported my choice to remain silent and offer what I knew only in written work.

As a Gestalt practitioner, I am interested in the lived experience of a child or adolescent with learning difficulties. An adolescent who has experienced the disconnection of non-support within his environment, for whatever reason, can carry the experience of shame--a feeling of being not okay or of being less than and of not fitting in the world of peers and adults. When asked about his experience, a thirteen-year-old client who was experiencing significant learning difficulties told me, "...the most embarrassing times for me are when I am asked to stand up and read...or give a report...or a speech." Describing his frustration when required to express his thoughts in words, he disclosed "...and I sometimes sit at the computer and sit and sit and sit and nothing comes out...so I tab over four, type in my name, date, tab over and type in the subject and nothing comes...I can't get my thoughts together, even though I have all the information inside..." Being different can lead to feelings of isolation, to a yearning to fit in coupled with the helplessness of not knowing how to bridge the gap. For many learning disabled students, being different is to know for sure that I will never make it in the world of adults and peers who are perceived as normal. This shame-based organization defines the field as one that is unsafe, where one is unsupported.

The experience of being different is loaded with meanings that can be negatively charged. This experience of being different and of feeling unsupported in this difference--which defines the shame-based style of organizing and interacting--is excruciatingly painful and poignant during adolescence. At this time when self is tentatively reorganizing itself, the danger of destructuring is ever present (McConville, 1995). To carry this burden of negatively charged experience is like carrying a load of dynamite onto a building site. It is dangerous, but also offers the opportunity of rebuilding or restructuring, and thus is a time when support for divergence is essential.

Adolescent development is characterized by an intensification of sensory experience. This increased sensitivity heightens the adolescent's vulnerability to shame based experience. As the child disembeds or differentiates from the family milieu, the self reorganizes (McConville, 1986;

1995). It is during this time that one begins to develop a workable sense of ownership of one's experience. At this childhood/adolescent boundary, meaning making, questioning, and sensory experience take on heightened significance. Emerging from the family field, the adolescent becomes acutely aware of her effect on others and how she thinks that others perceive her. It is a time when ground and figure seem to be illuminated with contrasting neon lights. This heightening awareness of sensory experience--this renewed sense about how one is received in the world--increases the learners vulnerability to shame.

For me, school became a place where my strongest learning was how to avoid the experience of shame. In my family field where my verbal expressiveness was valued, and my opinions encouraged, I talked unabashedly. In my current graduate school classes, where dialogue and discussion is valued, I experience the familiar encouragement that I knew in my family field, and readily become more vocal and spontaneous. In my public school experience this was not so, and consequently I appeared less capable than I did (and do) in more supportive learning environment. Was I, in fact, less capable?

I believe, along with Lee (1995), that "...without the voice the person is in fact less capable" (p. 10). When an empathic or interested listener comes along, one feels worthy of being heard. But "shame is triggered when one believes he or she has been observed doing something that is considered inappropriate" (Lee, 1995, p. 14). There is a direct link between how one feels about oneself and how one risks expressing oneself. Safety in the environment promotes support or acceptance based organizations of self, which in turn makes for fluid, spontaneous, and yet choiceful expression. Clearly then, a child's level of academic capability is related to her experience of safety and support.

As with most children, my early organizations were based on unaware choices. I learned to value my nonverbal knowing. The classroom field prompted my organizing perceptions and expectations of danger and non-support for spontaneous verbal expression. Shame, the regulator of the boundary, promoted patterns of interaction or contact style that were, in Gestalt therapy's language, retroflective. I held onto my verbalizations and spontaneous expressions, at least in situations where I expected critical feedback. In addition, the experience of knowing that other students could be received in their verbalizations, but that somehow my own might be unacceptable, led to feelings of social disconnection from my teachers and from many of my more articulate peers. I surrounded myself with friends who

159

were similar to me, expecting that the verbally fluent students would find me uninteresting. I was sure that something was wrong with me, and concluded that others must certainly know this. This was the manner in which I constructed meaning from the information I gathered from my own senses and perceptions.

If, as an adolescent, I had been evaluated by a learning specialist according to today's criteria it might have been determined that I was Attention Deficit Disordered or deficit in oral expression or in listening comprehension. (Notice the reification of the problematic style as a deficiency inside me.) As my spontaneity diminished in selected academic settings, my retroflective style of contact may have made it appear that I was not attending to the business at hand. In addition, my reticence to talk out in class, my holding back, might have been perceived as an inability to articulate my acquired knowledge through verbal expression. And if I did not consistently express myself, the learning expert might have questioned my intelligence, or at least, my ability to take in information by listening. Yet, this was my developing mode of interaction, my developing self, negotiating my school environment in response to some very specific interactions in the field.

In my own assessment of my adolescent learner-self, I would say that I was problem solving; i.e., creatively adjusting to the challenges presented by the field. And if my learning was indeed disabled, it was disabled as much by a field that was unable to meet and support me in my difference, as by my retroflective response to that field. In my opinion, this is a view that is under-appreciated in the contemporary assessment of learning difficulties: namely, that learning disabilities are not just phenomena occurring, or failing to occur, within the child, but represent, at least in part, a child's creative adjustment to a disabling learning field.

My Experience in the Field as a Professional

I am privileged to have had the opportunity of knowing many young students in a variety of school settings. Some of these young people have experienced learning difficulties; some have been diagnosed as having learning disabilities. During my nearly twenty years of experience as a school psychologist in public, parochial and independent schools, and in day treatment settings for severe behavior handicapped students, I have had the opportunity to assess the learning potential and needs of many children and adolescents and to collaborate with school personnel about how to best serve these students.

The Classroom Milieu

I have been privileged to witness a range of classroom experience with respect to learning difficulties. And I have learned through first hand experience that the behavioral profile or interactive style of any student is context dependent. It is always within a multi-dimensional social-cultural field that the student learns and demonstrates learning. It is precisely that social environment, in interaction with the child's or adolescent's native capabilities, that determines how that child appears to an observer. In one instance, observing students in a private school for students with special learning needs, I found that it difficult to identify learning problems at all, as the teachers taught to large classes but appeared to individualize so that no one child seemed to have more difficulty than any other. I have also observed classes where students stood out like squeaky clarinets in a string ensemble when asked to stand and read aloud, or were called on to respond and couldn't organize an oral response.

I remember being especially impressed when, as an invited partic-ipant in a regional special education assessment team, I observed a neigh-boring high school psychology class. I was informed by the teacher that his class of twelve included three learning disabled students who had been iden-tified with varying written, listening or oral language difficulties. He sug-gested that I attempt to identify those specific students while I observed the class discussing his presentation on Piagetian concepts. I was stunned. First, the presentation was similar to (but much more understandable than) those offered in my graduate courses. The discussion that ensued was high level and included participation by each student. The only unusual thing I noticed in the process was that only one student was intently involved in taking notes. I could not identify learning disabilities per se. All students were actively engaged in creative expression.

After class, this talented teacher explained that a class scribe was assigned to take notes for the class and would photocopy notes for each stu-dent. The teacher made himself available to help any student in integrating the material. Evaluation was done through a variety of processes including participation in class discussion, written work, oral work, or any other means necessary to determine integration of knowledge.

This observation as well as many others of this nature has rein-forced my belief that the conceptualization of learning disability as a reified condition of the learner is misleading. As in Winnicott's statement, "There is no such thing as a baby...one sees a nursing couple" (Winnicott, 1965), I believe there is no such thing as a learning disabled student. There is only a social field, a classroom environment and a learner. Learning is an interactive process that is co-constructed in the interpersonal field.

This experience stands out for me as an example of environmental support, which in this case included a teacher whose flexible style of organizing the field allowed for a multiplicity of interactions and connectedness. There was little opportunity for organizing shame based perceptions. I believe it is environmental support that contributes to our construction of meaning. It is what influences the meaning we make of our learning style, that is, of our own particular constellation of learning abilities. Environmental support, as offered by this gifted teacher, took the form of providing a milieu, a field in which each adolescent learner, whether labeled, disabled or abled could dynamically organize new gestalts or figures, could begin to create new maps for negotiating future experiences.

Working With Parents

I have spent many hours talking with parents, attempting to share with them results of integrated assessments of ability level measures, achievement testing, classroom observations and child interviews. I have collaborated with parents over their observations of their child's processes in attempts to make meaning. We have worked together with school personnel, attempting to identify supportive services. I have experienced the wide range of parent response from denial to acceptance, from over-concern to lack of concern. Most importantly, I have learned that parent response is not just a reaction to a learning disability, but part of the co-constructing field in which the learning disability manifests itself. Parent response is part of the field condition that constitutes the very meaning of the child's idiosyncratic manner of learning. It is not simply a question of whether the child is learning abled or disabled, but whether the child's environment--parents and school personnel--serve to able or disable the child in that specific growth process called learning.

Two examples from my work with parents in the educational setting illustrate what I mean by learning disabilities being part of a field condition. The first experience happened many years ago. A new student entered the public school where I was serving as the school psychologist. This twelve-year-old boy was pleasant mannered and drew little attention from his teacher. The boy's mother requested a conference with me, expressing concerned about her son's school progress. She described her son as affectionate, bright, creative and talented. Her concern was focused, mainly, on her perception of his difficulty in maintaining attention and focus.

I evaluated this young man through the standard process of parent and child interviews, observations, and standardized assessment tools. My structured observations revealed information that this boy did, apparently, attend to teacher input and task demand less frequently than other students in his class. He read and performed math functions as well as others in his class and at a level commensurate with his measured ability, which was within the very superior range when compared to age peers. His writing ability, however, was significantly below average. He could barely produce a coherent paragraph in response to structured testing conditions, and thus his scores on a standardized measures of written expression was significantly below his measured ability. Accordingly, he qualified for identification as a learning disabled student.

At the same time, his mother contacted his pediatrician who prescribed medication for Attention Deficit Disorder. There is a good deal of information that suggests that an attention deficit disorder can affect cognition, in general, and that ADD will exacerbate any learning disability (Hallowell & Ratey, 1994). Unlike some parents, this mother thankfully did not perceive medication as the sole answer to the learning difficulties, and gave permission for him to receive twice weekly half-hour sessions with a learning disabilities tutor.

The tutor worked creatively in allowing for written flow of ideas in areas of interest to this boy. In addition, the classroom teacher offered exceptional assistance in the context of routine help to all her students. Both parents were accepting of this child's learning style and appreciated his strengths and weaknesses. He responded by accepting the help available to him, and his written work quickly showed the benefits of these efforts. Tutoring was discontinued at the conclusion of the school year, and medication by the following year. This young adolescent boy found his niche and continued to be a successful learner.

An important question for any professional who works with learning difficulties concerns the use of psycho-stimulant medications. Perhaps the medication enhanced this boy's capacity to receive and integrate new information, thereby influencing interactions in the field and augmenting his capacity for contact and learning. Perhaps just knowing that this boy was taking medication supported teachers in reorganizing their perceptions in the field and influenced their actions toward him. Nonetheless, the manner in which parents and professionals provided environmental support and were flexible in their interpersonal interactions afforded this creative and sponta- neous boy the opportunity to grow and learn in connection.

In cases like this one, where medication seems to help, it is impor- tant to understand that effectiveness from a field perspective. What does it mean when we say that a medication works or doesn't work? Certainly, Ritalin and other medications have some affect on the central nervous sys- tem. However, any neurological event, from the earliest moments of life, does not occur in a vacuum. Like all phenomena, neurological events occur in a multi-layered social field. In the case of the teenage boy mentioned above, Ritalin seemed to reinforce, and be reinforced by the collaborative efforts of the child, parents, teacher, and specialists. In contrast, I have also witnessed cases where medication had its intended effects on the chemistry of the brain, but its meaning and impact were quite different. Not infre- quently, a prescription for medication helps to further disable the existential field process called learning. I have seen, for example, children for whom Ritalin was like a death sentence--a confirmation of a shameful abnormali- ty. I have also seen warring parents for whom Ritalin was a battle line drawn in the sand, a catalytic magnification of deep-seated marital disabilities. The point here is not to dismiss the importance of pharmacological intervention, but to stress that in working with these children, we must never lose sight of the larger social field in which psychological reality is constructed.

Support for Difference

I would like to share a second story; one that highlights the need to acknowledge the learning disability or learning difference. As Linda Davenport (1991) found, when she studied learning disabled youths and adults, the students who had been able to name their disability and accept responsibility or experience agency with respect to their difficulties did bet- ter than those who had not been labeled. Those who did not have others con- firm that they learned differently from their peers, that their styles were mis- matched with the environment, frequently held the belief that there was something wrong with them, that they were stupid or dumb. They often car- ried a sense of hopelessness about their ability to achieve in a culture that valued academic prowess. In other words, these young people and adults had organized their perceptions from a shame based perspective. The author, John Irving, said it well: "I wasn't diagnosed as learning-disabled or dyslexic... I was just plain stupid... I still can't spell... if you were a poor student at Exeter, you would develop such a lasting sense of inferiority that you'd probably need a psychiatrist one day..." (Hallowell & Ratey, 1994, p. 166). So, here's the other story. I had the privilege of evaluating a verbally articulate, creative, high school boy with a history of academic difficulties. I worked with this young man and found that although he demonstrated cognitive abilities within the superior range, his writing was almost unintelligible. In addition, this individual was feeling extremely depressed.

I invited this young man to meet with me alone before giving the assessment feedback to his family and school to personnel. I asked him if anyone had ever mentioned the term "learning disability" to him. He said that no one had, but acknowledged that an older cousin was severely disabled and was in a special school for learning disabled students in another city. The cousin had achieved success and was preparing to enter college.

I asked him how he felt about my naming his learning difficulty to school personnel. He began to cry in relief saying that he had always known that there was something wrong but that no one in his family had named the problem as a learning disability. He thought the problem was that he was dumb and that something was really wrong with him. Like many of Davenport's (1991) population, this young man was the victim of silence, a purposeful avoidance of certain matters that confirms the shameful nature of that which is unconfirmed. In reality, children find themselves immersed in the social/cultural/educational field onto which the shame of the adults in the field is projected. Such is the nature of the silence of not naming--it is our own shame that prevents us from naming the problem in the field.

When I met with this youth's parents, I began to understand what had transpired. His mother was well-versed in learning style problems in academic settings. She was a teacher, working in another school system with "special needs" children. His father had a history of learning and behavior problems for which he had compensated. He was a very successful businessman who used his creative capacities to adjust to a world that did not well receive him. Both parents adored their son and wanted him to feel good about himself. The father's style, which was figural and dominant in this family's field, involved praising his son for his creativity and implicitly blaming the academic environment for not recognizing this. The mother attempted to be confluent with his style by tutoring the young man and editing his work. She attempted to help him compensate for his learning style, but did not fully help him to acknowledge and accept (emotionally, if not academically) the drawbacks of his style.

165

Heart of Development

When this young man and his family joined a different environment, entered another context or field (the school community) they met with dissonance and a sense of disconnection. The family projected the learning difficulties onto the school personnel who "didn't acknowledge the creative abilities" of their son, attributing his learning frustrations to the "incompetence" of his teachers. In this way, they blamed the school for not being able to teach their son properly, thus covering their own shame.

For this boy, the effectiveness of educational interventions was entirely dependent upon the meaning made within his family field, and the relation of his family's meaning to that of the school's. My primary interventions with this case were to meet with his parents in order to neutralize the underlying shame that surrounded the father's learning history and the son's current difficulties. Only when we succeeded in re-framing these learning problems in ways that allowed for support in the field for acknowledged differences--only then did the school's special services begin to have a positive impact on this youth's learning performance.

Gestalt's Re-framing

I would like to offer a reconceptualization of learning disabilities that is consistent with Gestalt developmental theory. I believe that learning abilities and disabilities are expressions of the comprehensive field in which the process of learning takes place. Most contemporary thinking on learning disabilities targets the neurological functioning and internal information processing of the individual child, both of which are certainly relevant and important factors. But the comprehensive field includes the neurological functioning and information processing of all participants in the learning situation - the child, her parents, teachers, and even school administrators, educational scholars, and political architects of educational funding and policy. (What would happen, I wonder, if instead of writing an Individualized Educational Plan [IEP] for the child alone, we wrote a Comprehensive Educational Plan that addressed the needs of the entire learning field, parents and teachers included.) For the learning style of the individual child derives not only from the internal field of cortex and cognition, but also from the family context of contacting and valuing, as well as from the family's contact boundary with a particular educational system and a social/cultural value and belief system.

In the current literature of learning disabilities, Hallowell and Ratey (1994) go the farthest in the direction I am suggesting here. These authors state that the meaning of a learning disorder is inherently derived from the experience within the family field. Gestalt theory shows us how this meaning and experience within the family field is embedded in larger fields, and how the experience of being unable to meet environmental expectations has ramifications within the family and within the educational environment. Our commonly held cultural value on academic excellence and competence is quite skewed, such that we are inclined to presume that a diploma from Harvard or Yale or Stanford somehow implies a better human being. Certainly, this is madness. But it is a madness that surrounds and embeds the learning efforts of every child in our culture.

The experience of not being received or accepted by those in relation is one of disconnection and shame. "The pain of a learning disorder resides not only in the strain one feels in trying to function but in the disconnections one can suffer, a disconnection from language and from thought, from expression and creativity, from books and from words, as well as from people and from feelings" (Hallowell & Ratey, 1994, p. 161). When children or adolescents are earmarked as different or disabled, others may have a tendency to project their own feelings of inadequacy onto these students. In other words, adults' own experiences often result in their organizing their perceptions around deficit expectations.

As young children are embedded in their family field, they internalize the family beliefs and interactive processes (McConville, 1986, 1995; Stern, 1985). These processes and internalized beliefs are influenced by the historical context and cultural values available in the environment in which the family grows. When these beliefs and interactive processes or contact styles are out of awareness they can become stable patterns of interaction, limited in flexibility for each and every one of us. Children and adolescents with learning disabilities are especially vulnerable to contact disturbances if these processes are not named, brought into awareness, and then supported.

The experience of a child with a severe learning difficulty can be similar to that of a gifted child, or in fact, to that of any child who engages in an environment in which the field is not available for reception. Max Scheler's (1961) concept of *"ressentiment"* is a concept that comes to mind. Scheler wrote about teachers, who due to their own lack of giftedness held resentment for their gifted students and displayed this by being critical or non-accepting. Now again, we are reminded of the minority position, one of diverging from the norm and becoming a vulnerable target on account of one's differentness.

The converse is true, as well, as there are many gifted teachers who

167

are able to meet their students where they are and engage them in relationship so that reciprocal learning occurs. And, clearly, there are many families in which acknowledgment of strengths and weaknesses is explicit, and where unique and diverse styles of communication and learning are shared and embraced. It seems that the problem in the field of learning disabilities research is not in its extensive description of sub-optimal intra-cognitive processes that currently dominates the thinking in the field, but in its failure to describe how our most successful students are abled to learn. What are the processes of support and connection that enable the divergent among us to learn, to overcome our fears of being different or unique, and to fulfill our potentials for growth?

Conclusion

So it is within our specific cultural embeddedness that we tend to reify diverse learning styles as cognitive deficits that reside inside a person rather than as a condition of the social/psychological/cultural field. If learning disabilities are viewed in relation to field conditions, it seems relevant that we consider learning difficulties to be interactive challenges rather than a disability residing only inside a child or adolescent. Just as the goal of therapy is the transformation of the experience of shame into the experience of connection in the field, so, too, can learning experiences for children and adolescents with a variety of interactive styles be lived in connection rather than in isolation.

Support is defined by Gestalt therapy as interpersonal connection in the field. It is the backbone of therapy and of learning or change processes. The aim is not to be rid of shame but to live it in connection rather than in isolation (Lee, 1995). Gestalt therapy and the understanding of the development of the self within a context of relation and cultural/historical influence, can support the attention to valuing all learning styles, bringing these interactive patterns into awareness, and acknowledging the similarities and differences in various contexts.

Most of all, by being open to what is, by being available in the field we can continue to challenge the cultural introjects that invite disconnection, marginalization, disenfranchisement and the self construction of inadequacies. We can continue to influence the meaning making in our families, schools and communities through our own awareness of process and by supporting others in their endeavors.

References

Ainsworth, M. (1969). Object relations, dependency and attachment: A theoretical review of the infant-mother relationship. *Child Development, 40*, 969-1026.

Bowlby, J. (1969). *Attachment and loss: Vol. 1. Attachment*. New York: Basic Books.

Davenport, L. (1991). Adaptation to dyslexia: Acceptance of the diagnosis in relation to coping efforts and educational plans. Unpublished doctoral dissertation. Santa Barbara, CA: The Fielding Institute.

Hallowell, E., & Ratey, J. (1994). *Driven to distraction*. New York, NY: Simon & Schuster.

Latner, J. (1992). The theory of Gestalt therapy. In E. C. Nevis (Ed.), *Gestalt therapy: Perspectives and applications*. New York, NY: Gestalt Institute of Cleveland Press.

Lee, R. (1995). Gestalt and shame: The foundation for a clearer understanding of field dynamics. *British Gestalt Journal, 4*(1), 14-22.

McConville, M. (1986). The Gestalt phenomenology of adolescence. *Gestalt Institute of Cleveland Review, 1*.

McConville, M. (1995). *Adolescence: Psychotherapy and the emergent self*. San Francisco: Jossey-Bass.

Perls, F. S., Hefferline, R., & Goodman, P. (1951). *Gestalt therapy: Excitement and growth in the human personality*. New York, NY: Crown Publishers.

Scheler, M. (1961). *Ressentiment*. W. W. Holdheim, (Trans.). New York: Free Press of Glencoe.

Stern, D. N. (1985). *The interpersonal world of the infant*. New York, NY: Basic Books.

Wheeler, G. (1991). *Gestalt reconsidered: A new approach to contact and resistance*. New York, NY: The Gestalt Institute of Cleveland Press.

Wheeler, G. (1997). Unpublished lecture. Cleveland, OH: Gestalt Institute of Cleveland.

Wheeler, G. (1998). Towards a Gestalt developmental model. *British Gestalt Journal, 7*(2), 115 - 125.

Winnicott, D. (1965). *The maturational processes and the facilitating environment*. New York, NY: International Universities Press.

Part II:

Applications in the Field

6

Coming Out of the Shadows: Supporting the Development of our Gay, Lesbian, and Bisexual Adolescents

Allan Singer

The Dawning of a New Age

Several years ago my colleague, Fraelean Curtis and I attended the Boston Lesbian, Gay, Bisexual & Transgender Youth Pride Parade.[1, 2] On that warm, mid-spring day, several hundred "kids" from the city and the suburbs gathered their youthful enthusiasm, marching proudly, visibly, some arm-in-arm, some carrying placards such as, "How dare you presume I'm heterosexual" or "Brookline High School Gay-Straight Student Alliance." Many kids waved rainbow-colored banners, occasionally chanting a slogan or just whooping it up with glee; others walked more quietly, purposefully. And at the rally following the parade, we listened to a young woman, probably about seventeen-years-old, speak to the crowd about her experience in high school after coming out as gay in a school newspaper article on discrimination faced by various minorities. She recounted how scared she had felt that first day in school after her article's publication, and how she willed herself to be courageous and to stand up to anyone who gave her any grief. And when someone passed her in the hallway corridor and yelled, "You're a dyke!" she mustered her courage and yelled right back, "That's right; now deal with it!"

We stood with frequent amazement that day, quite moved by this assemblage of youth gathered together, supporting each other and celebrating the diversity of their sexual orientations. We asked ourselves, in a reflective moment, what enabled these boys and girls to be so self aware of the possibilities of their own sexual orientations, let alone to be so "out," so public, at so young an age? Wistfully, we recollected our own experiences of adolescence and 'coming out. It was a different world then, in the 1960s--a world opening up in many ways to the voices and experience of ethnic and racial minorities, to dissident political views, and to a more open sexuality for straight identified young people. But it was much less inviting and open for GLB experience and identity. Newspaper or magazine articles related to homosexuality were few and far between, and often pathologically focused. Occasional movie depictions (*Tea and Sympathy*, *The Children's Hour*, *Staircase*, *The Killing of Sister George*, *The Boys in the Band*) typically focused on stereotyped characteristics, with self-loathing as the integral by-product of being "queer;" often culminating in death or abject humiliation as the inevitable outcome of public exposure. With work, family, and community lives to protect, no public figures announced their homosexual inclinations. I recall at sixteen going to the public library to do research for some school paper, diverting my attention briefly to check out the card catalogue listings for "Homosexuality," and finding a scant few references, mostly old texts framing homosexuality as a form of pathological "sexual inversion." Those references, which I viewed quickly, furtively, with an anxious, vigilant awareness of who might be standing nearby, were not encouraging, offering no hope or suggestion of healthful possibility.

No, indeed, thirty years ago, parades like this one did not exist, and coming out certainly was not a fashionable option. As Fraelean and I reflected upon the day, we shared a mixture of pleasure and pride, but also a wisp of sadness as we thought of our own histories of coming out. In many ways, these parading adolescents seemed to inhabit an utterly different world from the one that we had known. Certainly they have benefited from the intervening years of social and cultural change, from the beginnings of the sixties' cultural revolution, through the emergence of the Gay Rights movement in seventies and eighties, to the emergence today of mainstream media representations of well-adjusted gays and lesbians in television and movies. And certainly they have benefited from the progress made in the increasingly public and political debate concerning Gay, Lesbian, and Bisexual (GLB) dignity and rights, which has accomplished among other things, the passage of the Safe Schools Act in my home state of Massachusetts, with its commitment to creating safe school environments for all students, regardless of sexual orientation.

But at the same time, and for all the changes that have begun for GLB individuals in our culture, Fraelean and I felt a great deal in common with these youth who paraded so proudly, as well. For, as much as our society has changed over time, we recognized that certain themes of adolescent development--such as the exploration and discovery of identity, and the challenge of finding support for this process--remain critical and problematic in spite of societal and cultural change. What is different today, and what remains the same, we asked ourselves? And how do these changes, or indeed, how does culture generally, enter dynamically into the identity--and particularly the sexual identity--of the developing adolescent? How does the experience of the gay/lesbian/bisexual adolescent differ from young people with a heterosexual orientation? And how are they the same?

As Gestalt therapists, we recognize the intrinsic and dynamic interrelationship of figure and ground. And certainly, the figural development of sexual orientation, whether it is GLB or straight identified, occurs against the ground of prevailing cultural norms, supports, ambivalence, negations, and outright punishment. How can the Gestalt approach help us to clarify these interrelationships? And then, how can this perspective guide all of us--straight identified and GLB identified alike--as we work with young people seeking to define themselves and their worlds, in the crucial arena of sexuality and sexual orientation?

These are the questions that began to emerge for me as I watched and reflected upon the wonderful spectacle of young people parading through the streets of Boston that Spring afternoon. In the chapter that follows, I will present my effort, from a Gestalt developmental perspective, to begin to answer some of these questions. In doing so, I'd like to begin by describing my own starting point as I began to think through these issues--my recollections of my own experience of coming out a generation ago, and what this revealed to me concerning the larger developmental themes of self-discovery, self-awareness, and identity, and of the intrinsic connection of these developments with the field processes of support and shame.

Coming Out: Then

Allan's Personal Reflection

As I walked through the corridors of my suburban school at the age of 12 or 13, going from one class to another, my primary objective was usually to stay as unnoticeable as possible. Since grade school, I had become intimately acquainted with words like "queer," "faggot," "sissy," "girl," and similar references intended to highlight my failure measure up to some perceived scale of male adequacy. I never knew which of my 'shortcomings' might have evoked such targeting at a given moment; was my voice too high? Was I not athletic enough? Was I somehow participating in my nomination to social ignominy? Certainly I didn't know how to protect myself very well, except through humorous deflection. Today I know that I was far from alone in these types of boyhood encounters of social abuse. In the years since, I have come to understand that many of my fellow males, regardless of sexual orientation, grow up with some core anxiety about male adequacy and whether we're "good enough"--based on performance measures such as early athletic ability or how well we defend ourselves from other boys' aggressive behaviors (which may themselves be motivated by insecurity and shame). Fortunately for me, I generally managed to form a close friendship with at least one other boy, or with a small circle from my fellow social outcasts. Nonetheless, I had learned and introjected from early boyhood that somehow I was different and not okay; consequently, social invisibility became the safest option.

The experiential fact of my attraction to (some) other males had also established itself from my earliest conscious memories. So it came as no surprise when, around this time, I developed a "major crush" on another boy, longing to sit near to him when in class so that I might gaze upon his beautiful countenance, admiring the contours of his form, the fine line of his nose, those beautiful eyes... Alas, how I hoped that he might notice me, my heart racing whenever our paths crossed, secretly gazing at him out of the periphery of my vision. At the same time, I dreaded his notice with equal force, terrifyingly aware as I was of the constant potential for peer group terrorism. After all, while I knew that boy-girl crushes were the increasing order of social conversations, ("Who's making out with whom this week?"), I equally knew that boys were not supposed to be falling in love with other boys. No songs on the radio pleaded the passions or heartbreaks of same-sex lovers. Neither movies nor television shows portrayed the existence of same-sex romance. Rather, in the dank mustiness of school locker rooms and hallways, verbal projectiles of "faggot" and "queer" permeated everyday conversation, not necessarily as a matter of construing sexual orientation, but as a means of derogating and attacking personal adequacy through an all-purpose, gender insult. I certainly believed that any disclosure of my own affectional inclinations would consign me permanently to a new level of social disgrace, with consequences I could not imagine surviving. No, indeed, the longings of my heart would remain hidden, transformed into endless romantic, occasionally masturbatory, fantasy and dreams of an imagined life

During those lengthy days, months, and years of adolescence, as I retroflectively cultivated my yearnings, I clung to the hope that my life would someday improve after leaving home for college (having projected in a creatively adaptive way that my personal problems were related to the deficiencies of the local population). I never once identified myself as homosexual, let alone, "gay" (the newly-adopted reference of self-pride). At 16, when I fell in love (once again from afar) with my Scottish English teacher, infatuated with the sound of his voice and the pronunciation of his words, I did so without a label for my love, other than love itself. Like many an infatuated adolescent, I sought solace in the privacy of my darkened room, listening to Barbara Streisand sing of love almost found, inevitably lost, and lucky people needing other people. I found a mirror for my heart in that music, drawing inspiration from the image of a star who had made it against the odds of public convention. When I noticed the rare reference to homosexuality in the newspapers or magazines, I poured over every word, absorbing each reference with hunger, never once telling myself; "I am one, too." I recall moving a portable television into my locked bedroom, lights off, during my fifteenth year in order to watch a CBS network special "White Paper on Homosexuality," which featured interviews with homosexual men in shadow, to protect their anonymity, as they discussed their hardships, their attempts to change, and their needs to stay hidden from view. Somehow, I knew that I needed to watch that program, to witness the reality of their lives. While I still I had no label for my feelings, my sexual attractions, I instinctively knew that I was not ready to know any more than I did, certainly not without more support from within and without.

Apparently no one in my family or personal network picked up on anything unusual: my "ups and downs" apparently seemed within the ordinary range of adolescent moodiness. At one point, another English teacher, sensitively noticing the desperation reflected in my writings, insisted that we meet to talk. I both appreciated and avoided his invitation, and when he finally insisted, I managed to conceal the true underpinnings of my depressed sensibilities. Still, I drew strength that he noticed and seemed concerned. And I determined that I would participate in school dances and proms, just like everybody else, not wanting to exclude myself or seem different, perhaps in part defying what I projected that others expected of me.

In the end I did not begin to label my own sexual orientation until my sophomore year of college. I once again had fallen in love, this time with a fellow student who had become my trusted friend. Deciding to come out to David and risking losing his friendship was probably the hardest thing I have ever had to do. That he tried in earnest to support me by asking; "How do you know for sure, Allan?" didn't comfort me in the way that I truly needed, but his follow-up phone calls reassured me of his continuing interest. My worst fears of rejection and renewed isolation abated. I didn't learn until much later that David was struggling to come to terms with his own sexuality. As it happened, we took a sociology course together entitled "Deviance and Respectability," subsequently scouring the Washington, DC gay community in the interest of thorough research. As I entered my first gay bar with anxiety-laced excitement and noticed a dance floor filled with multitudes of men, some of them appearing directly from my years of cultivated fantasy, I could hardly believe my eyes... the strangeness... the rightness... the visibility of it all actually happening. Years of masking, of hiding, of imagining and hoping, and now seeing that I had not been alone, after all, even as I had felt so alone for so long. I didn't accept David's invitation to dance with me that evening; I didn't believe that he meant it at the time, but in truth, I was too anxious, too excited, too disbelieving in the face of this wonderful revelation.

It would be several years and numerous college gay research papers later into the next phase of my coming out process, into my twenties, before I would feel ready to experiment with my first sexual encounters. This would occur only after I had begun to consolidate the validity and goodness of my sexual orientation. This I accomplished through my own increased self-understanding and acceptance (with the help of a good, non-judgmental therapist), and through selectively disclosing my gayness to friends and family in a considered and considerable effort to build my ground of support. I didn't realize then that coming out, as a process, would continue in some form throughout my life; each time I let someone know that I'm gay, or mention my spouse's name, or even state that I write and speak on GLB topics, I come out anew, sometimes stirring the anxiety of unmasking that I experienced as an adolescent when I didn't have a choice. I'm glad that I do now. And I'm moved that more adolescents today experience that choice and that sense of possibility to create a life. It's what I'd always hoped for, and more than I'd dreamt possible.

Fraelean's Personal Reflection

I grew into adolescence in a small New England town during the early 1960s, where I attended parochial school. I first remember feeling different at age 13 when my best friend became interested in boys. I felt her focus shift away from the two of us towards spending time with boys, and I clearly understood that my friend's behavior was "normal" and that my longing to remain her special friend was "abnormal." This experience informed a long, lonely journey of feeling abnormal, ugly, and not fully human, because I was not interested in spending time with boys. I harbored a deep, emotional longing for my girlfriends, which I experienced as a persistent emotional ache. I loved my girlfriends, but I had no sexual feelings for them. Sexual feelings were not available to me at all until I was in my late 20s.

During my teens and early 20s, I looked for evidence that caring between two women could be fulfilling. I went to movies hoping to see relationships between women that lasted and remained important throughout a woman's life, regardless of career and marriage. I felt alone and separate from the excitement of dating and sexual attractions that my friends were experiencing. In my mid-20s, I went into therapy because I wanted to be "normal," which meant to date men and to feel sexually attracted to them. The therapist I worked with agreed that I indeed needed to do just that. Through the course of this therapy, I developed sexual feelings but they were for women. This terrified me and I spoke of my feelings in therapy in an unimpassioned way for fear that I would have to consider myself as more disturbed than I already had thought I was. My therapist responded that I was finally going through "adolescent same sex attraction" and that soon I would be interested in men. I changed from this therapist eventually and saw another therapist with whom (I believed) I could discuss my sexual attraction for women. However, he seemed clearly invested in supporting any heterosexual interest that I mentioned. Eventually I saw an openly lesbian-identified therapist who gave me full permission to explore all of my feelings for women. As I look back upon my coming out journey, I regret the years of confusion, loneliness, isolation and fear, and I regret the time spent in therapy with professionals who were not able to support and appreciate my attraction to women. I feel fortunate to live in a time when GLB youth can be understood and supported both in therapy and in social organizations.

Emerging Figure Formation: Adolescent Developmental Tasks & Their Complications for GLB Youth

McConville (1995) presents a Gestalt framework for understanding adolescent development, describing the shift in how children receive and organize awareness and experience as they move into adolescence. On the one hand, there is the child's enlarging capacity to organize his/her field of experience at more and more complex levels. On the other hand, the child faces a growing exposure to wider, more diverse fields of information and influence apart from the family environment. As McConville elaborates, these dynamic factors mean a *reorganization of the self* in adolescence. The childhood organization of self, while a collaborative, relational, co-construction from a Gestalt point of view, relies heavily upon introjection--the direct absorption of a whole worldview, particularly mediated by the family field--to provide structure and meaning (p. 29). The child is an active participant in this creation of meaning, but essentially within the framework of an introjected worldview. With the evolution of neuro-cognitive development, social learning, and parental/educational/environmental support, the growing child progressively plays a more active role in determining the outcome of this process. As natural propensities for curiosity, exploration and awareness-formation emerge, particularly as adolescence gets underway, the individual shifts increasingly away from the mode of introjecting-without-awareness towards a mode of questioning, analysis, and the beginnings of critical thinking and judgment formation--i.e., the perceptual and cognitive equivalents of chewing with discernment.

As children introject and absorb prevailing cultural beliefs, messages, and cues from their family and wider environment, in the process they are assimilating the multiplicity of everyday images of "appropriate" gender behavior expected from boys and girls and emulated through adult male and female representations. Messages about same-sex versus opposite-sex expressions of affection and the expected boundaries of physical/sexual intimacy are held in the whole system of a given culture and expressed through varied means such as the family, the school, peers, religion, the legal system, and the media. This multiplicity of messages, then, represents the external organizing context within which children organize and ascribe meaning to their experiential data, including their developing awareness of internal sensations in response to their interpersonal attractions.

Many, though by no means, all GLB adults recall experiencing same-sex attractions from their very early memories of sexual attraction in childhood. However, children do not generally possess a language or an internal or environmental reference system to distinguish their attractions by labeling them "gay," "lesbian," "bisexual," or "transgender." By way of example, recall what I shared of my personal experience earlier in the chapter: while I was aware of sexual attractions for males from my earliest memories, I did not assign a label to my experience until later adolescence, when I had accumulated enough experiential data about my sensations, and felt internally supported enough to bear the anxiety and excitement mobilized by reflectively knowing myself. Sensations, attractions, and desires typically are held within the child's experiential world as "raw material," perhaps phenomenologically experienced as merely benign awareness, or creatively energized as fantasy and dream material. Given the relative absence even today of images of same-sex intimate pair-bonding in the environmental surround, it seems likely that GLB children with pre-figural experience of same-sex attractions learn early on to experience themselves internally as just "different." For those many GLB adults who become aware of same-sex attractions later into their chronological and emotional development, the pre-figural awareness of feeling somehow different may likewise be their initial experience, until the point in time when internal and external resources are sufficiently evolved to support figural experience of same-sex affection, attraction and response.

McConville (1995) elaborates how adolescence involves the process of *maturation of the contact boundary*--the boundary that defines the self and at the same time organizes and regulates its intercourse with the environment, allowing both closeness/connectedness and separateness/differentiation. In this schema, three significant processes contribute to the emergence and transformation of the contact boundary over time:

1. Disembedding from the family field.
2. Increasing capacity for interiority.
3. Integration of inner and outer changes in new, richer modes of contact/engagement.

In the Gestalt developmental model, the development of self and the maturation of the contact boundary are one and the same process. For McConville, the concrete manifestations of this developmental process are the adolescents efforts to re-negotiate the boundaries of important relationships (disembedding), the growing sensation and awareness of a personal and private inner world (interiority), and the implementation of these discoveries and accomplishments in the form of new, richer behavioral and relational commitments (integration). In his model, McConville correctly and usefully conceives these tasks as recursive, or back and forth, rather than rigidly sequenced. We encounter adolescents, in other words, sometimes focusing their energies on interpersonal boundaries (as when distancing from parents, for example); sometimes focusing on inner experience (as when cultivating sexual arousal and fantasy, for example); and sometimes focusing their energies on new modes of behavior and/or relationship which integrate both (as when trying on a new identity, or establishing a romantic relationship, for example). And these three tasks are pursued recursively, each serving as a backdrop and a support for the others.

The defining characteristic of this Gestalt model is its recognition that development is a matter of engaging, transforming, and being transformed by the surrounding social and cultural field. As Paul Goodman wrote, the psychological self cannot be understood independent of the field that it attempts to resolve (Perls, Hefferline, & Goodman, 1951). Elaborating upon this insight of Goodman's, Wheeler (1998) has written that the surrounding society and culture "...are not just 'the environment of the child's self' but *are the dynamic material which is actually being integrated*" (p. 118, emphasis added). Political and social conditions, in other words, and certainly a society's attitudes toward sexual orientation and identity, "become something more than the background: they are integrated into the self-structure of the developing subjective person" (Wheeler, 1998, p. 118). What the Gestalt approach teaches us therefore, is that we cannot appreciate the self development and sexual identity formation of any youth without looking first at the social context of that development. And because our current societal and cultural context creates entirely different possibilities of shame and support depending upon sexual orientation, the developmental tasks described by McConville are significantly complicated for GLB adolescents. The point I wish to make, and which the Gestalt model helps to explain, is that the developmental process of *becoming a self*, that is, of disembedding from the family field, discovering ones interiority, and integrating these discoveries in the form of identity and relationship, is significantly different for GLB youth. In the remainder of this chapter, I will describe the nature of this difference. It is my hope that a clearer description of the tasks and challenges faced by GLB adolescents will enable caregivers, straight and GLB alike, to better understand and serve the developmental needs of their adolescent clients. (Here, as throughout this chapter, I recognize that gender orientation considerations implicit in transgender identity development may not be adequately described in this presentation, and again deserve their own careful consideration, though this is beyond the scope of this chapter. Likewise, I make no attempt here to speak 'for' Lesbian experience, which will certainly both resemble and differ from gay male experience in many important ways.)

Increasing Interiority While Masking the Emerging Figure of Self

Gay, lesbian, and bisexual youth experience the aforementioned developmental schema but with additional significant considerations. The tasks of normative adolescent development are inherently more complicated for the GLB youth because the field itself is more troubled and contradictory. In particular, the emergent sense of oneself may often be of *a self that needs to hide from contact in order to survive*. Generally, adolescent intrapsychic movement involves increasing awareness of internal experience (interiority), even as the onset of puberty and hormonal production is precipitating an often volcanic emergence of sexuality informed by the intrapsychic and biochemical aspects of sexual and interpersonal attraction. Within this potent intrapsychic/biochemical mix of pubescence, the orienting function of sexual orientation begins to emerge. Depending on the individual adolescent, homosexual attractions often enter as pre-figural awareness, i.e., as a broadened awareness of sensations and attractions that may focus upon or merely include others of the same sex, but without necessarily being labeled by the individual as such. The adolescent boy or girl not yet ready to support a clearly-defined awareness of same-sex attraction inhibits, suppresses, or otherwise retroflects consciously experienced or clearly focused sexual attraction. In this earlier developmental stage, the adolescent may experience an intensified "crush" on someone from afar, or entertain in fantasy romanticized same-sex adventures, or perhaps experience him/herself as somehow "different" in a vaguely unsettling way while remaining unsure as to the actual nature of that difference. Some GLB adolescents note their differentness as their friends speak of opposite sex interests, with or without noting same-sex attractions at that time. The absence of opposite sex attractions may become increasingly unsettling, or framed as just "a stage" that will pass. For bisexually-oriented adolescents, opposite sex attractions may become figural prior to same-sex attractions, or the reverse may apply, or attractions to both sexes may co-exist figurally. The adolescent who develops internalized supports and flexible contact skills cultivates a readiness to sustain the anxiety of self-revelation without threatening the integrity of the self-boundary. Pre-figural awareness of sexual attraction gradually coalesces into a sharpening boundary of self-awareness, perhaps sharpening the sense of being different from the others, and often crystallizing in an increasing intensity of same-sex attractions, or in an attraction to a particular other. The movement toward claiming figural awareness of GLB orientation culminates in the process of self-identification through labeling, or "coming out to oneself." Again, this moment of self-revelation reveals itself uniquely for each GLB individual and, as with all processes of development, needs its own time and contextual support with which to emerge.

The process of moving from unlabeled sensory experience to an emerging figural awareness of GLB orientation typically unfolds against a childhood background of introjecting the prevailing messages about homosexuality held in the environmental surround. Attitudes and beliefs about sexuality and gender roles have been introjected through interaction with family, peers, and the institutions of culture: educational, religious, political, social, and legal. Media representations of "Who we are supposed to become" have typically saturated the adolescent sensibility throughout the preceding years of exposure to television, radio, music, talk shows, cartoons, and now the computerized "info-world." Whether homosexuality has or hasn't received much press and publicity for the specific adolescent at hand, the overwhelming mass of messages and images supporting notions of heterosexual outcome drench our culture, and these introjects have been absorbed into the cellular psychological tissue of our GLB adolescents. Historically (and presently still), the sheer valence of these cultural messages regarding same-sex sexual attraction and orientation has either negated, disparaged, or discouraged the sense of affirming life possibilities for the gay, lesbian, or bisexually-identified person. Thus, the adolescent emerging into figural awareness of GLB orientation typically experiences some degree of the accompanying shame surrounding her/his incipient sense of difference.

Figural awareness is that moment of self-revelation and surprise (or shock) when an individual self-labels what has heretofore been a less clearly delineated experience of sensation and awareness. Figural, bounded self-definitions might include; "Oh my God, I must be gay!"; "I love another girl; I wonder if that means I'm lesbian?"; "I like her, but I also like him; maybe I'm bi." Gestalt theory teaches us that we need to have enough *support* from within and/or from without in order to tolerate novel figural awareness and the corresponding anxiety. Hence, until the GLB adolescent builds enough ground of internal and/or external support with which to manage a figural awareness of sexual orientation, the emerging process of awareness is typically managed through retroflection, or holding back. The adolescent keeps awareness of the meaning of his/her same-sex feelings and attractions as undefined and held back as necessary to maintain her/his self-integrity and to avoid being threatened by totalizing, shame-bound, "bad self" feelings. Through private containment and through confluence, acting as if one were the same and felt the same as a projected *Heterosexual-Everyone-Else*, the

183

adolescent protects him/herself from becoming affectively overwhelmed.

Once again, the developmental movement towards increasing interiority and heightened awareness of internal experience nourishes the defining, boundary-making figure of sexual orientation during adolescence. The GLB adolescent with a healthy-enough sense of her/his contact boundaries, including the ability to sustain anxiety and to assess environmental support, typically masks awareness of sexual orientation from exposure in contact, either intra-personally (keeping one's figure of sexual orientation internally unlabeled) and/or interpersonally (keeping one's sexual attractions and orientation a secret from others). The adaptive aim of this resistance to contact is to protect the emergent self from environmental disconfirmation and to prevent the surfacing of potentially overwhelming anxiety and shame.

The adolescent who discloses homosexual inclinations without adequately developed internal and/or external supports risks volatile consequences, including potential emotional lability, peer and/or familial rejection, or even suicidality. Indeed, over forty percent of all homeless adolescents have been identified as GLB (Governor's Commission, 1993). Other prevalent risk factors include alcohol/drug abuse and unsafe sexual behavior. Developmentally, adolescents often experience an abbreviated perception of time combined with a distorted sense of their own invulnerability when in the throes of an excited state. An increasing capacity for interiority does not immediately translate into the development of perspective. Hence, adolescents are often more prone to acting on impulses and seeking immediate gratifications without thinking through the consequences of their actions. In the age of AIDS, unsafe sexual behavior is of particular concern. So high-risk adolescents, such as those who seem in a particular rush to come out without discrimination or without thinking through their resources and needs for support, in particular, need to be carefully evaluated diagnostically in terms of their overall contact functioning and risk for self-destructive behavior.

Re-Embedding the Self Within a Social Closet

Adolescents shift their introjective field of influence increasingly away from parents and family, moving in the direction of their peer group for a sense of relatedness and identification. Behavioral influences and cues from the peer group and its representations in the world of media and marketing begin to assume greater import. The world of one's family transforms into a holding ground of varying degrees of restriction and supervision, perhaps a guaranteed shelter, perhaps an emotional sanctuary with (or within) a room of one's own, including free meals, a hot shower, and a mirror to scrutinize one's daily appearance and bodily changes. The adolescent reconstructs her/his perceptions of parents and siblings, reconfiguring the family constellation into a background springboard for diving into the foreground of social and school life. In normative adolescent development, there is an attempt to stand apart from the milieu of parents and family, separating oneself from one's "uncool" or prehistoric founding dinosaurs in order to define one's own evolutionary next step. Concurrently, the adolescent remains exquisitely sensitive to other's opinions and approval, including parents and other family members. Yet, as the adolescent works to explore, define, and assemble her/his own unique identity, uniqueness is often measured paradoxically in terms of the peer group mores and acceptance. Adolescents want desperately to belong and to be accepted as part of their group. Without bathing in enough peer group social acceptance, adolescents dis-embedding from their family field and re-identifying their identity within their peer world risk their foundations of self-esteem and self-confidence, risking being overwhelmed by a menacing sense of isolation and loneliness.

For GLB youth, once again this task of adolescent development, that of re-embedding in a re-defined context, is conflictual in that the move away from the family of origin precipitates a concurrent move both toward and away from the peer group. As with any adolescent, GLB youth need to join and experience belonging with their peer group, or some part of it. At the same time, GLB adolescents in increasing figural awareness of their sexual orientation recognize their singular difference from heterosexual peers and the related (heterosexist) cultural surround. School socials, locker room conversations, and weekend dates all become markers for the GLB adolescent to notice his/her difference. The prospect of being "discovered" raises intensified projections of shaming and derogation by peers, particularly critical at a period when acceptance, when who is "cool" and who is not, is at a premium. The adolescent who privately begins to figurally identify her/himself as gay, lesbian, or bisexual typically experiences heightened anxiety and fear, sometimes terror and panic, at the possibility of being "found out," even if she/he is already targeted and taunted by peers. Many GLB youths simply 'pass' invisibly, not appearing gender discrepant in their presentation or behavior, often engaging in heterosexual talk and dating. For some, the effort to mask same-sex attractions by heterosexual involvement reflects a genuine exploration and experimentation with sexual identity and fluidity. For others, this effort to "pass" is a survival strategy in the face of potential social disgrace. Some GLB adolescents become hyper-vigilant, trying to erase any vestiges of similarity or association with homosexuality, including "identifying with the aggressor" by taunting or telling "fag jokes" or gay-bashing. Occasionally, some GLB youths become heterosexually promiscuous or go so far as to create pregnancy in order to prove their heterosexuality in the face of threatening internal sensations which suggest otherwise.

A more recent, encouraging development in some contemporary communities are those GLB youth, usually of high school age, who do decide to come out to their peers and/or families. After all, the times really are changing, gender roles and representations are expanding in variety, and information about diversity in sexual orientation is more openly discussed than in previous decades. Boys wear their earrings, and girls play athletics, and appearances that formerly called someone's sexuality into question may no longer automatically do so. In some adolescent circles, gay is "cool" and bisexuality is fashionably "in." But let's not kid ourselves; it's still a big deal for the GLB youth who decides to come out. The risk of social rejection remains paramount except perhaps in the most enlightened of communities. Still, more GLB youth are tolerating the risk of being socially marginalized, harassed, or even endangered, by identifying themselves openly. Some have told me; "It's no big deal." "My friends, if they're really my friends, accept me for who I am." There are occasional stories of a gay youth taking his or her same-sex date to the school prom, sometimes after battling the school authorities for that right. Some communities offer "alternative dances/proms" specifically to provide a safe and "normalizing" context for their GLB youth. In several major cities, special alternative high schools like the Harvey Milk School in New York have opened to serve those GLB youth who could no longer tolerate the harassment that they faced in their previous school settings. Likewise, there are an increasing number of community social groups serving GLB youth, such as the *Alliances for Gay & Lesbian Youth*, which offer groups, counseling, and places to "hang out." In some enlightened guidance counselor's offices, posters or pamphlets visibly display the existence and implicit acceptance of GLB concerns by displaying a positive image or by indicating local resources. Some public libraries stock local or national GLB periodicals.

Since many youths exploring their identities may experience some confusion about their sexual preferences, such social change allows adolescents to consider themselves with a more open sense of possibility. Granted, confusion about one's sexual orientation heightens anxiety and requires permission and support to be unsure, to explore, and to avoid rushing into labeling identity prematurely. Psychotherapists, in turn, need to respect an adolescent's pace in exploring his or her sexual orientation without an investment in a particular outcome or a rush to label out of some well-meaning intention to assure the adolescent of the therapist's enlightenment and acceptance. Tolerating uncertainty and its traffic signal of anxiety is an intrinsic part of any exploration, for both therapist and client. As always, the social context, the "ground," informs and interfaces with the figure of GLB identity formation, and profoundly so when considering the developmental task of re-embedding within one's peer group.

An affirmative, all-inclusive context, such as a "gay/straight student alliance" potentially offers an invaluable "holding environment" for the GLB or self-exploring adolescent, who may experience a sense of belonging and safety with peers otherwise unavailable to him or her, regardless of whether they are ready to come out explicitly. For others, though, the mere thought of entering a room hosting a "gay-straight alliance" group might be tantamount to an act of self-disclosure and an intolerable level of exposure. No one can ultimately judge an adolescent's readiness to experiment with re-embedding her/himself in such a context, except the adolescent him/herself.

The impact of the larger social field and its visibly available supports cannot be overstated in determining whether GLB adolescents decide to come out at this stage of developing figure formation. However, even in the most supportive social fields, the process of coming out (for anyone, and certainly for adolescents in particular, given developmental issues) heightens anxiety around fears of rejection and loss of love. Self-esteem in this early process is often on the line and subject to extremes of variability. Prospects for feeling okay about oneself and for the possibilities of leading a "happy life" are necessarily perceived from the adolescents' limited base of experiential knowledge; therefore projections are often skewed. The adolescent ready to come out may feel major anxiety, dread, or despair; or conversely, may experience a "pink cloud" of euphoria, or a heightened sense of personal power combined with rebellious motivations or anger-laced, "in your face" self-declarations. As with any person, each adolescent mobilizes into action based on whatever mix of internal and external forces provides the fuel of her/his excitement. Ideally, coming out publicly results in an accepting-enough response, which enables our given adolescent to experience support rather than shaming, and accompanying relief from the years of retroflected energy and the intensified projections preceding the coming out disclosure. There are certainly no guarantees that anyone can offer an individual about what actually will occur in response to coming out publicly. Since adolescents often don't fully consider or think through the consequences of their decision-making, a therapist can provide support by helping them to consider the "*what if's.*"

- What are they expecting from coming out?
- What do they imagine the other person's reactions will be?
- What if they do not receive the reactions they hope for?
- How do they imagine they'll feel in that event?
- How would they ideally like to react ?
- What and whom might support them if things do not go according to their hopes and needs with family or with friends?
- What resources are available to them, as well as to the person/people to whom they plan to come out (including reading materials and national group support resources such as: *Parents and Friends of Lesbians and Gays*)?

All of these questions help orient adolescents for whom publicly coming out as GLB has become figural, not only to their awareness of present excitement and mobilization, but also to their need to define adequate support in the face of possible negative consequence. Adolescent development requires self-expression, acting out the self, as a means of experimenting with new behaviors, trying on new roles, and ultimately defining a deepening, expanding sense of identity. The delicate balance between providing supportive acceptance while encouraging awareness and discretion in acting out is part of artistry of therapeutic intervention with a GLB adolescent at this stage.

Keep in mind that at this point of history, even with tremendous strides in greater public awareness and increasing visibility of GLB youth, the majority of GLB adolescents with emerging or figural awareness of their sexual orientation do not come out to anyone during their adolescent years. As concerned, well-intentioned care-providers, we must not be in a hurry to rush the coming out process. Closeted awareness is certainly defining and, while it may also be confining, the darkened, secret confines of a hidden self may be the safest alternative available to a given adolescent depending on the strength of inner and outer supports. That's why the light seems so incredibly bright, sometimes even momentarily blinding, when we finally open up that closet door to reach out, to reveal, to make contact.

Identity Integration and The Postponement of Acting Out

Exploration... experimentation... taking metaphorical bites from the world of experience and chewing on it, with increasing capacity to reach out and seek from the grab-bag of possibility: the world of adolescence suggests opportunities to move from a deepening inner life to sampling from an expanding outer world. As previously cited, McConville (1995) addresses the need for adolescents to act upon their world as a developmental imperative, as a movement from childhood reliance on introjection to more active, integrative processes as a primary means of relating to experience. For GLB youth, certain forms of acting out which heterosexuals take for granted are put on hold. How many times a day, for instance, do teenagers talk together about whom they find cute, who's got a "nice bod'," who's developing in what way, whom they "like," whom they'd like to ask out for Saturday night, or by whom they'd like to be asked out. How many endless telephone calls tie up the lines with talk of who's going out with whom, who's in love with whom, who made out with whom, who broke up with whom, etc. These things are part of developing social skills. Certainly, experiencing the panoply of excitements, tensions, rewards, and angst in discovering mutual attraction is part of developing self and self-confidence during adolescence.

For GLB youth in the closet however, social skills practice in addressing intimacy needs with same-sex objects of affection and/or lust is typically delayed. Making that anxiety-ridden phone call to ask someone for the first date; learning to handle acceptance and rejection; traversing the pleasures, pratfalls, and frequent awkwardness in dating contact, in deciding when to meet and what to do, in reaching over to hold the other's hand, and then figuring how and whether to move on from there; experiencing the awakening emotions which arise when keeping company with someone special, and then being able to talk about it with your best friend (or maybe the entire public school assembly). All of these things, talked about between friends and classmates in the hallway corridors and in furtively-passed notes during algebra class, are the stuff of blossoming adolescence in our culture, the maturing no-longer-child playing with the newly accessible, forbidden fruits of adult life.

All of these things--these tempting foodstuffs of intrapsychic and interpersonal development and the associated social skills--are held inside, retroflected, gestating deep in the hearts and fantasies of our GLB adoles-

cents occupying their closet. What happens to those yearnings to belong intimately when the postponement of dating and peer discussion of dating lasts
throughout adolescence? Does the yearning to belong to an intimate other
necessarily intensify when it gets held in secret for so long? Does fantasy
life become more creatively essential? Do defenses or resistances to contact
develop in heightened ways in order to manage retroflected or deflected
desire?

For instance, if remaining hidden in the culture is a form of confluence, a conforming to an imposed social norm, how does that inform the
GLB individuals' later capacity to express an individuated voice? What then
are the potential impacts for GLB adults, when adolescent social skills practice and identity development through acting out the self in order to explore
same-sex orientation, are not possible in the same way? I pose these questions here without pretending (or wanting) to offer generalized answers, certainly not in the absence of adequate research. I do offer my conviction,
grounded in the phenomenological premises of Gestalt theory that any
knowing ultimately comes from contacting each person's actual experience
and felt reality.

Concluding and Continuing Visions

I want to conclude this chapter with a vision of hope. I hope for a
world which embraces each human being's uniqueness and which places an
ultimate value on our ability to get along with each other by knowing our
communalities, and respecting our differences. I hope for a world which
supports our capacities to form sustaining and supporting attachments, in
which our capacities to love and to care for one another are celebrated. In
this world an individual's given sexual orientation is a non-issue--or rather,
it is held as a vital, meaning-inspiring and organizing aspect of a fully complex being, to be witnessed and understood and treasured. I hope that gay
men, lesbian women, bisexual women and men, and transgendered people
of whatever sexual orientation, as well as heterosexually-identified men and
women, shall all have nothing less than complete and equal civil liberties,
for full human participation and development. I dream that each and every
child shall grow up feeling supported in discovering his/her own delights in
living, including attractions and interests and excitements, so that in the passage from adolescence to mature adulthood, our children shall learn to
embrace their sexuality fully in their own time, to enjoy their sensuality as a
part of their capacities to belong intimately, and to act responsibly in order

to maintain mutual health and well-being. I hope that each person shall find enough love in the world for nourishment and love across a lifetime. Love between men; love between women; love between men and women; love across the span of gender identifications; in whatever manner of sexual and affectionate expression feels right, which no one of us can ultimately determine or judge for another.

Meanwhile, for this vision to become real, each of us has a role to play. For the therapist of whatever sex, gender, or sexual orientation, that role is to educate ourselves and the parents and other caregivers we work with on the specific challenges and developmental dilemmas of GLB identity formation, and then to work to support each adolescent in his/her own unique developmental course. This chapter provides one Gestalt exploration as a frame for understanding these issues, and hopefully for stimulating your awareness and thinking. This planet's a big place, and at the same time from another perspective, it's a tiny circumference. Still it's big enough to hold all of us, all of our experience and all of our dreams

References

Alyson, S. (1991). *Young, gay, & proud*. Boston, MA: Alyson Publications.

Bernstein, R., & Siberman, S. (1996). *Generation Q*. Los Angeles, CA: Alyson Publications.

Chandler, K. (1995). *Passages of pride: True stories of lesbian and gay teenagers*. Los Angeles: Alyson Publications.

DeCrescenzo, T. (1994). *Helping gay and lesbian youth*. New York, NY: Huntington Park.

Due, L. (1995). *Joining the tribe: Growing up gay & lesbian in the '90s*. New York, NY: Doubleday.

Governor's Commission on Gay and Lesbian Youth (1993). Making schools safe for gay and lesbian youth, Boston, MA.

Heron, A. (1994). *Two teenagers in 20*. Los Angeles, CA: Alyson Publications.

Hetrick, E., & Martin, A. (1987). Developmental issues and their resolution for gay and lesbian adolescents. *Journal of Homosexuality, 14*(1/2), 24-43.

McConville, M. (1995). *Adolescence: Psychotherapy and the emerging self*. San Francisco, CA: Jossey-Bass.

Pollack, R., & Schwartz, C. (1995). *The journey out: A guide for and about lesbian, gay, and bisexual teens.* New York, NY: Penguin Books.

Reed, R. (1997). *Growing up gay: The sorrows and joys of gay and lesbian adolescence.* New York: W.W. Norton.

Wheeler, G. (1998). Towards a gestalt developmental model. *British Gestalt Journal, 7*(2), 115-125.

Footnotes

1 "GLBT" is an acronym for "gay/lesbian/bisexual/transgendered." In this chapter, dealing primarily as it does with young men and women who are sexual orientation issues rather than gender identity per se, the term "GLB" will be used to refer to the experiences of gay, lesbian, and bisexually-identified or identity-exploring youth. It is understood that many of these reflections do apply to the experiences of young people with transgender issues or identity, whereas others may not.

2 I wish to thank Fraelean Curtis for her written contribution to this chapter and for her support as a colleague and a friend.

7

A Gestalt Approach to the Treatment of Adolescent Eating Disorders

Beverly Blaney and John Smythe

Introduction

Eating disorders are prevalent in all developed nations. Their diagnosis is usually apparent given the characteristic core symptoms with which these patients present. As outlined in the *Diagnostic and Statistical Manual of Mental Disorders, Fourth Edition* (1994): anorexia nervosa is defined as the refusal to maintain adequate body weight, an intense fear of becoming overweight, a disturbed body image, and amenorrhea for three or more months. Bulimia is defined as episodes of binge eating, regularly engaging in self-induced vomiting or use of laxatives, and an undue preoccupation with weight and body shape.

The treatment of anorexia nervosa, unlike its diagnosis, is often extremely challenging. We would like to describe an evolving approach, based on Gestalt therapy and Gestalt developmental theory, for the management and treatment of these disorders. In this chapter we will briefly review the current understanding of the origin and treatment of these disorders. The remainder of the chapter will focus on the following three issues:

1. The value of the Gestalt model in the development of a program for adolescent eating disorders.

2. The clinical application of the Gestalt model in identifying and clarifying issues arising during treatment of adolescent eating disorders.

3. The importance of experiential work in the treatment of eating disorders.

Current Psychological Approach to Eating Disorders

The conventional psychodynamic theories of eating disorders have evolved from simplistic symbolic interpretations of eating refusal to a contemporary multi-determined model incorporating social, familial and individual factors. A number of authors have attempted to define these factors.

Bruch (1974; 1982) maintained that anorexic patients have poorly developed identities and a pervasive sense of inadequacy as a consequence of having over involved mothers. She postulated that anorexics therefore use their eating disorders as a means of gaining autonomy and self-respect.

Crisp (1974) asserted that parents of anorexic patients have avoidant coping styles and often suffer from low self-esteem and sexual conflicts. He postulated that anorexia nervosa represents the adolescent's phobic avoidance of the normal developmental changes of puberty, in particular with regard to sexuality and separation from the family, as these threaten to destabilize the family.

Palazzoli (1988) and Minuchin (1978) have also placed great emphasis on the role of the family in the pathogenesis of eating disorders. Minuchin states that these families are unable to resolve or tolerate conflict within the family and therefore become rigid and unable to adapt to changes, such as a daughter's onset of adolescence. The struggle to maintain order may provoke a convergence of anxiety and concern on the adolescent that may help to generate and support his or her illness.

Palazzoli suggested that certain alliances are formed between generations within families that allow them to use strategies that avoid the expression and resolution of conflict. These families often emphasize external goals such as educational and social achievements, without attending to their internal psychodynamic issues.

The work of these authors has helped give rise to the widely accepted multi-determined model of anorexia nervosa (Garfinkle & Garner, 1982). This model is incorporated into the current multidisciplinary approach to treatment, in which treatment programs focus both on weight restoration, employing behavioral and cognitive therapies, and psychotherapy. Behavior therapy, which involves providing graded rewards and privileges for weight gain, must be supported by cognitive therapy so that the patient learns about the nature of the disorder, including nutritional factors, medical complications, and the origin and effects of dysfunctional thoughts regarding weight and self image. After weight is restored, the psychological and relational aspects of the illness are addressed with individual, family, and/or group psychotherapy. Some studies suggest that family therapy is more effective with adolescents, whereas adults respond more favorably to individual psychotherapy.

The multi-determined model of eating disorders with its emphasis on family is compatible with Gestalt's emphasis on context, in which the individual is viewed as inherently inseparable from her environment. The Gestalt model of adolescent development defines and incorporates the transitional stages of the individual's maturation within the familial field, as will be illustrated in the next section.

Management and Treatment of Eating Disorders: An Evolving Approach

The treatment program on which this chapter is based has been developed in the context of a group-oriented outpatient program for the management and care of adolescents diagnosed with Anorexia Nervosa and Bulimia Nervosa. Patients may receive one or more of three therapeutic interventions: family therapy, individual therapy and group workshops. It is from the group workshops that we have developed a Gestalt inspired treatment model for adolescents with eating disorders.

Group Workshops: A Gestalt approach

When our program was established in 1993, we discovered that adolescent treatment program models were not readily available. As a consequence, we followed the existing norm of adapting adult programs for the treatment of adolescents. These programs, which have proven effective in treating adults, have two standard components or steps: psychological education, and behavior change. We incorporated these standard components in the form of Psychological Education Seminars, which are devoted primarily to education, and Recovery Groups, which are devoted primarily to behavior change.

Psychological Education Seminars. These seminars begin by helping the individuals to discover self-image. Patients are helped to examine ways that they may have incorporated aggressive and devaluing messages from society, their family of origin, and other personal experience into their self-image. This involves exploring many factors, both cultural and personal, including the stereotypes in media, social norms, and childhood experiences from which the self-image is derived. In particular the ideal of "thin-

195

ness as beautiful" is examined.

Recovery Groups. The second step is to help patients develop an awareness of the conflict created, and the self-injury experienced, when sacrificing oneself to the ideal of thinness. Providing individuals an opportunity to consider other, preferably gentler and saner, ways of regarding and treating themselves supports behavior change. New behavioral goals are negotiated on a weekly basis within the group. These include eating and non-eating objectives (e.g., wearing shorts, not weighing oneself, etc.).

Our early work in the Psychological Education Seminars and the Recovery Groups was based upon standard methods and objectives of Cognitive and Behavior Therapy. We noted as a result of these methods that the awareness and behavior change achieved tended to be primarily conceptual and somewhat superficial. We felt that for treatment to be genuinely effective, therapeutic awareness and behavioral goals needed to be more deeply rooted. If new learning is to be fully integrated into an individual's sense of self, the conflicts generated by our culture of thinness must be clearly perceived as a sensed experience. It is not enough merely to think a situation is wrong, one must taste the truth of the issue, feel the effect of it in one's being. The therapeutic process, we concluded, must be one of self-experience in which learning is grounded in being, in personal awareness, rather than in concepts; (e.g., "I feel better; I have more energy now that I'm eating more, and I like this feeling," versus "It is a good idea to feed my body.") As a result of our own growing awareness of the limitations of traditional treatment approaches, and our belief in the therapeutic value of experiential referencing, we turned to the challenge of integrating the insights and practices of Gestalt Therapy into our treatment program.

The discovery of self through awareness, as opposed to abstract thought and directed behavior change, is a fundamental aspect of Gestalt therapy. Gestalt therapy not only honors the individuals perceived reality as ultimately valid, but it also sees the emergence of this self-awareness as an essential component of adolescent development. The Gestalt approach aids the individual in this task by redirecting her sense of self back towards her own immediate experience and encourages the individual to accept ownership of that experience.

Patients learn that anchoring themselves in more authentic, personal experience is healing. In contrast to the ultimately destructive effort to create or perfect oneself by living up to an image or ideal, self-acceptance through self-discovery becomes a pathway to recovery and wholeness. Therefore, we have come to believe that incorporating a Gestalt approach into the treatment of eating disorders can deepen its therapeutic impact, and help to promote substantial change.

Group Workshops: Emerging Adolescent Issues

In the Psychological Education Seminars, group participants explore factors within themselves and society that generate and support the ideals of thinness underlying eating disorders. They also examine the personal consequences of following these adopted ideals at the expense of their health and well-being.

During these seminars, adult patients often begin their first steps towards recovery. They recognize that their behaviors are motivated by their conditioning and begin to consider that there are other ways to act and respond in their lives. Our data however, indicated that although adolescent patients often enjoyed the educational seminars, they were frequently unable to utilize the information to achieve any improvement in their symptoms. It was suspected that the workshops were not recognizing and addressing particular adolescent developmental issues.

For the majority of adolescents in our clinic, the motivation to seek treatment is external. An external authority figure--parent, school counselor and/or doctor--arranges for another set of authority figures (the treatment team) to provide a solution to the identified patient.

In contrast, adult patients generally initiate their own entrance into treatment. Adults are usually motivated to change their eating disorder behavior out of a personal, internal dissatisfaction with the effects that it is having on their lives. Their desire to seek treatment arises from their aware sense of illness and pain. Through their suffering and despair, they discover a personal voice with which to challenge the introjected ideals of our culture of thinness, and the eating disorder can thus be identified as a problem to eliminate. Consequently, adult treatment programs move their participants directly from psychological education groups into recovery groups, where specific behavior change strategies are promoted.

Many adolescents, however, still tend to identify positively with their eating disorder, particularly in the initial stages when the associated behavior is less disruptive to lifestyle. In fact, the eating disorder may provide them with a useful tool by which they can gain some control in a world in which most authority is external. As a consequence, many adolescent patients are not ready at this early stage of their treatment to initiate committed behavior change. Caught as many adolescents are in the struggle to develop a functional identity, the eating disorder may become an integral part of that identity. Adolescents who tend to develop eating disorders struggle to gain autonomy and control through the adopted perspective that to be thin is to be beautiful and happy. Thus their efforts to create their own happiness are directed through weight control and self-denial.

This has a number of consequences, including the development of a pervading sense of guilt and inadequacy. Unable to enjoy life, these teenagers blame themselves for being failures. The embedding culture of thinness has given them the formula for happiness, and rather than question the validity of the formula itself, they assume that somehow they are at fault.

Often, it is not until the eating disorder behavior seriously disrupts their lives that they begin to question its underlying principles, and look for other ways to be in the world. Ironically, it is this growing awareness of personal suffering that ultimately opens the possibility for real healing. Dismantling an eating disorder requires, in addition to the corrective information of the educational seminars, a discovery of personal authority and desire to challenge the perspective of the surrounding culture. In other words, the adolescent both needs a new map and a new authority, one that is no longer externally referenced. She needs to develop autonomy. This begins with the acknowledgement and ownership of psychological pain. This ownership gives birth to the desire to end suffering.

Gestalt theory supports the view that change is guided by the individual's awareness and ownership of experience, which in turn mobilizes a desire to *feel better*. This subjective viewpoint becomes the foundation from which the adolescent can challenge objective references. The painful anorexic and bulimic behaviors then become part of the recovery process by drawing the adolescents' attention to areas of inner disharmony. The individual discovers personal authority and responsibility by honoring internal experience and values, as opposed to incongruent, external ones.

If we assume that the developmental capacity for this personal perspective is already established, as many traditional, adult treatment models seem to assume, we may unwittingly jeopardize the recovery process. The adolescent may identify the treating professional merely as another external authority, in competition with existing authority figures. The therapeutic endeavor, however, is not to replace one external authority with another, but to help the individual access and appreciate their own voice.

Gestalt theory equates ownership of experience with healthy functioning, and recognizes adolescence as a time when ownership of experience is an important developmental issue. McConville (1995) refers to this as the development of *interiority*. We decided to specifically address this issue in a separate workshop, designed specifically for our adolescent population. The Making Choices Workshop was created to meet this need, and to address this work from a uniquely Gestalt perspective. The creation of the Making Choices Workshop was a deviation from the adult model of treatment, and allowed us to more appropriately address the developmental processes of adolescence.

Gestalt Model of Adolescent Development

The recognition, appreciation, and actualization of one's individuality occur gradually in the developing adolescent psyche. McConville (1995) presents a Gestalt model of this developmental process in terms of a reorganizing of the adolescent-environment field, the field where contact is made between self and other. According to McConville, this reorganization involves three recursive and interrelated developmental tasks: *disembedding*, *interiority*, and *integration*.

The first task, disembedding, arises as the individual begins to experience a discordance between emergent and intensifying inner life, (which is felt as uniquely one's own) and outer, adopted persona, (which is embedded in the surrounding cultural context). The adopted persona includes the values, rules, and ideals that the child-adolescent has inherited from family and society. These seem during childhood to be indistinct from one's own values. In adolescence, however, the individual may begin to sense a lack of fit between these codes (which begin to feel more external than internal), and inner, intuitive life. Embeddedness within family and society provides an important context within which children can learn, grow, and obtain support. However adolescents may begin to sense an alienation from self if their adherence to "adult" context requires them to ignore their own emerging authority. If they are encouraged to disown their own experience in favor of society's interpretation (e.g., hunger = thin =good; e.g., satiety = fat = bad) their development will be thwarted. Disembedding requires the adolescent to first become aware of this social context, and by doing so, to feel herself beginning to stand apart from it.

Closely related to disembedding from family and social context is the task of interiority, an emerging awareness and ownership of one's own experience. Personal meaning, instead of adopted meaning, naturally arises when experience is owned. This gives rise to the adolescents' appreciation of his or her own reflective capacity to make personally congruent choices, and actions become meaningful more so for their personal relevance than their compliance with environmental expectations.

With integration, the third task and overarching aim of adolescent development, the individual begins to respond in each circumstance and relationship in a way that excludes neither the contextual ground of experience, nor the inner sense of meaning and authority. She engages in the world free to use the knowledge bequeathed by parents and society, but not constrained by it. Societal values may be re-embraced, but only if they accommodate the internal meaning the adolescent has discovered.

These developmental tasks are not separate or independent of one another. Rather, they are related in a recursive and mutually defining fashion. The first task, disembedding, is not actually distinct from the second, interiority. Discovering one's embeddedness highlights one's distinctness from the field of embedded conditioning but, at the same time, it enables the discovery and exploration of one's inner world. A fish is unaware of the water in which it has its existence; should it hypothetically become aware of its environment *qua* environment, it would simultaneously intuit itself.

Similarly the achievement of integration, at least in a penumbral sense, is involved in the tasks of disembedding and interiority. The appreciation of self and other includes a sense of their interdependence. Fish and water create a wholeness of experience. To the degree that either pole, self or other, is suppressed or ignored, a corresponding disharmony will emerge. From a Gestalt perspective, self dwells at the boundary of organism and environment. It originates in the interplay between interior and exterior. Self arises as a transitional awareness of each shifting moment in which one is capable of interacting and responding in a way that feels integral

There always remains the tendency to phenomenologically concretize the shifting moment into predominantly internal states or external structures. There is always the habit of fixating, trying to define the moment and separate it into distinct outer contents or inner feelings. This may give one the belief in a solid boundary between Me and Not-Me, but this solidity is a myth. The transitional moment is fluid. In the moment one discovers neither an independence from, nor a pure dependence upon, other. Rather, an inter-dependence with other is experienced. The relationship of interdependence is not defined according to the fixed roles and needs of two separate objects or subjects. It is perhaps best described as a relationship in which there is a commitment to remain honestly open, present, and available. Paradoxically, this provides a quality of stability, bringing a steady, integral resonance into one's life. The paradox that the healthy adult must hold is that to live with integrity requires one to be present but not inflexibly solid; to care about a situation without demanding that it look a certain way. This is the work of integration.

If the adult has successfully begun these developmental tasks, despite the natural tendencies to fixate and solidify experience, he will be capable of utilizing these contact skills as the situation demands. That is, he will be capable of disembedding (differentiating from his environment, as well as seeing his introjects and pre-judgments), interiority (sensing his inner world and trusting his intuitive understanding) and integration (staying with whatever arises with a fluid awareness of inner and outer realities). Essentially what we are describing here is opening: opening to oneself in situations, rather than shutting down, and letting situations speak instead of prejudging them. In the Gestalt developmental model these tasks are rooted in adolescence; once begun they are never finished.

The Gestalt model of adolescent development provides a scaffold on which we have organized and developed our eating disorders program. There are at least two distinct reasons for using this model. First, the model provides a clearly articulated model of adolescent development. Second, the Gestalt model's emphasis on the role of context in the development of the emerging adolescent self, is compatible with our own emphasis on the role of context--family and society--in the development and treatment of an adolescent eating disorder

Initially, we began by using the Gestalt model to critique our program, contrasting the Gestalt model of adolescent development with our existing approach. This comparison confirmed our experience that adult program models do not adequately address the critical developmental work of interiority. Adult groups move directly from information seminars to long-term recovery groups, the central focus of which is the provision and practice of more adaptive strategies requisite for recovery. The adult program models did not anticipate nor adequately explain the response of our adolescent patients to educational information concerning eating disorders. Adult patients tend to absorb this information readily, and to use in support of their resolve to defeat their disorder. Our adolescent patients, on the other hand, were often still struggling with the development of centered, internal reference, and thus were unable to grasp the destructive nature of externally referenced messages regarding thinness. Rather than the grounded resolve of many adult patients, they responded to educational input about their eating disorder with intense ambivalence. Many of our adolescent patients, still identifying with their eating disorder and clinging to its false promise to solve their misery, were not ready to utilize the Psychological Education Seminars.

The Gestalt model offered a theoretical explanation for what we were experiencing. The adolescents did not realize that this clash of authentic self and external culture was personally relevant, because they had not yet done the developmental work of disembedding and interiority.

This insight led us to the conviction that the Gestalt model could provide a reliable blueprint for the creation of a more comprehensive and developmentally appropriate adolescent program. If the model of adolescent development were actually embedded in the structure of a treatment program, this could ensure that the ongoing work of adolescent development

Table 1
Adolescent Developmental Stages and Corresponding Workshops

McConville's Developmental Tasks	Workshops		
	Psychological Education	Making Choices	Making Changes and Beyond Body Image
Disembedding	+++++++	++	++
Interiority	++	++++	++
Integration	++	++	+++++++

would be addressed. We concluded that disembedding, interiority, and integration, could become the thematic foundations of a structured therapeutic approach to adolescent eating disorders (Table 1).

Application of the Gestalt model to an Eating Disorder Program

Consistent with McConville's model of development, our program views these developmental tasks both as an evolutionary sequence and as a growth process that occurs recursively throughout the process of treatment. Thus each workshop supports the entire process of field reorganization and disembedding from culture, developing an interior experiential reference, and integrating these learnings in the form of committed behavior change. But, by the same token, each workshop emphasizes the work of one particular developmental task (e.g., the Making Choices Workshop addresses the specific task of developing an interior point of view).

Disembedding: Psychological Education Seminars

The intention of the educational seminars is to support the process of adolescent disembedding in three specific ways. First, we attempt to explain the predisposing, precipitating and perpetuating factors of an eating disorder that have been identified by existing psychological models (see Bruch, 1982; Crisp, 1974; Minuchin, 1978; Palazzoli, 1988). Thus, patients are made aware of the psychological dynamics of identity formation, autonomy development, low self-esteem, sexual conflicts, separation issues, and family conflict.

Second, we encourage the patients to examine the familial and cultural messages regarding the "beauty ideal" and its promise of success and happiness. Parents often encourage intake restriction in their daughters at very early ages, hoping to protect them from the weight-prejudice of the dominant culture. This potentially supports the development of an eating disorder and explains why many adolescent girls begin eating disordered behaviors before the onset of puberty. By encouraging their daughters to restrict their food intake, parents unwittingly give them two damaging messages:

1. They unwittingly support the culture's message that there is something wrong with the child's natural weight.

2. They support the suggestion that the child can and should do something to "correct" this physical imperfection.

Within this belief system, restricting and purging can become necessary means for "correcting " physical imperfections. The physical discomfort of living below set point becomes compulsory for those adolescents conditioned to believe that they are only going to gain acceptability through these forms of self-denial.

In these seminars, patients are encouraged to examine their acceptance of these values and the effect that upholding these values has on the quality of their own lives. The patient begins to discriminate between the cultural appeal of thinness and her own experience. If in this comparison the patient notices that the costs of engaging in eating disorder strategies outweighs the benefits derived from these strategies, she invests in her recovery and continues on to the next workshop. When this disparity is not realized by patients there is a correspondingly low desire to continue with treatment.

A third goal of the educational sessions is to alleviate some of the inevitable anxiety experienced by members of the patient's environment. To address this, a concurrent seminar for the parents, siblings, friends, and significant others is presented. Although this seminar presents much of the same information the patient receives, it also discusses the impact of an eating disorder on the patient's environment. Watching a child engaged in voluntary starvation usually produces extremely high levels of anxiety in their environment. In an honest attempt to help, family and friends often engage in behaviors that may actually aggravate an already difficult situation. Our contextual intervention often results in creating a less hostile environment in which self-reflection is more possible.

The process of disembedding that occurs at this stage occurs on all levels of relationship (i.e., with self, family, peer group, and the culture at large), as the adolescent struggles to discover radically new and different possibilities of being. Unfortunately, these ways of being are rarely modeled in the surrounding world.

The Psychological Education Seminars teach the patients to recognize the cult of image that dominates our culture. Seeing the familial and cultural context is itself a therapeutic intervention. It loosens the defining grasp of external authority, while opening the ground of experience to the possibility of personal meaning. This is the task of interiority.

Interiority: Making Choices Workshop

Nurturing the development of interiority is delicate work. Our impetus for creating the Making Choices Workshop was to respond to the realization that this work was not addressed in adult programs. The goal of this workshop is to help the teenagers understand the power that they already possess for directing their own lives as well as the directions that are open to them. We believe that the recognition of both personal responsibility and the capacity to exercise that responsibility is essential to developing the will and ability to overcome an eating disorder. In fact, the eating disorder itself provides a useful and poignant tool for these adolescents to realize and to demonstrate their ability to take control of their lives, and thereby institute positive change in themselves and their world.

Interiority requires self-discovery. One means of allowing the adolescent to discover his inner world is to cultivate the experience of a personal dilemma (McConville, 1995). In this workshop the adolescent is encouraged to confront and hopefully resolve the dilemma that characterizes eating disorders:

Is it more important for me to be accepted by others for how I look, than to be accepted by myself for who I am?

Can I exchange the external image that I have created for others, in favor of accepting my own unique, internal experience of self, even though it may not be legitimized in the culture around me?

Danger lies on both sides of this predicament. The obsessive attempt to emulate our culture's idealized standard of beauty often brings sickness. Occasionally it brings death. On the other hand, if one abandons this endeavor one must confront the perceived possibility of loss of status, or even social isolation. Internal self-acceptance may be at the expense of external, social acceptance. The recognition of this dilemma requires an awareness of a personal interior, an authentic self. Interiority is equivalent to the discovery of this authenticity, from which personal choices can be made. Interiority is awareness: awareness of experience, awareness of self.

To reconcile this dilemma the adolescent must shift from valuing external referencing to internal experience. It then becomes more possible to shift away from the behaviors that seek external reinforcement.

Treatment motivation based solely on external authority will be counteracted by other external pressures. Trying to eat to please one's parents, to be the "good girl," will be unsuccessful because it does not eliminate the competing introject that thin = good and weight gain is not culturally acceptable. Even positive suggestions (such as developing a nurturing acceptance of oneself) rarely work if they come only from some outside authority, such as a parent or a treatment professional. But if self-acceptance is realized as an authentic desire and need, that is, as a dimension of interiority, then it can generate the motivation necessary to challenge destructive cultural introjects.

Having begun to evolve a sense of interiority, the motivation to treat the eating disorder can arise from internal authority instead of external authority. Once this process begins the adolescent can start to integrate external forces and skills into a self-willed process of recovery.

Ironically, one outcome of our work with adolescents has been to recognize that many of the adults we treat are also struggling with issues of personal authority, and have not yet completed their own adolescent voyage. Adult programs begin with the assumption that the work of adolescence has been completed. The development of an eating disorder however, is often a response to being unable to successfully complete the work of adolescence. Adults may have become stuck with a particular developmental task (e.g., disembedding) and this often needs to be addressed in treatment. As a consequence of this we are presently planning to incorporate some aspects of the Making Choices workshop into the adult program.

Integration: Making Changes Workshop

In the Making Changes Workshop the work of integration is addressed. The adolescent patient, having anchored a sense of self in internal experience, is now ready for the work that adult programs relegate to Recovery Groups--the work of committed behavior change. We focus on two areas primarily: (a) the physical, bodily relationship to food and (b) sinterpersonal relationships with other selves. In both areas, these relationships have previously been characterized by imbalance, with interiority typically sacrificed to the felt demands of the environment. In this workshop, we support interaction with the environment that makes space for interiority, such that personal meaning can become the driving force of behavior. Personal meaning is not discovered in isolation, but reached through the process of engagement between self and other. The interplay of these two domains is already, by definition, integrating. When meaning is allowed to emerge through the interplay of self and other, rather than defined by purely internal or external authority, the inherent validity of each interaction is respected.

Western philosophy and culture define the body as an external object. In developing interiority, an individual learns to experience the body neither as isolated from the environment, nor as wholly defined by the environment. The relationship between self and environment can become stifling or abusive if either of these poles is invalidated by the authority of the other. Recovery is not served by replacing an external tyrant with an internal one. Instead what is needed is both: (a) a suspension of the attempt to truncate one's experience into either outer or inner and (b) permission for both the individual and the environment (including others) to interact fluidly and respectfully without either grasping or rejecting the other in immediate awareness. This allows the individual to act not as dictator, focused only on his own interests regardless of the other, but as an agent, an author of integrating transactions between self and environment.

Integration is not a step to be taken but a shift in experiential referencing. That is, neither "I" as the experiencer, nor "That" as the experienced, is the sole focus. Rather the experience "Itself", which includes both self and other in a comprehensive context, is attended to. The eating disordered adolescent, having witnessed the danger of taking introjects as reality (disembedding) and having discovered the validity of internal experience (interiority) is invited to enter into this process.

This workshop gives them the opportunity to practice integration in their relationship with food, its acquired meaning and their body's needs. The simple act of putting food into their mouths triggers strong emotional reactions associated with challenging thoughts and interpretations. We encourage our patients to self-nourish while remaining aware of these reactions. Remaining open to their thoughts and feelings creates space in which a healthier relationship with nourishment and food can arise. Although this healthy relationship is the accepted goal of this work, the task which is being introduced is of broader relevance to the individual's life--that of developmental integration, and the discovery of one's inherent healthiness. In this workshop, developmental integration takes the specific form of committed, self-supported, behavioral change in eating patterns.

A second way that the Making Changes Workshop addresses the task of integration is by teaching patients to experiment with new transaction patterns between self and the interpersonal environment. Participants are challenged to try on new modes of communication, such as becoming more assertive, which can serve to transform the quality of contact in important relationships. As with food, our participants are encouraged to make interpersonal contact in a way that takes in the other fully and respectfully, without sacrificing the fullness and integrity of the self's own emerging voice.

Experiential Work: The Beyond Body Image Workshop

Most traditional eating disorder treatment programs utilize individual and group skills developed within the framework of cognitive behavioral therapy. In our work with adolescents however, we have discovered that the use of experientially based group exercises significantly enhances the recovery process.

A major advantage of experiential work is that it gets people out of their heads and into their bodies. Experiential work provides an opportunity to attend to the body. Attention to the physical develops a renewed sense of self, creating a foundation for the reconciliation of the body-mind, the division of which lies at the heart of eating disorders. It can be revealing to examine the adolescent patient' s concepts of human embodiment. A typical response from one teenage girl was, "My body is just something that my mind walks around in." This utterance succinctly encapsulates the attitude necessary for the creation and maintenance of an eating disorder; my body is subordinate to my mind, my feelings subordinate to my thoughts. Shifting this attitude is the pivotal point for recovery and has prompted the creation of the Beyond Body Image Workshop.

Many treatment centers incorporate body image workshops into their eating disorder programs. These generally teach patients to develop a more accepting, caring attitudes toward their physical image. Our work has not only been to change the cognitive attitude towards the body image, but more significantly to change immediate body experience itself. Much of this workshop is based upon the writing and teaching of Kepner (1987), who has pioneered the development of body oriented methods in Gestalt Therapy at the Gestalt Institute of Cleveland.

The Beyond Body Image Workshop places a heavy emphasis on experiential work. It is essential that the patient establish (or re-establish) a mindful awareness of her own physical experience and learn to value this way of relating to herself. This often involves a radical shift in how these young women understand themselves and what they choose to value in their experience.

Many adolescent girls have never experienced a peaceful coexistence with their bodies. Rather, their bodies become sources of shame, embarrassment, and humiliation. Rejection of the body becomes for many the only possible escape and finally, they declare war on themselves. In this war against the body, all physical experience is ignored, minimized, invalidated, or reinterpreted. Intense cramps for example, when noticed at all, become symbols of success that demonstrate super-human levels of self-control.

Experiential work provides the eating disordered patient with an opportunity to begin to rediscover her physical experience, facilitating the work of disembedding, interiority, and integration. This workshop attempts to go beyond simply helping young women make the best of a bad situation (i.e., spiritual entrapment in a fleshy form). By attending to experiences in which the physical body is an integral aspect of being, and by encouraging our patients to trust the knowledge arising from this experience, we help them appreciate that acceptance of their body is possible, sensible, and in fact, essential. It is through the physical body that we make contact with the world and experience ourselves. It is within the physical, and not despite it, that we meet the spiritual.

The workshop powerfully challenges the dominant dualist ideology of our culture by teaching that a personal, non-conceptual, and existentially referenced selfhood is the source of authority. By further awakening their interior sensory experience of body as a source of self-experience, this workshop heightens their capacity to reference from authentic bodily experience and it's inherent wisdom. Reclaiming ownership of bodily experience is a means of both disembedding from the culture's grasp of the body and reconnecting with one's ever-present interiority. This is one of the defining tasks of adolescent development: the reclaiming of one's body. When treatment accomplishes this learning, eating disordered behaviors begin to fade; when it does not, eating disordered behaviors inevitably persist.

Recovery and Relapse: A Case Report

Although the thematic structure of our program progresses from disembedding to interiority and then integration, this is not to imply that this work occurs in exclusive or successive stages. Recovery patterns, like development itself, are often cyclical, and relapses are an expected part of the process. Behavior may lag somewhat behind cognition, reflecting the patient's struggle in integrating new understanding. This pattern of progress was evident in Andrea, a fifteen-year-old referred to our program for treatment of her anorexia nervosa.

When Andrea first presented to clinic she was unable to provide any explanation for her recent and drastic weight loss. She had a "perfect" family and enjoyed a "very close" relationship with her mother, whom she described as "very supportive." While in hospital, Andrea completed our Psychological Educational Seminar and also made rapid progress in regaining weight. She developed a perspective independent of her family that highlighted the struggles out of which her eating disorder arose. However upon discharge she resumed previous eating patterns, and experienced subsequent weight loss.

During the Making Choices Workshop Andrea began to identify areas of conflict with her family (particularly her mother). She felt that her eating disorder was the only thing in her life that her mother could not control. During this workshop Andrea's eating once more improved as self exploration gave rise to an appreciation of her own needs and values. In many cases these values differed from her mother's. Andrea began to develop her capacity to see and say what mattered to her, and began understand that this was different from what she had been taught to accept as important. Meaning began to be referenced from her own experience. Nourishing herself, she discovered, felt good.

At the conclusion of Making Choices Andrea negotiated to attend eight family therapy sessions to focus on her relationship with her mother. Treatment was provided by one of the psychiatric residents. During this period, Andrea struggled to articulate her desire for more privacy from her mother. Although Andrea's mother made a number of attempts to accommodate her daughter's concerns, Andrea still did not perceive herself as sufficiently autonomous in her relationship with her mother. Consequently Andrea's eating behavior again began to deteriorate as she succumbed to her mother's view of appropriate behavior. At the completion of the family therapy Andrea once again re-entered the sequence of group workshops.

The Making Changes Workshop provided Andrea with an opportunity to explore and practice her fragile sense of self-authority and responsibility. Within weeks she regained her previous eating goals. At this time, however, she began to identify patterns in her behavior, making meaningful connections between specific emotions and eating behaviors; (for example she realized that she often binged after confrontations with others, especially her mother). The communication skills and assertiveness training taught in this workshop helped Andrea find alternative coping strategies for dealing with conflict. She was able to establish some autonomy and has been successful in eliminating her binge/purge behavior in many contexts. Unfortunately Andrea still continues to employ this behavior at home where her autonomy is more readily compromised and where she occasionally feels she must subordinate her own truth to that of her adult caretakers.

Despite the obvious gains Andrea has made in implementing alternative strategies and despite the increased insight into her behavior, Andrea's eating behavior continues to fluctuate. Unfortunately, Andrea's up and down response to treatment is not uncommon. This reflects the adolescent's ambivalent embeddedness in social context, and continued struggle to free herself from social conditioning. Environmental social structure does in fact meet many of the adolescent's needs, such as food and shelter. Most are still reliant upon their family in many ways. It takes courage and an emergent capacity for independent functioning for adolescents to authentically challenge parental authority. Our workshops attempt to give them a center from which to confront that authority; that is, an appreciation of their own experience and a correspondingly strengthened sense of self. Skills for articulating their views and the confidence to remain faithful to their own truth are important objectives of our program.

At the time of this writing, Andrea's next step is to participate in our Beyond Body Image Workshop. This workshop will allow her to further develop an appreciation of the validity of experience referenced meaning, supporting her development of personal authority. The anorexic's body, as we have said, is deeply embedded in the culture. In a sense, the culture owns it, reinterpreting its experience and defining its purpose. The adolescent must take ownership of the body back from the culture in order to heal. This is accomplished by reconnecting with bodily experience, by letting one's body awareness create its own meaning. When Andrea learns to trust the wisdom of her bodily experience over the embedding forces of her cultural and social context, only then will the simple, self-defining value of hunger and satiety finally and completely displace the oppressive seduction of starvation and physical exploitation.

Conclusion

Central to this work, regardless of where one is in the journey, is both the courage to drop externally referenced guidance and the willingness to open to the immediacy of one's bodily experience. This can be frightening and painful as one faces the fear of rejection and also experiences one's pain and suffering. Yet it is only by feeling the pain we cause ourselves through ignorance and misguidance that we become open to the possibility of healing.

The layers of social and cultural conditioning are like concentric circles in which the adolescent's sense of personhood seems embedded. Each has to be traversed, often more than once, in the process of becoming disentangled from their hold. Relapses occur as the adolescent moves through the levels of her life from which she is not yet liberated by self-awareness and self-authority. However, relapses are often opportunities for successively discovering increasingly larger degrees of selfhood and thus are not necessarily therapeutic failures.

A tenet of Gestalt therapy is that symptoms are resolved through the achievement of self-support. A loving and respectful attitude toward oneself is incompatible with an eating disorder. Learning to trust and cherish the body decreases the probability of defilement. This requires disembedding from the family and culture that has defined us, and reorienting back towards our own immediate experience. This necessarily includes a thorough embrace of physical experience. Unconditional acceptance of the body arises from simply attending to one's experience without judgment. This becomes the foundation from which integrated living and action originate. It is a natural ability to attend to oneself with an open mind. The initial stage of our work is to help adolescents unlearn and discard the suppressive messages that they obey, and then to simply look with fresh eyes at themselves and their world.

For adolescents with eating disorders, the path away from self-criticism and injury, and toward self-acceptance and health, requires the initiation of this process of growth. The Gestalt Model provides a framework for understanding the concrete developmental tasks that contribute to this growth in developing a treatment program based upon this model, we have tried to support this growth by assisting our patients within the context of their adolescent journey.

Along the way, we have learned a number of lessons that have contributed the effectiveness of our program. These lessons include:

1. It is valuable to incorporate a model of adolescent development in adolescent treatment programs.

2. The Gestalt model provides an excellent framework for the creation of an adolescent eating disorder program because it emphasizes both context and experiential work.

3. Experiential work has a crucial role to play in the developing awareness and interiority.

4. Recovery, like development itself, is rarely a linear process and relapses often reflect a cyclical pattern of progress.

These discoveries have guided us in creating a treatment program that is uniquely shaped not only by the pathognomonic features of eating disorders, but also by the specific developmental needs of our adolescent population.

References

American Psychiatric Association (1994). *Diagnostic and statistical manual of mental disorders, fourth edition.* Washington, DC: The American Psychiatric Association

Bruch, H. (1974). *Eating disorders.* London: Routledge and Kegan Paul.

Bruch, H. (1982). Anorexia nervosa: therapy and theory. *American Journal of Psychiatry, 139,* 1531-1538.

Crisp, A., Harding, B., & McGuinness, B. (1974). Anorexia nervosa: psychoneurotic characteristics of parents' relationship to progress: A quantitative study. *Journal of Psychosomatic Research, 18,* 167-173.

Garfinkle, P., & Garner, D. (1982). *Anorexia nervosa: A multi-dimensional perspective.* New York, NY: Brunner-Mazel.

Kepner, J. (1987). *Body process: A gestalt approach to working with the body in psychotherapy.* New York, NY: Gestalt Institute of Cleveland Press.

McConville, M. (1995). *Adolescence: Psychotherapy and the emergent self.* San Francisco: Jossey-Bass.

Minuchin, S., Rosman, B., & Baker, L. (1978). *Psychosomatic families: Anorexia nervosa in context.* Cambridge, MA: Harvard University Press.

Palazzoli, M.S. (1988). *Self starvation.* London: Human Context Books.

8

Assertiveness and Conflict Resolution: An Integrated Gestalt-Cognitive Behavioral Model for Working with Urban Adolescents

Iris G. Fodor and J. Christopher Collier

Preface

The interest in Assertiveness training in the United States developed out of the human potential movement of the 60s, and the development of Cognitive Behavior Therapy (CBT) both of which were a moving away from the Psychodynamic/Freudian influence that permeated American psychology and psychotherapy. Instead of being weighed down by our early childhood experiences that had to be excavated and analyzed, there was an emphasis on self-actualization, growth, working on ourselves and taking charge of our lives.

Individualism and self-determination and assertion are core American values. Until the 1960s, they were mostly for men. With the women's movement and movements of disadvantaged and minorities, each person could take charge of life, grow, and become more self-assertive. Furthermore, in the mental health field, assertiveness underlies another value--being in touch with feelings and being able to express them to get one's needs met. In this was the belief or assumption that people who were unassertive were thought to be self-denying, likely to be depressed, and to develop psychosomatic symptoms, and perhaps left behind in achieving self-actualization and life's satisfaction.

In the past ten years, the growing edge for assertiveness work has a new thrust in the area of education. This work features social skills development, social competency, and conflict resolution. Schools and educational systems focused on adapting this assertiveness work into social skills programs for children and adolescents. While adapting and beginning a foundation for this work with adolescents, it appeared that this concept fit mainstream American views of adolescent development.

Following Erikson's (1968) theory, which is still a strong influence, there is the view that the essential task of adolescence in our culture is to move away from family and to find/forge one's identity. However, as this work with adolescents and work in schools is increasing in popularity, there is now a recent spirit within the psychotherapy community to shift away from the prior individualistic focus. Modern psychoanalysis and experiential Gestalt therapy have adapted a relational theoretical perspective; a concern with self/other relating and a concern with self in community. The thrust of this work is to highlight the person's self-actualization in the flow of relating with others. The tension between meeting ones own needs for self-expression and assertiveness while recognizing and appreciating the needs of others is central.

The purpose of this chapter is to present a structure for learning assertiveness, with an emphasis on self-expression, but within a relational framework. The focus is on teaching about the nuances of social interactive experiencing and behaving. This work emerged from a cognitive behavioral perspective for training in assertiveness, but is integrated into a framework for a Gestalt-experiential perspective, emphasizing the teaching of assertiveness as highlighting styles of making contact with others and for dealing with interpersonal conflict.

This model has some similarities to that presented by Goleman (1995) in his best selling book *Emotional Intelligence*, where he speaks of "schooling the emotions." He proposes that students learn emotional competence by attending to emotional self-awareness, learning to manage emotions, as well as learning empathy and the handling of relationships (p. 283-284). Assertiveness involves open, honest communication. It is essentially a matter of risk taking, being direct, and putting the facts on the table. This philosophy reflects the underlying assumption that unassertive people lead a self-denying life that causes them to suffer in interpersonal relationships and sometimes leads to emotional and physical consequences.

Personal Ground
Iris G. Fodor

Long before I became a Gestalt therapist, I was involved in the development of cognitive behavior therapy and its application to assertiveness training. As a trainer of School Psychologists in a university setting, I also adapted the cognitive/behavior model for training graduate students to work with adolescents on social skills. This ongoing collaborative work with graduate students resulted in an edited book on adolescents' assertiveness (Fodor, 1992).

My interest in Gestalt training resulted from comparisons made by Gestalt trained participants in my Assertiveness Training groups who saw compatibility with Gestalt therapy. I began training in the summer residential program of the Gestalt Therapy Institute of Los Angles more than 20 years ago and became a Gestalt therapist. Until recently, these two worlds were separate domains for me; I taught cognitive behavior therapy to my graduate students and I continued training in Gestalt therapy and worked as a Gestalt therapist in my private practice.

Recently, I have been working on integrating these two approaches in my teaching and practice. I have presented workshops and written about such integration for the cognitive behavioral (1987), integrative (1993) and, most recently, for the Gestalt therapy community (1996, 1998). This chapter written in collaboration with Christopher Collier completes the circle of articulating the clinical integration in the realm of assertiveness which I have been practicing all these years.

Personal Ground
J. Christopher Collier

As a high school English and theater educator I became very interested in adolescents and how their socio-cultural experiences impacted their behavior and interactions with their peers, both inside the classroom and out. Following a psycho-educational model for my classroom interventions, I subscribed more to cognitive behavioral frameworks that seemed quite effective in teaching social skills, conflict resolution, and other important classroom elements. During this time, I was also provided the opportunity to work with homeless adults, adolescents and families living on Los Angeles' skid row shortly after the Los Angeles riots in 1992.

Through my work with the Los Angeles Poverty Department, I began to see the striking connections between the cognitive processes of these individuals and their heightened awareness as a result of the experiential psychodramatic work we were doing. Rather than focusing solely on their appraisal and evaluation of their experiences, living in such a violent and impoverished environment, the psychodrama focus emphasized the awareness of their personal experiences in the here and now. It was this focus on the now that seemed to provide much greater awareness, catharsis, and, in turn, empowerment.

While pursuing my doctoral studies in the Professional Child/School Psychology program at New York University I was introduced to Gestalt therapy and the Gestalt community by Dr. Iris Fodor. Concurrently, I was also working as an extern in an inner city school in East Harlem. It was there that we had the opportunity to collaborate in developing a model for assertiveness and conflict resolution training that would bring the cognitive behavioral and Gestalt frameworks together.

Framework for an Integrative Model for Teaching Assertiveness and Conflict Resolution

In working with adolescents in schools, an integrative, Gestalt/cognitive, psycho-educational model is presented to teach adolescents assertiveness and conflict resolution. To accomplish this objective, we utilize a basic cognitive behavioral framework for assertiveness training. However, in addition to highlighting the cognitive beliefs associated with relevant aspects of interpersonal relating, so central to the cognitive approach, we move beyond the traditional cognitive-behavioral approach to learning assertiveness to feature the contact functions inherent in learning to be assertive.

Our experience with this work has taught us that cognitive learning, by itself, is not enough to generate growth and behavior change in adolescents. Adolescents are natural experiential learners. Hence, our model adopts a Gestalt lens to highlight self-awareness process and awareness of contacting in interpersonal interactions as a foundation for assertive and conflict resolution skills. Using experiments and role play, this model provides a framework for teaching adolescents to experience their own styles of relating, as well as providing experiences for learning different ways of self assertion and resolving conflict with others.

In working within this model, in contrast to a strict cognitive behavior therapy approach, our primary goals include increased awareness of self and other, sensitivity to the socio-cultural field, and a sensitive/experiential approach to learning new behaviors. We are not focused on change as a goal in itself, but rather on exploration and experiment. In promoting this kind of growth experience, we have found that Gestalt therapy's contribution is indispensable.

In this chapter, we will first outline the basic model for teaching adolescents the skills of assertiveness and conflict resolution. Following this, we will present an application of this model with a group of urban adolescents in an inner city school.

The Socio-Cultural Field of Adolescent Development

Adolescence is clearly a time for change--biologically, emotionally and cognitively. In order to effectively cope with the stressors of these unpredictable and conflict-laden experiences, it is essential for adolescents to develop a broadened repertoire of contact skills. In Gestalt theory, contact--the organism's engagement of its environment--involves the polar processes of joining with and separating from the other. The successful negotiation of adolescence requires the individual to further develop both of these capacities, and one of the most important expressions of this development is the growing ability to assert oneself and to handle conflict. On a daily basis, adolescents are confronted with situations that call for social interaction. Adolescents still live with their families, spend most of their day in schools, and are expected to participate in peer culture. Often in peer interactions, adolescents deal with the jockeying for status, as well as the pressure to succeed in dating relationships. When adolescents do not function competently in these interactive situations, they are noticed, singled out, or suffer social ostracism and humiliation. When faced with problematic social interactive situations, many adolescents withdraw, act immaturely, inappropriately or aggressively, and must then face consequences resulting from this behavior (i.e., social disapproval, punishment, lower self-esteem). As adolescence is a particularly difficult time for many people, and because so many adolescents report problems with authority, not having the skills to turn toward peer culture for support and friendship makes this time of development even more stressful and lonely.

Further, given the multi-cultural character of many urban settings in our country (i.e., as we find in New York City with the influx of new immigrants and the resulting diversity--racial, cultural, and socio-economic--of its population), adolescents often have conflicting cultural identities and differing styles of managing difference and conflict. They may not feel they fit into the so-called mainstream American culture. Additionally, they may be subjected to prejudice, discrimination, or scapegoating. Adolescents who did not fit into the heterosexual dating mode may also suffer as well. Learning assertiveness skills to cope with these transcultural issues is essential for inner city adolescents. For too many adolescents, the lack of awareness of the nuances of social interaction or the lack of interactive skills contributes to the development of emotional problems. Further, longitudinal research suggests that adolescents with poor social skills are high risks for serious emotional disturbance as adults (Seltzner, 1989).

During the past decade, mental health professionals working with adolescents, both in the community and in schools, have become interested in addressing these problems. Cognitive behavior programs for teaching social skills and assertiveness have proliferated. From our experience at New York University, we have discovered that most clinicians, teachers and personnel working in clinics and schools need to hand tailor the standardized cognitive behavioral assessment and treatment programs to suit their particular populations (e.g., adolescents who are recent immigrants have issues in acculturation; second generation adolescents may have inter-generational cultural issues with their families).

As the incidence of violence, racism, and inter-cultural conflict escalates in the inner city, conflict resolution training programs are becoming increasingly popular (Sadalla, Henriquez, & Holmberg, 1987). Acknowledging this, conflict resolution skills training has now become part of the curriculum in many high schools. This training is often conducted in classrooms by teachers or volunteers who have attended a weekend conflict resolution workshop, and who follow a packaged educational curriculum. The standard conflict resolution model follows from mediation training, focusing on conflict resolution skills, working with the two parties involved in conflict, and utilizing a mediator. Usually, it is assumed that once the two parties sit down with a mediator, tempers will be cooled and rationality will prevail.

In our observations of these school-based mediation sessions, it appears that they too often provide only a surface, band-aid approach to these still simmering disputes. The emphasis, based on an educational model, attempts to address the specifics of a particular conflict. Some of the most effective programs also feature a psycho-educational model where a one-to-one approach is utilized in teaching adolescents needed skills to become aware of themselves and others in these emotionally laden and conflict filled interactions. In practice, however, and when carried out in the classroom, the focus remains on more practical problem solving and techniques for conflict resolution, with self-awareness and relational issues tak-

219

ing a back seat. From a Gestalt viewpoint, these programs can be said to rest upon an introjective model of teaching and modeling, and in so far as they do this, fail to accommodate to the highly experiential nature of adolescent learning and development. Adolescence, after all, is more than an accumulation of new skills. It is a reorganization of contact, a transformative process of learning to experience self and others in new ways (McConville, 1995). Consequently, our emphasis on heightening awareness and learning about differing styles of contact is an important step in making conflict mediation training more congruent with the realities of adolescent development.

When we examine the components of these packaged educational training curriculums, we see that they are put together from the older, psychological literature developed by cognitive behavioral psychologists under the rubric of assertiveness and social skills training (Alberti, 1970; Eisler & Frederickson, 1980; Lange & Jakubowski, 1976). These older cognitive/behavioral programs focus on a training model which features education about assertiveness, identifying cognitive underpinnings of assertiveness problems, and teaching, modeling, coaching, and practicing new behaviors (Fodor, 1980). Even so, with therapists no longer doing the training, the conflict resolution curriculum lacks depth and focus.

The model presented here attempts to update some of this older cognitive/behavioral work by integrating it with a Gestalt perspective. This integrative approach to conflict resolution and assertiveness training highlights awareness by focusing on triggers to conflict and the cognitive processing of experience (how the person constructs their awareness of the experience). One of the goals of this approach is to help adolescents develop behaviors that are congruent with their developmental challenges at this stage of life, helping them become aware of self-other dialogue and the social context in which these social interactive problems occur.

In this chapter, we will describe an integrative cognitive and psycho-educational model for training adolescents in assertiveness and conflict resolution. This work features components of the cognitive behavioral framework for such programs. However, we will feature a Gestalt focus on awareness of self and awareness of self in relation to other, as an essential aspect of assertiveness training. In addition, we will also attending to contextual features of the field.

In trying to integrate features of cognitive and Gestalt therapy, it is important to note important differences between the two models that may hinder or foster an integration of the two therapies. We have developed a model that uses much of the standard CBT approach, but in a way that reflects the insights and methods of Gestalt therapy. (See Appendix for a fuller discussion of issues that facilitate or hinder such integration.)

Assertiveness and Social Skills: The Intervention Package

Most cognitive behavioral assertiveness trainers use some variant of a flexible treatment package that includes assessment, learning to distinguish assertive, aggressive and non-assertive behavior, and a focus on skills training using cognitive restructuring, behavior rehearsal, modeling, and homework assignments. Continuous monitoring of behaviors is typically a central part of the program (Gambrill and Richey, 1976; Lange & Jakobowski, 1976; Fodor, 1980; Eisler & Fredericksen, 1980; Michelson, et al., 1983; Goldstein, et al., 1980; L'Abate & Milan, 1985; Hazel, 1990).

In adapting the basic assertive and social skills format for adolescents, we found that school environments and classrooms provide ideal opportunities for these group interventions. The assertiveness and social skills curriculum can be presented in a structured psycho-educational format. The situations that occur naturally in a group reflect the broad range of real life situations that adolescents cope with. For example, a peer group provides for shared problem solving among adolescents with similar concerns (e.g., coping with anger, getting along with one's parents, dealing with dating etc.). A group also provides a natural laboratory for the assessment of assertiveness problems, for working with ongoing interpersonal conflicts among group members, and for facilitating experiments in changing reactions and behaviors.

Tasks in Learning Assertiveness

In this chapter, we will highlight assertiveness and conflict resolution with adolescents in peer relations. By bringing in a Gestalt perspective, learning to be assertive can be viewed as a schematic process--each new learning building upon the other, with new organizations emerging as the adolescent encounters new challenges. Unlike the standard CBT approach, our model focuses on sensitivity to each adolescent. While we adapt the three styles of communication featured in CBT programs--assertive, unassertive, and aggressive--we highlight these communication styles as modes of contact.

The central feature of our program utilizes these three modes of contact to learn conflict resolution skills by assessing each person's style/mode of approaching conflict, and teaching the adolescents about these modes and alternative ways of contacting. When a conflict with a friend arises, how does the adolescent behave? Is she assertive? Does she express her feelings and thoughts to the other? Is she unassertive? Is she passive and avoidant in dealing with the situation? Or is she aggressive to her friend? That is, does she angrily confront and blame her friend for the conflict?

Included in our model is an assessment about how the adolescent construes the conflict situation (what story does she tell herself and believe about the conflict?) What are her rights in the situation? How does she handle her feelings? How good is she is at listening to her friend's point of view? How well developed are her social/conversational skills?

The techniques used in this psycho-educational assertiveness program include role play, behavioral rehearsal, individual and group feedback, decision making, and reinforcement to enhance self esteem. Homework assignments are often given as well.

In the integrative CBT program, the role of the trainer is that of teacher/coordinator, feedback giver, and facilitator for group process using the interactions among the group members to facilitate the learning about assertiveness. Additionally the trainer is there to provide support in the field for the experiential exercises, and to promote the development of self-support for new learning, self acceptance of setbacks, and an appreciation of the difficulty of the work.

We begin the program with education about what is and is not assertiveness. Next, we attend to the construing process--learning to listen, clarifying feelings and self talk, rights clarification, and setting goals. Following this, we focus on skills training that includes learning to dialogue and working out solutions to conflict. We end with a discussion and self-appraisal of the individual and the group's learning and growth. We will now examine these components in greater detail.

Education: Introducing New Cognitive Schemata

We typically begin the program by highlighting styles of communication--learning to talk about and distinguish assertiveness, aggressive, and unassertive passive behaviors. In Gestalt language we view these ways of behaving as contact modes. We typically provide an example of a conflict and ask the group for volunteers to role play friends engaging in these various ways of handling interpersonal relating and conflict. Out of these discussions, the group as a whole develops a consensus on their own definitions of these styles of contact.

We define assertive behavior as involving a direct, open, honest communication that is self-expressive, but respectful of the other (Alberti & Emmons, 1970; Lange & Jakubowski, 1976). In Gestalt language, assertive responding involves knowing what you feel, giving yourself the right to experience and voice these feelings, clarity in what you want to say, sensitivity to the impact of what you are saying on the other, and willingness to dialogue, hear the other side, and see the others point of view. Assertiveness involves holding on to your own ground, while appreciating difference.

Following some demonstration role plays in the group, we next discuss and distinguish between assertive, aggressive, and unassertive/passive behaviors. Each social group is different and by beginning with these role plays--which are often fun and engaging--the group typically realizes that it is not easy to achieve consensus concerning the definitions of assertive, aggressive and unassertive/passive behavior. In our experience most members can agree on aggressive behavior--which they typically do not like--and extreme passive behavior. Understanding and developing consensus concerning assertive behavior requires more work, however. The differences between assertive, unassertive/passive, and aggressive behaviors are illustrated in the material adapted from Alberti and Emmons (1970) in Table 1. Though this discussion and role playing, it is then possible to attend to how the group members frame these concepts and organize their experience

Table 1
A Comparison of Passive, Assertive, and Aggressive Behavior

	Passive Behavior	Assertive Behavior	Aggressive Behavior
Characteristics of the behavior	Emotionally dishonest; indirect; self-denying; inhibited	(Appropriately) emotionally honest; direct; self-enhancing; expressive	(Inappropriately) emotionally honest; direct; self-enhancing at the expense of the other; expressive
Your feelings when you engage in this behavior	Hurt; anxious at the time and possibly angry later	Confident; self-accepting at the time, and later	Righteous; superior; deprecatory at the time, and possibly guilty later
The other person's feelings about his or her self when you engage in this behavior	Guilty or superior; annoyed	Valued; respected	Hurt; humiliated
The other person's feelings about you when you engage in this behavior	Irritation; pity; disgust	Generally, respect (but possibly also resentment)	Anger; desire for revenge; resentment

Modified by Patricia Jakubowski-Spector from Robert E. Alberti & Michael L. Emmons, *Your Perfect Right: A Guide to Assertive Behavior*. San Luis Obispo, CA: Impact, 1970.

along these dimensions.

Role Play and Discussion

For the purpose of role play and discussion, we introduce examples that are close to group members' experience, allowing them to grasp the concepts in a personally meaningful way. For example, to teach about the differences between unassertive/passive and assertive behavior, we might introduce the following scenario: a teenager and her best friend are experiencing unexpressed tension over anger and rivalry for the affections of a male classmate. An assertive response would involve the teenager stating directly to her friend. "I think we better talk, I feel a lot of tension between us because of Jim." Or, "I am angry that you are dating Jim, you knew I wanted to date him." Essentially, assertiveness involves ownership of one's experience and a willingness to express it to the other. If a teenager is able to communicate assertively, she typically reports feeling good about herself.

In contrast to assertive behavior, unassertive behavior can be defined as inhibited, avoidant, or passive behavior. In Gestalt language, we speak of deflective, retroflective, and confluent modes of contact. The adolescent who utilizes confluence, for example, opts for accommodation to the other, rather than risking separation or a breach in the relationship. There is often no willingness to dialogue or voice a point of view that another might not like. In unassertive behavior, differences are blurred over and conflicts are avoided. Often the unassertive teen is unaware of what she feels or wants, or perhaps believes she has no right to express what she feels.

In the disagreement with the friend mentioned previously, an unassertive teenager would hold back feelings, avoid eye contact, avoid groups where they might run into each other, or drop out of a shared activity group without ever discussing the matter. Unassertive behavior is indirect, a withholding of feelings and an avoidance of dealing contactfully with the issues. Usually, because unexpressed feelings are hard to keep under control, these feelings do indeed surface, often in the form of sadness, depression, or anger. For the most part, unassertive adolescents do not feel good about their lack of assertiveness and will criticize or shame themselves in a fashion that creates additional bad feelings.

Our focus on skills training for the unassertive mode features giving the adolescent the right to his or her own feelings and voice while teaching skills in self-expression. Additionally, we help the adolescent to handle the anxiety that comes with breaking confluence and addressing difference.

Often, indirect or passive aggressive behavior may also be part of the unassertive style. In our example, the teenager discussed above may not express her anger at her friend, but the anger may be expressed, indirectly, and often out of awareness. She may forget to bring back notes she borrowed before an exam and/or, she may criticize her friend to other people and complain about the friend's flirtatious behavior. Again, the teenager may not even be aware of experiencing anger and the impact of her behavior on others. If confronted by another who labels the behavior he or she may become ashamed and berate his or her self.

Another form of unassertive behavior is aggressive behavior. Aggressiveness and assertiveness have been very much confused in the literature. It is considered assertive to be able express anger directly (i.e., "I'm angry at you"). However, aggressive behavior typically emanates from a projective mode of contact. The individual may project his or her own anger, construing the other as threatening or hostile in their intent. This projection promotes defensiveness and may lead the individual to adopt an aggressive, attacking stance in which can only escalate the confrontation. Often, aggressive behavior arises when the person is threatened by a difference and fears a loss of confluence. Ironically, aggressive behavior is often a coercive attempt to maintain power over the other in a misguided effort to maintain connectedness.

In the example introduced above, an aggressive adolescent may project her own anger and accusingly blame her friend. "You've been awful to me, you've betrayed our friendship. What kind of friend are you?" she might say. The projection is self-enhancing at the expense of the other, insofar as it locates the responsibility for the conflict entirely in the other person. "You should have known I was waiting for him to ask me out. You should have known how hurt I'd feel if you started dating him." In the projective, aggressive mode, angry feelings drive the behavior. There is no grasp of the conflict as a matter of differences, and thus no willingness to dialogue.

Most people do not like to deal with someone in this aggressive mode. With adolescents, arguments and fights can escalate from aggressive responding. Too often, unassertive people retreat further when confronted with an aggressive onslaught, which invites another round of projection and further infuriates the aggressive person. Regardless of whether the aggressive person achieves what they want, they too often end up like the unassertive person, feeling badly about themselves after aggressive encounters. They are frequently ashamed of their inability to control their temper and are often shunned by their peers. According to Seltzer's (1989) research, aggressive adolescents are ranked lowest in popularity by their peers.

In some instances, an unassertive person will suddenly become aggressive. The person is initially unassertive and there is a buildup until there is a "last straw" kind of provocation and then a blowup. For example, the teenager in our example might try to overlook her friend's dating someone she had wanted to see. Later, however, when she sees them together, she may blow up out of control. She then berates her friend, spilling out all the resentments in a hysterical, angry fashion.

Sometimes, the non-assertive adolescent engages in a process we call "grievance collecting;" silently compiling a list of perceived injustices and eventually presenting them in an aggressive, accusing manner. Often, the person who is the target of the tirade is caught completely unawares, experiencing the response as grossly out of proportion to the provocation. Furthermore, aggressive behavior often has unpredictable consequences. It can trigger withdrawal, avoidance or an aggressive response in return. Frequently, the person under attack discounts what the other is saying, brushing them off with "She's gone mad!" or "He's acting like a child."

Socio/Cultural Aspects of Assertiveness: Culture and Gender Issues

The preceding discussion reveals an Anglo-European bias in assertiveness training that reflects mainstream American values. In the United States and Europe, for the most part, we value self expression, standing up for yourself, and working out disagreements by dialogue. Different cultures might label these modes of relating differently and the behaviors may have different connotative meanings depending on the cultural context. (See Canino & Spurlock,1994; Cheek,1974; Hsu,1992; Knox,1992; and Plannells-Bloom,1992 for a fuller discussion of these issues).

Furthermore, even within our own culture, gender issues are too often intertwined with these modes of relating. The literature reports robust male/female differences connected to assertive, unassertive and aggressive responding (Jakubowski-Spector, 1973; Phelps & Austin,1975; Osborn & Harris, 1975; Wolfe & Fodor, 1975). In western culture men and women have been socialized differently in regard to assertive communication. Males have been trained to see assertiveness as part of the masculine role from early childhood on. They often confuse assertive, aggressive and competitive. Often when a male behaves in an assertive/aggressive manner, he engages in controlling, bullying or loud dominating actions. Typically, he is not criticized because this behavior is considered role appropriate.

Researchers report an additional male characteristic of inhibiting public displays of vulnerability or helplessness. So, if a male needs help or is feeling upset, it is difficult for him to ask for help or show the pain, particularly from another male (Lange & Jakubowski, 1976).

Females are typically socialized in the more traditional female role that stresses niceness, gentleness, taking care of others, not making waves and not expressing anger. Women have been socialized to inhibit or feel they have no right to their own voice. Furthermore, they also are reinforced for acquiescent, accommodating, and avoidant reactions in conflict situations. In traditional female socialization, confluence is preferred to the breach of separation.

Furthermore, angry women are particularly castigated in our culture and many females still feel they are behaving aggressively when in fact they are asserting themselves appropriately. Many people will label appropriately assertive behavior on the part of a woman as aggressive (Rich & Schroeder, 1976; Solomon & Rothblum, 1985; Fodor, 1987). Consequently, women often will inhibit their experience or expression of anger. In problematic and abusive male/female interactions we often have the extremes of the male aggressive/female unassertive patterning.

One of the main contributions of the women's movement was the development of mainstream assertiveness training programs for women that is still ongoing. However, today, too many adolescents still adhere to the more traditionally defined male and female roles and their struggles with assertive issues are inherently tied up with their own sex role definitions. (See Duggan-Ali, 1992 and Plannells-Bloom, 1992 for a fuller discussion of these issues).

Developing Awareness: Teaching a Phenomenological Perspective

In traditional conflict resolution programs, there is an assumption that the parties to the conflict are experiencing a misunderstanding and can be taught to process the experience in a new way by sitting down with a mediator. Left out or in the background is the actual dissection of the components of the misunderstanding. Central to our work in conflict resolution is an attempt to deconstruct the elements of the conflict by trying to understand the conflict from the perspective of the other. However, before on can appreciate the perspective of the other, an understanding of one's own awareness process is needed. Hence, the training we do includes attending to the individual's own construing process, highlighting self talk and clarifying feelings associated with these constructs prior to the focus on dialogue (Fodor, 1998).

Attending to the Construing Process

From a phenomenological perspective, individuals are rooted in their schematic way of organizing experience following their own social history and experience. People vary in their own awareness of how much they are construing their own experience and the recognition that reality is constructed. Too often, people, believe their own reality and do not or cannot view the situation from another's perspective. Central to so many conflicts is the "I-know-I-am-right-and-you-are-wrong" organization of the experience. Mediation training addresses these conflicts by bringing in an outside person and getting the parties involved in the conflict to talk in the hopes of being able to see things from another point of view.

In the combined Gestalt/CBT model, it is important to begin with the triggers and the construing process by teaching adolescents about their own cognitions and beliefs about a particular situation. It is vital to teach these adolescents that they are actively constructing their own take on the situation and that there are other possible alternatives in viewing the same situation. Raising awareness of their beliefs (i.e., cognitive appraisals, self statements, stories they are telling themselves about the situation) is central to this learning process.

Identifying Triggers

Imagine the following scenario similar to the one described earlier: two males are in conflict because one of them has gone out with the girlfriend of the other. They are very upset at each other and the conflict appears to be escalating.

The first step in working with these adolescents would be to identify the triggers--the red flag words--that are organizing their experience. Next, the boys would be shown how these words, beliefs, and cognitions are connected to feelings. In previous work by Wolfe and Fodor (1973; 1977), cognitions identified with assertive, aggressive and unassertive behaviors have been defined.

Constructs such as, "My best friend asked my girlfriend out" frequently contribute to an aggressive/angry reaction. For example, if an adolescent organizes his view of the conflict situation by telling himself a "How

dare he?" story, construing himself as righteously aggrieved, this organization of experience will almost certainly generate anger. In other words, the adolescent organizes his view of the situation around core beliefs such as:
  - The world should be fair and just.
  - Friends should not ask out one's girl.
  - My friend should think about me instead of being so selfish.
  - I'm gonna get even.
  - I'll show him he can't treat me this way.
  - People have to, and should do, what I want them to do.
  - I can't control my anger.
  - When I talk with my friend, I'll just let him have it.
  - How dare he do this to me? and so on.

In adolescents, low frustration tolerance and the implicit belief that "this is more than I can possibly stand" often accompanies out of control angry feelings. Cognitive schemata unfold along the lines of "If I can't stand feeling this way, I must do something." All too often these beliefs are tied into stereotypical beliefs about male gender roles (e.g., there is a belief in a need/responsibility to "get even" and show the other who is the "real man").

If the adolescent has an unassertive style of contact--a conflict-avoider--he will appraise and organize the situation differently. Constructs that contribute to an unassertive (passive, avoidant) reaction can take the following forms:
  - I can't talk to my friend about it, it would upset him too much.
  - Don't make waves.
  - It's easier to avoid hassles than to face them.
  - Why get upset over this, it's not worth it.
  - Maybe if I say nothing, he'll back off.
  - Why pick a fight? and so on.

Similarly, the adolescent may deny that he or she is upset, deny that his or her needs matter, or become anxious about the consequences of assertion:
  - He's my friend; his needs count more than mine;
  - I'm helpless;
  - If I asserted myself, it might be awful or catastrophic--my friend might get in my face, or even get a knife or gun and get me.

Clarifying Feelings

Moving beyond self-talk, is it is important to clarify the feelings being elicited by a particular situation and to look at the link between feelings and self talk. Once the cognitions--ways of construing the situation--and the stories the adolescents are saying to themselves are identified, it is helpful to heighten the awareness of the affective process.

Typically, in such problematic conflicts, there are three affective/cognitive behavior processes we work with corresponding to the modes of contact discussed previously. Unassertiveness (passive, avoidant behavior) is typically linked with an unawareness of feelings. In the case of aggressiveness, there are often impulsive outbursts in which anger is so intense that thinking is lost and potential harm could occur. Our intervention model helps adolescents to develop awareness of these non-adaptive modes of responding, and uses this awareness to strengthen feelings, beliefs, and behaviors that contribute to assertive responding. It is this final component that much of the intervention model focuses on. Central to the training is a focus of awareness of schematic patterning and recognition of how one's thoughts, feelings and behaviors are linked.

Adolescents are all too often unaware or unclear of their own feelings, or have only a vague notion of being upset. Many remain unaware that they are upset until some time later. Emotional awareness training might focus on feelings related to triggering incidents, as well as learning to distinguish anger, excitement, anxiety and general feelings of being upset. Furthermore, the linkage of feelings to the contact processes of separation/joining is also clarified for the adolescents. Anxiety often accompanies a break in confluence or feeling of separation. Anger may occur when hearing about a difference, particularly when the person believed that he or she was more in control of the situation.

Often, the initial stages of a workshop concentrate on clarification of feelings. Similarly, in various role plays throughout the workshop, work may also be continued on awareness of one's feelings. Various other emotional reactions for the adolescents to identify and clarify include being scared of the anger and retreating, failing to feel their own anger when they are party to aggressive behavior, or starting to get anxious, withdrawing, and then wondering why they are upset.

In developing awareness, an unassertive adolescent might learn to slow down and study his internal process in action, identifying and clarifying both his anger and the retroflective self talk that inhibits its expression. For example, in recognizing that angry feelings override thinking and that people often go from becoming aware of being angry to feeling out of control, deconstruction of the feeling process can begin by asking the adolescent. What is anger? What happens when you feel angry? What are the physical sensations of anger? What feelings of satisfaction or dissatisfaction occur when you express anger? Training in processing the expressive, as well as the retroflective process is useful in understanding variations for venting oneís feelings. Whereas some adolescents need to learn to undo the retroflective process, others need to learn how to create it, for example by identifying and practicing such cognitions as "Think before acting," "Calm down," "Count to ten," and so on.

When anxiety is figural and associated with fear of assertive responding, relaxation and imagery is often utilized. "What happens when you imagine yourself asking someone you like for a date? Where do you feel the anxiety? What's happening to your breathing? Can you imagine yourself breathing slowly and calming down, and then imagine yourself talking to a person you'd like to date?"

Behavior Change

There are a number of component behaviors that adolescents must learn if they are to improve their assertiveness and conflict resolution skills. In our program, we address these components through the use of teaching, awareness-raising, and role playing interventions.

Setting Goals

Adolescents often need help in identifying, clarifying and adhering to assertive goals. Understanding what he or she wants to achieve is frequently problematic for many urban youth. For example, in the previous example of a disagreement over dating, does the adolescent really want to engage in fighting to show that he or she is right. Or does he actually want some setting of rules or boundaries for dating between friends? Here the group can be particularly helpful in providing exploratory dialogue and work on appropriate goals for specific situations. Dialogue about goals is another way for adolescents to see things from another's point of view.

Rights Clarification

Together with goal setting, the clarification of rights is an important element of an assertive style of contact (Alberti & Emmons, 1970). For example, if an adolescent believes she has a right to her feelings, and a right to give them voice, she is more likely to insist on being treated fairly and expect to have her issues heard. In other words, she is more likely to risk assertive responding.

In our group work, we raise important questions related to this issue of personal rights: what types of rights do adolescents have in schools, in their families, with their friends? Do girls have fewer rights than boys in self-expression? What about the rights of minorities? What about adolescents who don't fit into normative culture? Do best friends have to agree on everything? Do they have a right to be different and still be able to be close? Some rights that group members might identify include freedom to make choices, to express themselves, to not be labeled, to be different from the crowd, to make mistakes, and the right to be included in the decision making process in school, as well as in their family.

An early assignment for an assertiveness group is to work together to discuss rights. What rights go with respect, increased self-esteem, the rights of friends in relationships, and so on? What happens when rights are violated? How does one feel? Put down, humiliated, upset? How often is anger connected with a violation of one's rights? Can one channel anger into assertive action to correct rights violations? Adolescents learning to take charge of their lives and to address school and community issues are often an outcome of assertiveness training.

Learning to Dialogue

The development of pro-social skills is the core of an assertiveness training program. In effect, we are teaching these adolescents micro-counseling skills, what Nevis (1998) calls modes of conversation and dialogue. This includes owning ones experience, reporting it to others, and engaging in an intersubjective dialogue with equal emphasis on talking and listening. We try to teach good will in interpersonal relating, respecting the feelings, and points of view, unique experiences, and cultural backgrounds of others.

Learning to Listen and See the Other's Point of View

Many people are so preoccupied with making their own points they neglect to focus on what it may be like for someone to be on the other side of an issue. A Gestalt perspective on dialogue addresses the following questions: Can the adolescent put herself in the place of the other? After articulating one's own position, can the adolescent listen to the other's point of view? Can he or she tolerate and respect assertiveness in others?

Awareness and Conflict Resolution

From a Gestalt viewpoint, dialogue requires a capacity to empathize with the other's experience and a willingness to allow for multiple realities. This requires the adolescent to acknowledge that the other also has a right to his or her experience, and to learn the skill of listening without anger and defensiveness.

In actual practice, however, the conflict often reemerges in the process of listening. The adolescent says to himself that the other person has no right to construe the situation in the way that they do. This problem in listening and accepting difference is a major obstacle for many adolescents. This is an arena where so much intercultural misunderstanding can occur. Crucial to overcoming this hurdle is for the adolescent to learn to remain quiet, listen and take in what the other person might be saying, even if they disagree.

To aid in skills acquisition, we focus on the communication styles tied to assertive, non-assertive, and aggressive responding. (See Lange & Jakubowski, 1976; Fodor, 1980; McKay, Davis, & Fanning, 1983 for further examples). We teach our group participants to attend and reflect on body language associated with assertiveness responding e.g. strong stance, steady voice tone, steadiness, eye contact etc. We contrast that with the body language associated with unassertiveness (e.g., low, wavering voice; e.g., eyes pointed toward the floor; e.g., stooped over, etc.). Role playing can be a key instrument in facilitating body awareness. What does it feel like when someone is talking to you with a strong assertive stance? How do you feel when you can respond in kind?

Using scenarios like the one of the dating conflict, we encourage participants to experiment with clear, open communication, making direct, honest "I statements," and attending to voice tone, body language, and eye contact. In role playing, we support teens to identify and clearly state their feelings, and to ask assertively for what they need and want.

In work with angry adolescents, dialogue work needs to address the projection and blaming. Blamers usually are not willing to own what they are feeling or to take responsibility for their emotions and behavior. In our groups, we heighten the participants' awareness of the words, tone, and body language of aggressiveness, and have them role play being angry, blaming, and projecting. This helps angry adolescents to develop more awareness of their style, and to learn about the impact this style has on others. Also, through reverse role plays, angry adolescents become aware of what it feels like to be on the other end of the interaction.

We work on teaching the adolescents to practice these skills via

233

role play and behavior rehearsal in the group, and after sufficient practice to try them out in their real life situations. We also teach support--self support when one is engaged in learning to confront rather than avoid, and group support for the process to facilitate experiment and change. For two people to be able to talk about what is happening between them might be the most challenging part of learning assertiveness. We are also sensitive to the support in the field for these new behaviors. For example, an authoritarian teacher might not appreciate a previously accommodating student pointing out what she does not like about the class.

Self Expression: Managing Emotions

As adolescents work towards assertion they must learn to express their thoughts and feelings clearly while keeping feelings of hurt, discomfort, anxiety, anger and rage under control. Sometimes people know what they want to say and as they start to talk they are overwhelmed with anxiety or anger. Naturally, most people feel some discomfort in charged encounters, but for some people the anxiety and anger interferes with effective responding. We use relaxation training, guided imagery, and anger control training to work on managing emotions. For example, in a role play where a teenager wants to ask a girl out for a date, but is overwhelmed by anxiety, we might have him or her utilize breathing and relaxation to counter the knotting sensations in the stomach and the quivering voice.

Appreciating the Work

Whether or not assertive goals have been reached, is it possible to be pleased with how one dealt with the situation? Is it possible to thank or appreciate others when they do listen or respond to assertive requests? If the friend agrees to sit down for mediation can the adolescent let him know he appreciates this way of working the conflict out?

Solution, Compromise, or Impasse?

Acquiring assertiveness skills often leads to a higher degree of satisfaction in conflict situations. But even a full repertoire of appropriately assertive responses does not guarantee the achievement of one's goals. In some instances, being assertive leads to the direct achievement of personal goals, while in others it serves to clarify the need for compromise. And certainly, compromise is much more readily achieved when both parties have acquired the assertiveness and dialogue skills that we have described above. Nevertheless, even adolescents who have worked at their assertiveness and compromise skills will experience conflicts that prove irresolvable. Learning to tolerate and accept these genuine impasse situations is itself an important skill for adolescents who encounter conflict.

What happens to the boy in our earlier example if he is assertive with his friend about their dating conflict, but his efforts to state his feelings and engage in productive dialogue lead nowhere? Certainly, for many adolescents, this sort of frustration often leads to an escalation of aggressive behavior. He may drop his good intentions for conflict resolution, and shift into an aggressive contact style, projecting responsibility and blaming his friend: "This is all your fault, you're just thinking about her and waiting for me to let down my guard; you can't be trusted." For this person, the experience of impasse is intolerable, and his escalating anger reveals an unyielding insistence that things be other than what they are.

An impasse is a signal that there is insufficient support for the individuals involved to resolve their conflict, and that additional resources should be brought to bear upon the situation if they are available. For example, this would be an opportunity to initiate the mediation phase of conflict resolution, by bringing in a neutral outsider to aid in restating the positions and working on listening skills.

On the other hand, assertiveness sometimes leads to a clearer picture of how irrational or rigid the other person truly is, and thus the impasse may reveal the real impossibility of change. By learning to accept these situations as part of life, the adolescent can then begin to look elsewhere for satisfaction. At the very least, learning to accept the inevitability of impasses helps him to avoid the wasted time and energy of banging his head against brick walls.

Planting Seeds for Tomorrow:
A Case Example of Social Skills Intervention with Inner City Males

The following case example is based on an actual socials skills group implemented in a New York City public school during the spring of 1996. The model utilized in this chapter served as the guide for this particular intervention and was designed collaboratively by the authors of this paper. Please note that while the case example does follow the general framework we proposed, variations in scope and sequence do occur. In so doing, our intent is to further demonstrate the adaptability of our model for various populations, settings, and goals. Additionally, the boys in this example fall in the twelve to thirteen year age-range, on the border of pre and early adolescence, and the group strategies utilized were designed to adapt our model to their developmental maturity level.

Rationale and Group Selection

This social skills group was developed in an inner city school in Harlem after much consultation with teachers regarding disruptive and aggressive behavior in several of the males in the classrooms.

After discussions with one particular teacher, "Ms. Rodriquez," about various problems and concerns with several students in her classroom, she was very excited about the prospect of some of her students gaining social skills and assertiveness training. Specifically, she expressed concern over the students' problem-solving skills, interpersonal communication skills and conflict resolution skills. Following continued dialogue with Ms. Rodriquez, we decided to narrow the group down to a group of males whom she felt were having particular difficulty in these areas.

Initially, ten pre-adolescent and early adolescent males were selected from her classroom that could most benefit from a social skills intervention project. Each of these boys was identified as being either passive or aggressive. Included in this selection were also a few who displayed minimal disruptive behavior problems, but who seemed shy or apprehensive in social interactions with others. The leader then met with this group of students to explain and discuss the purpose of the group and to create interest in their participation. Of these ten students, all expressed interest to participate in the group and parental permission forms were sent home.

Group Dynamics and Profile

From the first meeting with the group members, the differing cognitive abilities and levels of communication skills and behaviors were quite clear. Although a homogeneous sampling of students may have made the focus of the group much more specific, the authors felt the diversity and varying abilities would provide an interesting chemistry to the group. Similarly, it was believed that this type of group would also foster appropriate behavior modeling exercises and role playing opportunities, as well as provide different viewpoints and experiences throughout group discussions.

Important to note, however, is that the group was mixed in that it consisted of both passive and aggressive boys. Following is a brief discussion of each of the six group members gleaned from teacher reports, self reports, and classroom observations:

Jermaine is an outgoing, friendly African-American male with a great sense of humor. He is interested in art and wants to be a professional artist. Although he is very talkative, he listens well to others and appears to be very sensitive and caring. When sharing experiences with other group members, he appears adept at describing his own feelings about his experiences.

Antonio is a shy and slender Latino male with dark curly hair. He is very reserved and frequently needs encouragement to actively participate in the group. Although he appears quiet, he admits to having difficulty fighting and arguing with his classmates and friends.

Javier is a tall, slender Dominican male. He frequently talks about being teased by the other children in his class and feels that people "always make fun" of him. He has difficulty expressing his ideas, and often has difficulty focusing on what the group is talking about. Still, he attempts to be the class clown and often does inappropriate behaviors to gain attention (i.e., disrupting class, making funny faces, etc.).

Roberto is a short, stocky Hispanic male who prides himself on being "hip." He is the "captain" of some school and community sponsored athletic teams and is known to frequently attempt breaking up fights. In his words, "It's not worth it to fight. You only get into more trouble."

T.J. is a very talkative and energetic African-American male. He always wants to be "first" and frequently tries to dominate his classmates and be recognized as "the best." Similarly, he is quick to point out what others may be doing inappropriately, but fails to recognize these behaviors in himself. At the same time, T.J. is very helpful and tries to be respectful of other people's feelings.

Carlton is a tall African-American male who initially appears very quiet and reserved. He enjoys playing sports activities, but often gets angry if the game cannot be played according to his rules and expectations. Similarly, he is quick to react and frequently is the center of many verbal and physical confrontations. Even so, he is very protective of his friends and is not afraid to "stand up" for someone in trouble.

Although the members of the group did not consider themselves "best friends," they did enjoy participating in the group and looked forward to their sessions together. Frequently, they would come to the leader's office to say hello or to find out what activities were going on that day. Throughout the sessions, they were very energetic and welcomed varying activities. As a result, the meetings tended to be very fast paced and activity centered. Likewise, the boys often had difficulty allowing one person to talk at a time as they were eager to share their own experiences.

Group Session Location and Duration

Since available space was extremely limited, the group meet in a small corridor next to the school's gymnasium. While the area is fairly narrow, it did provide some sense of privacy and isolation from the rest of the schools' activities. Similarly, there was adequate room to place each group member's chair in a small circle, as well as ample room to move about for role playing and dramatic activities.

The group met for approximately fifty minutes immediately following the students' lunch time. Since they would miss one class period per week to participate, their teachers agreed to allow the students to only participate for a series of six sessions.

Social Skills Assessment

To gain as much information about the individual group members as possible, a variety of assessment tools and procedures were implemented. Included in these measures were teacher interviews, student interviews, behavior observations, Social Skills Checklist (teacher and student scales) (Goldstein, et al., 1980), and the Children's Behavior Scale (Michelson, et al., 1983). Separately, each provided a very isolated view of each child, but when combined helped provide a more complete picture of each participant. Likewise, the various assessment measures aided greatly in determining the various components and activities in the project.

Teacher interviews, student interviews and various observations all helped support the usefulness of an assertiveness and conflict resolution training program for all of these students. Similarly, the teacher and student rating scales aided in pinpointing target areas for each individual, as well as helping formulate overall training modules for the entire group.

Overall, the various instruments indicated fairly consistent results and observations. Noteworthy, however, is that the students perception of his own adequate problem-solving behaviors differed considerably from those reported by the teacher and by observation reports. These discrepancies may be related to any number of reasons including the situation under observation, mood of the teacher or student when completing the form, or that the students did not want to reveal negative behaviors about themselves, etc. In addition, results from the CABS indicated a range of passive behaviors (i.e., Javier and Roberto) to more aggressive behavior patterns (i.e., Carlton and Antonio).

The following list outlines a few general goals for each individual in the group as indicated by a combination of assessment measures:

Jermaine: As indicated by the social skills self-report and teacher report, Jermaine appeared to have good social skills in terms of classroom survival skills and friendship-making skills. Likewise, teacher reports and observations suggested some difficulty with skills pertaining to conflict resolution and recognizing feelings. Similarly, his responses to the CABS indicated a tendency to be more passive than assertive. Program goals focused on learning to identify and express feelings, expressing his needs more effectively, and solving problems more assertively.

Antonio: Based on self-reports and teacher reports, Antonio seemed to have difficulty expressing his feelings without aggression. In addition, observations of him in various situations pointed to the need to learn how to get along better with his peers. Social skills training focused on relaxation techniques, identifying and expressing feelings, anger management, and communication skills.

Javier: Information from observations, teacher reports and self-reports all indicated difficulty gaining peer acceptance and dealing with stress. Specific goals of this program for Javier attempted to promote self-confidence, effectively identify and express feelings, increase interpersonal communication skills, and increase assertive behavior.

Roberto: According to all of the assessment tools used, Roberto appeared to have good social skills. Information on the CABS indicated that he may act passively in some situations and not identify his feelings. Therefore, social skills training focused on identifying and expressing feelings as well as increasing assertive behaviors.

T.J.: Although T.J. did not express or appear to react with violence in social situations, information from self-report and teacher report measures, as well as the CABS, all indicated tendencies towards aggressive behaviors. The focus of training elements for T.J. in this project focused on expressing ideas and feelings more effectively, developing relaxation techniques, and establishing more self-control over impulsive behaviors.

Carlton: As indicated by all of the collected data, Carlton seemed

239

to be very aggressive and experienced difficulty controlling his anger. In addition, as witnessed in several observation opportunities, he frequently used inappropriate language and physical means to assert control over people. Intervention strategies dealt with identifying and expressing feelings, utilizing relaxation techniques, improving anger control, identifying assertive and non-assertive behaviors.

Social Skills Training Modules

The following outlines the integrated Gestalt/Cognitive Behavioral model utilized in this intervention project focusing on assertiveness and conflict resolution. Each module filled a single fifty-minute session.

Module One: Social Skills Introduction and Assessment. Each of the participants arrived at the first session on time and was eager to begin. Having left some of their classmates behind who also wanted to participate in the group, they appeared to feel "special" as they left their rooms. Noteworthy, was the value they placed on being able to be a part of a group as evidenced by their statements to classmates, "He's only going to work with a few of us. This is our time!" Excitedly, they each selected a chair from the office, moved to the group "area" and formed a large circle.

In order to learn each member's name and begin to build a sense of "group," an icebreaker called the Name Game was introduced. Interestingly, all of the participants except Antonio were excited about the activity and enjoyed participating. Although everyone was given the option to not participate, Antonio decided to continue. Once he gained confidence in the experience, he began to relax and became very open in his interactions with the other group members. All were laughing and enjoying the "silliness" of the game.

As the initial activity was brought to a conclusion, a brief review of the group's purpose was discussed and guidelines for group participation were presented. These included mutual respect, listening to others, allowing one person to speak at a time, the right to "pass," giving eye contact to whoever was speaking, and respecting the agreement for confidentiality. Following this, the students were each given the Social Skills Assessment to complete. We read through the questions individually as each student recorded his own response.

When the group had completed the questionnaire, a discussion about social skills began. Several responses and examples defined social skills as "table manners" and "how to act with rich people." A general explanation was given of "social skills" as relating to the ways we act, behave, talk, and/or react with other people. It was then explained that the purpose of the group would be to work on ways to help them relate to people in "better" ways that might help improve relationships with friends and family. The group then discussed different ways people talk to each other (i.e., friends, family, teachers) in different situations (i.e., home, school, parties, church).

As time was about to end for the session, a final group activity was lead to help point out how important each individual member is to a group. The Spider Web was formed and the students each had a good time trying to "problem-solve." As expected, the members began to get rowdy and shout at one another. It was necessary to intervene and point out that it might be easier to solve the problem if only one person spoke at a time. When everyone is yelling, nothing was accomplished. Although it was difficult for them to control the urge to blurt out their ideas, they each did a nice job at "self-monitoring" and finding the solution.

When the time had ended, I asked them to think about the different situations they experienced throughout the upcoming week and to try and pay attention to the different ways they behaved depending on the situation.

Module Two: Understanding Feelings. This session began by reviewing their "homework" assignments from the previous session. Generally, they each noted how they tended to act differently in school then at home. In school, they tended to be more quiet and reserved, especially when they talked with their teacher or the principal. At home, according to the students, they were more apt to be rowdy, yell and get into arguments and fights with their siblings and friends.

After this brief discussion, some techniques for body relaxation and awareness were illustrated. They first began with some physical warm-ups, stretching and flexing various parts of the body, and then went on to talk about proper breathing. Initially, some of the group members found this work quite amusing and began laughing. As some of the others really focused their efforts and concentration, the "gigglers" began to follow their example. Amazingly, all of them were participating in the breathing exercises and a brief, guided-visualization experience.

When the relaxation exercises were completed, group members were asked how they were feeling. Responses included statements such as "really relaxed," "sleepy," and "real soft." They were then asked what other feelings they experienced in their lives and in what situations they related to these feelings. Similarly, they were asked to describe the various physical manifestations/sensations (i.e., stomach ache, tightness in the chest, sweaty palms, etc.) they associated with different feelings.

Each group member was then given a hand mirror. Different situations were explored and the participants were asked to make a face showing how they would feel in that particular situation. They enjoyed this activity and began to "ham" it up. Interestingly, many of the emotions they portrayed contained smiles even though they were sad, frightening, or painful feelings. This opportunity was utilized as a time to explain how emotions and feelings are often hidden, as well as the importance of our bodies and faces in telling our true emotions and feelings.

The group then talked about feelings they experienced and the importance of identifying and talking about feelings. Many expressed that they often felt anger, sadness, and happiness. They were then asked to describe if they ever had any other feelings (i.e., embarrassed, , humiliated, ashamed, proud). Several described experiences they had had in which they felt humiliated by a parent or teacher, or embarrassed by something they did in class and everyone laughed.

In order to prepare for upcoming sessions, the students were given the CABS to complete. As with the social skills assessment, each question was read aloud as they marked their own responses.

Module Three: Getting Along with Others. When the students arrived for this session they had just come in from having lunch and free time outside and were very rowdy. Hence, this was a good opportunity to do another relaxation and body awareness activity in order to get the group focused. This started with physical exercises involving stretching various body and muscle groups and concluded with a focused breathing and visualization exercise. The group had remembered the exercises from a previous session and worked without any nervous laughter or energy.

As soon as the body awareness activity was finished, the group began to discuss the issue of friendship, and the qualities each looked for in a friend. The group's responses included elements such as being friendly, humorous, trustworthy and honest. They then talked about how to maintain friendships through communication and listening. Each of the group members expressed the importance of spending time together and standing up for one's friends if they were in trouble.

The concept of "active listening" was then introduced and related to how it could be used in the classroom and in talking with their friends or other people. Also mentioned was how frequently ineffective listening is a problem in arguments and fights, as well as a factor in poor performance in school. In order to improve listening skills, they were instructed that they were going to do a project and given an opportunity to practice using their listening skills. They then went to another room that had been previously set up with clay flowerpots, paints, seashells and glue to use in decorating the pots. The students then used the materials in any way they wanted to decorate their own flowerpot. (They would be planting flowers at a later session.)

Throughout the activity, participants were instructed to pair up with a partner and to talk about their weekend. Before a student could respond, they had to restate what the person they were talking with had just said. Similarly, when they needed additional materials, they had to repeat what the person was asking for before passing the needed materials. The students had difficulty with this, but soon were able to listen and respond with few reminders to restate what had been said. Throughout the experience, they were asked how it felt to be communicating in that manner. Without exception, they each thought it was "very weird." Acknowledging their feeling of awkwardness and continued practice was suggested to help them be better listeners. Likewise, they were asked to use active listening when they got in an argument throughout the week and see if it was helpful to understand the problem better when they listened to each other more carefully.

Unexpectedly, the group participants were really excited and engaged in the process of making the flowerpots during this session. While they went through the seashells, they seemed as if their hands were filled with gold coins. They were extremely eager and enthusiastic as they looked through the shells and selected their paints. With only a few reminders, they began to use "please" and "thank you" when asking for materials.

Module Four: Assertiveness Training. Session Four began with a reading of a short story illustrating various themes related to assertiveness. This story was used as a springboard to talk about assertive behavior and asking participants to share their experiences of having to make choices about their behaviors. As each began to shout out their experiences, the sharing time was paused for a review of the group's "guidelines."

From this, the session went on to introduce the concepts of passive, aggressive, and assertive behavior. The students then role played some passive, aggressive and assertive behaviors and asked to "freeze" the action and then re-try other possible behaviors and responses to the situation. Interestingly, they frequently tended to act either very aggressively or passively in the various situations. For example, when asked about how to handle a situation in which "someone takes something that belongs to you," they all thought it would be best to "kick his ass!" They were then asked to think about the consequences this would have and to think of other ways they might handle the situation. As a suggestion was made, participants were encouraged to role play the suggestion to see what possible consequences that particular action might have. This was particularly important to do in helping them identify how various behavior "choices" bring about different consequences and responses, as well as an excellent opportunity to develop empathy and insight into other people's position or experience.

After several of these situations, the group again went to another room to plant some flower seeds in the pots they had painted in a previous session. A limited number of seeds and choices were provided in order to create an atmosphere for the group members to have to practice the assertiveness skills that had been discussed.

Upon first introducing the potting soil and seeds, they immediately wanted to start yelling out what they wanted and attempted to grab for the seeds. Modeling assertive behavior for them, they were told by the facilitator that it was very important that they work this out amongst themselves and suggested that they use the techniques that had been talked about.

For the most part, they were able to do so, with the exception of Javier who just sat back and let the others take whatever they wanted. As a result, he was left to use what remained. When asked how he felt about this he replied, "Okay," with little affect or eye contact. He was then asked by another group member if he got the seeds that he wanted for his pot. Javier just looked at his chair and shook his head "no." It was then suggested that the group might want to explore some ways to help Javier get what he wanted. Several participants made some very good comments including trying to trade with someone who had some of the seeds that he wanted. The facilitator asked Javier if any of the suggestions sounded like something that he might want to try. Javier thought that he could try the suggestion about trading. He said that he really wanted a few of the "purple flower seeds" and stated that he had a lot of the "orange ones" that he really didn't want. He then asked if there was anyone who might want to trade some of their purple seeds for some orange seeds. Antonio said that orange was his favorite color and that he would like to trade. It was pointed out how this helped both of them to get what they really wanted and suggested that this might be used in other situations in their lives.

Finally the session ended and they, surprisingly, suggested keeping the plants at school and taking them home the next week to their mothers for Mother's Day. All agreed that this would be a good idea.

Module Five: Resolving Conflicts. As fate would have it, two of the boys (T.J. and Carlton) entered the room for the session yelling at each other and insulting each other's "mother." Following this insult, T.J. picked up a chair and threatened to throw it at Carlton. The facilitator quickly intervened by positioning himself between the two boys, placing his hand on the chair, and firmly stating, "I need you to put the chair down now!"

Reluctantly, T.J. slowly lowered the chair to the floor and shoved it across the room. They were then told that this type of behavior would not be tolerated and encouraged them to attempt working the problem out in another way. If they wanted to fight and couldn't work their problem out with their words and not their fists, they would not be permitted to stay in the group for that particular day. Both said that they wanted to stay, but that they did not want to sit by each other. Respecting their wish, they were allowed to sit wherever they would feel most comfortable.

Because of this outbreak, the session immediately began to discuss conflicts and what happens when these get out of hand. A couple of the boys shared stories they had witnessed in their neighborhoods in which neighbors were arguing and then began using weapons and guns. They were asked how this made them feel, as well as how they felt when their own conflicts got out of hand. The essence of their responses indicated that they realized that many conflicts escalate because the people involved didn't want to "lose face or be disrespected."

Sensing that T.J. and Carlton were still really upset by the way their arms were crossed and the positions they were sitting in their seats, a decision was made to do some more relaxation and breathing exercises. As these progressed, it was explained again how these exercises can be helpful in reducing stress, tension, anxiety, and anger. Similarly, it was also pointed out that conflicts are often better able to be worked out when both parties are defused and not at their "peak" with anger.

Since the next portion of the module was to deal with communication, compromise and problem solving, the two boys who were fighting were asked if they would be willing to try and work their differences out during the group. It was very helpful, and valuable, to use "what was there and real" at that particular moment. Both agreed, so the following conflict resolution steps were presented on a large sheet of poster paper that had been attached to the wall:

1. Stop and think before you say or do anything.
2. Speak with the other person or persons to find out what the problem is.
3. Reach some agreement on how to handle the problem and come to some agreeable compromise.

4. Do what you have agreed to do.
5. Know that sometimes the conflict cannot be resolved and it is then best to stay away from each other.

Each step was broken down and applied to the problem between the two boys. For example, each took a turn explaining "their perspective" on the problem and then listening to how the other person heard what they had just said. As they began to talk to each other it became clear that T.J. was upset because he wanted to play basketball outside with Carlton. However, since Carlton was already in a game with another group when T.J. came outside, T.J. thought that Carlton would "disdain" him. As a result, T.J. decide to stick his foot out and trip Carlton when he ran past. By the end of this process, both had come to an agreement to try and talk to each other about how they were feeling before they reacted impulsively. Further, they agreed that they would wait to go outside the next day until each was done eating so they could start their own game together.

The session ended by reviewing the conflict resolution process.

Module Six: Putting it All Together/Closure. Session six began, at the request of the students, by doing the Spider's Web activity that had been done during the first session. When this was finished, they were asked to review the issues that had been talked about in the various sessions. Similar to the seeds which were planted, they were told to think of these ideas as "seeds" that--similar to the plants--could grow and grow and be used throughout their lives.

Next, they were asked to think about how they control their own behaviors and the ways they interact with people. When this was finished, the students then completed an evaluation form to express their feelings about the workshop (i.e., most/least helpful elements, suggestions for improvement, etc.) and were re-administered the CABS.

Interestingly, all of the participants' scores reflected more assertive behaviors than the first administration. In addition, the responses to the workshop evaluation questionnaire all indicated that the workshop was helpful and enjoyable to them. Their biggest suggestion was that they wanted the group to continue all year long. Similarly, during a post-workshop conference with the members' teacher, Ms. Rodriquez, she indicated noticing an improvement the behavior of all the boys in class. Specifically, according to Ms. Rodriquez, the students who participated in the group were not as aggressive with each other or their other classmates, and also seemed to handle their conflicts with one another in more effective ways.

Finally, a Coke and chip party was held to commemorate their active participation and completion in the group.

Case Example Summary and Conclusion

A six-session workshop was planned as a social skills intervention project with six, inner city, male, early adolescents. The group met in a small corridor next to the school's gymnasium once a week for fifty minutes for a series of six sessions. Topics addressed throughout the workshop included social skills, feelings and emotions, getting along with others, assertiveness training, and conflict resolution. Overall, the group was very enthusiastic and actively participated in the activities. Specifically, they seemed to really enjoy the role playing exercises and the hands-on activities involving the flower pots and planting seeds.

Results from the post-assessment indicated some positive growth in assertive behaviors in all of the students. In addition, observations and teacher reports indicated more appropriate social skills and conflict resolution techniques by the group participants. Similarly, responses to the written evaluations of the workshop were positive and indicated that the experience was helpful. Although group participants still experienced some difficulties solving conflicts, many helpful "seeds" were planted that will hopefully be utilized in the future.

References

Alberti, R., & Emmons, M. (1970). *Your perfect right: A guide to assertive behavior.* San Luis Obispo, CA: Impact Publishers.

Canino, I., & Spurlock, J. (1994). *Culturally diverse children and adolescents: Assessment, diagnosis and treatment.* New York, NY: Guilford Press.

Cheek, D. (1974). *Assertive black/puzzled white.* San Luis Obispo, CA: Impact.

Duggen-Ali, D. (1992). Social skills and assertiveness training integrated into high school sexuality education curriculum. In I.G. Fodor (Ed.), *Adolescent assertiveness and social skills training: A clinical handbook* (pp. 219-233). New York, NY: Springer.

Eisler, R., & Frederickson, L. (1980). *Perfecting social skills.* New York: Plenum.

Ellis, A. (1962). *Reason and emotion in psychotherapy.* Secaucus, NJ: Lyle Stuart.

Ellis, A. (1995). Reflections on rational-emotive therapy. In M. Mahoney (Ed.), *Cognitive and constructive psychotherapies: Theory, research and practice* (pp. 69-73). New York: Springer.

Erikson, E. (1968). *Identity: Youth and crisis.* New York, NY: W.W. Norton.

Fodor, I. (1980). The treatment of communication problems with assertiveness training. In A. Goldstein & E. Foa (Eds.), *Handbook of behavioral interventions* (pp. 501-603). New York: Wiley.

Fodor, I. (1987). Moving beyond cognitive behavior therapy: Integrating gestalt therapy to facilitate personal and interpersonal awareness. In N. Jacobson (Ed.), *Psychotherapists in clinical practice: Cognitive and behavioral perspectives* (pp. 340-410). New York: Guilford Press.

Fodor, I. (1992). *Adolescent assertiveness and social skills training: A clinical handbook.* New York: Springer.

Fodor, I. (1993). A feminist framework for integrative psychotherapy: Cognitive and gestalt perspectives. In G. Striker & J. Gould (Eds.), *The comprehensive handbook for integrative psychotherapy* (pp. 217-235). New York: Plenum.

Fodor, I. (1996). A cognitive perspective for Gestalt therapy. *British Gestalt Journal, 1*(5), 31-42.

Fodor, I. (1998). Awareness and meaning making: The dance of experience. *Gestalt Review, 2*(1), 50-71.

Gambrill, E., & Richey, C. (1976). *It's up to you: Developing assertive and social skills.* Milbrae, CA: Les Femmes.

Goldstein, A., Sprafkin, R., Gershaw, N. & Klein, P. (1980). *Skill streaming the adolescent: A structured approach to teaching social skills.* Champaign, IL: Research Press.

Goleman, D. (1995). *Emotional intelligence.* New York: Bantum.

Hazel, J.S. (1990). Social skills training with adolescents. In E. Feindler, & G. Kalfus (Eds.), *Adolescent behavior therapy handbook* (pp. 191-209). New York: Springer.

Hsu, C. (1992). Assertiveness issues for asian americans. In I.G. Fodor (Ed.), *Adolescent assertiveness and social skills training: A clinical handbook* (pp. 99-112). New York: Springer.

Jakubowski-Spector, P. (1973). Facilitating the growth of women through assertive training. *The Counseling Psychologist, 4,* 76-86.

Knox, T. (1992). A framework for understanding high-risk black adolescents' social interactive issues. In I.G. Fodor (Ed.), *Adolescent assertiveness and social skills training: A clinical hand book* (pp. 82-98). New York: Springer.

L'Abate, L., & Milan, M. (1985). Preface. In L. L'Abate & M. Milan (Eds.), *Handbook of social skills training and research* (pp. xi-xiii). New York: Wiley.

Lange, A., & Jakubowski, P. (1976). *Responsible assertive behavior: Cognitive behavioral procedures for trainers.* Champaign, IL: Research Press.

Lester, H. (1992). *Me first.* New York: Houghton Mifflin Company.

McConville, M. (1995). *Adolescence: Psychotherapy and the emergent self.* San Francisco, CA: Jossey-Bass.

McKay, M. Davis, M., & Fanning, P. (1983). *Messages: The communication book.* Richmond, CA: New Harbinger.

Michelson, L., Sugai, D., Wood, R., & Kazdin (1983). *Social skills assessment and training with children: An empirically based hand book.* New York: Plenum Press.

Nevis, S. (1998). Discussion of the New England Writers Group, Boston, MA.

Osborn, S., & Harris, G. (1975). *Assertive training for women.* Springfield, IL: Charles C. Thomas.

Phelps, S., & Austin, N. (1975). *The assertive woman.* San Luis Obispo, CA: Impact.

Plannells-Bloom, D. (1992). Latino cultures: framework for understanding the latina adolescent and assertive behavior. In I.G. Fodor (Ed.), *Adolescent assertiveness and social skills training: A clinical handbook* (pp. 113-130). New York: Springer.

Sadalla, G., Henriquez, M., & Holmberg, M. (1987). *Conflict resolution: A secondary school curriculum.* San Francisco, CA: The Community Board Program, Inc.

Rich, A., & Schroeder, H. (1976). Assertiveness training. *Psychological Bulletin, 83,* 1082 1096.

Seltzer, V. (1989). *The psychosocial world of the adolescent: Public and private.* New York: Wiley.

Solomon, L., & Rothblum, E. (1985). Social skills problems experienced by women. In L. L'Abate & M. Milan (Eds.), *Handbook of social skills training and research* (pp. 303-325). New York: Wiley.

Wolfe, J., & Fodor, I. (1975). A cognitive/behavioral approach to assertiveness training in women: Special issues on assertiveness.

Heart of Development

The Counseling Psychologist, 5, 45-59.

Appendix
On Integrating Gestalt and Cognitive Therapy

In attempting to integrate these different therapy systems it is important to keep in mind that there are important areas of compatibility and incompatibility. (For a fuller discussion of these issues, see Fodor, 1987, 1996).

Some differences between Gestalt therapy and Cognitive Therapy that need to be addressed in integrating these differing systems of therapy include the following. A good deal of Cognitive therapy, in spite of its stated phenomenological emphasis in its foundational framing by Kelly (1955) follows an objectivist scientific model for therapy. In particular, the emphasis is on so-called 'objective' measurement of systems and therapy outcome with a goal toward building a scientific basis for theory and therapeutic procedures. Gestalt therapy is built on an existential, field theory framework of viewing therapy through the subjective lenses of the client and therapist and posits a relativity perspective on so-called reality. Additionally, while, Gestalt therapy highlights process (what is happening), cognitive therapy focuses more on content (the problem). In contrast to Gestalt therapy which highlights sensory states and feelings, Cognitive therapy emphases thinking. Simply stated, "we feel what we think" (Ellis, 1962). In Rational Emotive Behavior Therapy (REBT), the most popular cognitive therapy, Ellis (1995) features dysfunctional or irrational beliefs as central to psychopathology. The clients are encouraged to report on their self-talk, their beliefs, assumptions and evaluations as a central aspect of the therapy.

In addition, Cognitive and Gestalt therapist view the role of the therapist differently. Cognitive therapy emphasizes a dyadic/consultant role for the therapist. For example in REBT, the therapist engages in a Socratic dialogue to argue the clients out of their dysfunctional beliefs, or presents behavioral experiments to foster alternative belief systems. Gestalt therapy is more dialogic. Following its existential foundation, and the emphasis on contact, Gestalt therapy tends to focus on the two phenomenologies: those of the client and the therapist. They highlight moment to moment experiencing, and the therapist's role is to facilitate awareness of this experiencing process. Furthermore, cognitive therapy often goes beyond the moment of immediate experience, by asking the clients to report on their self-talk focusing on beliefs, assumptions, and evaluations.

Finally an important distinction between the two therapies is the view of the nature of change. In Cognitive therapy the therapist actively works to help clients change their dysfunctional beliefs with the aim of changing dysfunctional behavior. Cognitive restructuring and re-framing is the goal of Cognitive Therapy. Change is actively measured by objective ratings, self report scales, and adherence to homework assignments (Freeman, Simon, Beutler, & Arkowitz, 1989). Gestalt therapy, following existentialism, has no explicit goals except increased awareness (Simkin & Yontef, 1984). Gestalt therapy posits the "paradoxical theory of change" which advocates having clients be fully where they are, in order to own and explore present experience (Beisser, 1970).

In spite of these important differences, there are some similarities between these two therapy systems that serve as ground for integration. They are both modern structuralist systems. Gestalt therapy evolved from Gestalt psychology and field theory, while cognitive therapy grew out of modern cognitive psychology. They both evolved from and contributed to the humanistic psychology movement. They are both health and growth-oriented. Cognitive therapy postulates a hedonistic base similar to Gestalt therapy's view of organismic self-regulation. They both claim to be phenomenological in varying degrees by attempting to understand what's happening from the client's frame of reference. Gestalt therapy is more interested in what's happening now, while cognitive therapists highlight the client's evaluations and appraisals or interpretations of what's happening now (e.g., the explaining, and evaluative functions.)

Both theories are essentially constructivist in that both see the client's story or viewpoint as his own constructive view of reality. In addition, they could also be said to consider process in that they both invite experiments to study the client's organization of experience as vehicles for trying out new behaviors or ways of being. However, in Gestalt therapy the aim is to foster awareness, while in CBT, the therapy often follows a programmatic format, with the explicit goal of changing behavior. In recent work, one of the authors has presented a theoretical model for the integration of the Gestalt therapy concept of awareness with a cognitive perspective, highlighting the construction of meaning making as an aspect of ongoing process. That theoretical perspective is beyond the scope of this chapter, but that work is a beginning to lay the foundation for integration of these two therapies (see Fodor, 1998).

References

Beisser, A. (1970). The paradoxical theory of change. In J. Fagan and I.L. Shepard (Eds.), *Gestalt therapy now* (pp. 77-80). New York: Science and Behavior Books.

Freeman, A., Simon, K. Beutler, L., & Arkowitz, H. (1989). *Comprehensive handbook of cognitive therapy*. New York, NY: Plenum.

Kelly, G. (1955) *The psychology of personal constructs*. New York: Norton.

Simkin, J., & Yontef, G.M.(1984) Gestalt therapy. In R. Corsini (Ed.), *Current psychotherapies, third edition*. Itasca, IL: Peacock

Yontef, G. (1993). *Awareness, dialogue and process: Essays on gestalt therapy*. Highland, NY: Gestalt Journal Press.

9

Shame and Support: Understanding an Adolescent's Family Field

Robert G. Lee

Kevin was 15 when I first met him. It was early in July when his mother called and scheduled the initial appointment. The school term had ended a few weeks previously, and he had barely made it through, having been suspended several times--kicked out of one program entirely--for oppositional behavior and failing grades. Although he was being allowed to continue in school in September, more than one school administrator, as I later learned, was on the verge of suggesting that Kevin be placed in a residential setting which could focus on his behavioral problems full time. His mother reported that he had been extremely verbally abusive at home--"a poor example for his younger sisters and brother"--continually disrespectful to his mom and siblings, hostile and combative when he didn't get his way, disobeying curfew.

How do we understand such behavior in an adolescent? Is it biological--perhaps some version of the bad seed theory? Perhaps a learning disability--his teachers had always said that he was smart enough but that he just wouldn't apply himself. Is it contextual or relational? How important are family dynamics? Is it developmental? Gestalt field theory with its constructivist, intersubjective foundation offers a unique lens with which to examine this puzzle. Gestalt field theory focuses on the combination of inner and outer components of life that influence behavior and development. In this sense, the field is one's mapping (one's construction) of inner needs, temperament, attributes, desires, skills, limitations, etc. in combination with the outer environmental set of resources and limitations. From a Gestalt perspective, these two elements of the field, inner and outer, are always connected; they are a unit. Our mapping or knowing of "self" is always linked to our mapping or knowing of "other." Both are created simultaneously from the same intersubjective, experiential data. Goodman (1951) saw that the site of self-process lay at the boundary between "self" and "other." A sense of "self" does not exist a priori to a sense of "other." Goodman called the meeting of "self" and "other," from which our experience and knowledge of each emerges, *contact*.

This positioning of the site of self process not only acknowledges that our sense of "self" is always wedded to our sense of "other" but, in addition through contact, that we intersubjectively influence each other's mapping of "self/other." We are not subjects operating on static objects in our environment. Instead, we are subjects that encounter other subjects, co-creating our sense of ourself and each other together as interactions unfold. It is Gestalt therapy's focus on contact that makes it a relational, intersubjective theory and separates it from individualistic approaches such as behavioristic and psychodynamic theories. (See Wheeler, 1996, for a fuller discussion of individualistic versus field-based paradigms.)

Thus, from a Gestalt perspective, in order to understand someone's behavior, we must understand the person's co-constructed map, the experiential context in which the behavior exists. The behavior itself may be figural, but to understand the meaning of this figure we must first understand the ground from which it emerges; i.e., the person's needs and perceived set of possibilities for connection/disconnection in the environmental field. What is *this* adolescent's perceived world like? What are his dreams, fears, confusion? What are his basic beliefs about himself and others? What are the experiments in which he is engaging to explore his world and further develop his map? And how do we get an entry into learning the answers to these and other questions? (Ask people who work with adolescents and their families and they will tell you how much they don't know at any one time.)

In Kevin's case I started by asking to see the entire family. This is my usual stance in treating an adolescent, since it allows me to begin by seeing the family context for the adolescent's mapping. Kevin, his younger sisters and brother, and his mother appeared for the first session. I was told that Kevin's dad, a carpenter and cabinet-maker, couldn't make it because he had to finish a job for a client. Kevin's mother reported that her husband ran his own small business with several employees, and was often up against delivery deadlines.

Kevin took the couch, kicking with disdain at his brother who attempted to get there first. Mom admonished Kevin, but he ignored her. I asked them to tell me about what they were like as a family. As they talked about themselves, two things stood out to me about their process. First was their sense of humor. In a Don Rickles style, they would systematically put each other down. I must admit the put-downs were funny and they often seemed to nonverbally convey both a fondness for the other person and a pride in the family, even if they also seemed to sting their target. Second, the occasional disputes and differences that arose, such as who sat where, who played with which toys, and who got to talk, were handled with quick bursts of blaming anger at each other.

When I reflected my first awareness to the family, the sarcastic, put-down humor toward each other increased. This then appeared to be a major family contact style--one which they had all developed with great skill. What were its defining characteristics? And what did this say about specific components of the family's belief system? These questions led me to suggest an experiment. I conveyed my appreciation of their collective skill in humorously roasting each other as well as my sense that they seemed to be showing me their fondness of each other and a piece of their family pride. They seemed pleased. I mentioned further that their roasting seemed to have a sting for the person on the receiving end and wondered about the importance of that part of their style. Could they also express their appreciation/fondness/liking of one another without the sting, I asked? They said of course they could. I suggested they try it just for the fun of it. Would they, one at a time, be willing to say to every other family member something they appreciated/liked about that family member? All agreed to the experiment, and each family member took his/her turn. The result: *No one could do it!* First, they reported that it was "strange" for them to focus on what they liked about the others; they said they felt somewhat embarrassed. In a number of instances they couldn't find anything without my suggesting a list of possibilities. Even when they could identify something they appreciated/liked about one of the others, they couldn't say it without finding some way of putting the other down, again humorously. They were amazed that the task was so difficult; they had thought that it was going to be easy.

Together we had learned something important about a major family contact style. But what was the significance of this learning? Again, what did this tell us about the family's belief system? And how did that relate to the problems that others had ascribed to Kevin? What we learned was that the family could not openly share their appreciation or fondness of one another. This might be developmentally appropriate to one extent or another for some of the kids, but it was true of mom also. It wasn't as if they didn't like each other. Their fondness of one another could be seen in the playfulness of their roasting each other. Nor could this be "just a family habit." While all families have "flat sides"--areas of low relational skills, where what is needed is simply to show a new way, and help them practice it--this family was unable to give positive feedback even with coaching. Instead, their inability to openly share this kind of information pointed to an unaware family taboo around engaging in this activity, an unaware family sense that expressions of fondness and appreciation must be disguised, camouflaged. When I think of the unaware compulsive hiding involved in a taboo such as this might be, as well as the collective loss of voice it suggests, I think of shame.

I have found in therapy that the signs of possible shame have served as a beacon, often lighting the way to hidden ruptures and vulnerabilities that otherwise might go unnoticed, and the avoidance of which are the unseen "rocks" that scuttle mutual sensitivity and flexibility. To understand why this is so, let's briefly review the theory on shame that I, Gordon Wheeler and many others have been developing (e.g., Lee, 1994, 1995, 1997; Lee & Wheeler, 1996; Wheeler, 1997).

Shame and Hiding

Let's start with a major function of shame, namely, that it enables us to hide. In this way it helps protect our privacy through out life. When we experience shame or sense even the possibility of shame, we tend to cover up, to camouflage our desire and/or behavior. This means that the experience of shame in others most often cannot be recognized directly; it does not come with a sign that says that the person is experiencing shame. Instead what is seen is the person's aware or unaware attempt to hide, avoid, and/or cope with his experience of shame. Common strategies for attempting to conceal and cope with the experience of shame include behaviors such as blaming another, flying into rage, controlling or using power, becoming perfectionistic, withdrawing, resorting to addictive or obsessive behavior, and humor (Kaufman, 1989; Lewis, 1971; Retzinger, 1987). Thus when we encounter these behaviors, it is possible that they are covering the experience or the anticipated experience of shame.

To this point in my experience with Kevin and his family there were several occurrences that might indicate camouflaged shame. One was the collective loss of voice around being able to directly express appreciation and liking of one another. Another was the way differences were dealt with in the session (quick bursts of blaming anger). And another was the absence of dad. Could dad's absence be an example of what Lansky (1985) called "professional preoccupation," an ongoing withdrawal from an intimate situation under the guise of "work demands," which is actually motivated by hidden shame? Indeed, I had noticed what seemed to be a longing for dad from all the family members.

But how can shame be so important and so powerful? To start with, the phenomenon of shame is much more complex than what we normally think of when someone says, "You should be ashamed of yourself" to indicate some moral wrong doing. When we begin to understand shame, we find that it is much more ubiquitous than is commonly understood. It takes many forms, and in fact there is a cluster of affects with shame at their core--shyness, embarrassment, chagrin, shame itself, humiliation, feeling vaguely "lousy" or depressed--all helping us to hide in some way.[1]

The affect theorists have given us another way to view shame's major function of enabling us to hide; one that starts to understand the interpersonal complexity of shame. Tomkins (1963), the father of affect theory, recognized that shame is a regulatory affect. He grounded his theory in Darwin's notion that the emotions provide an important social function. Tomkins stated that shame's specific function is to regulate the positive affects of interest and enjoyment.[2] That is, shame pulls us back when we perceive that acting upon our interest or enjoyment (our desires, hopes, yearnings, urges, dreams and the like) might be inappropriate or socially dangerous. Thus, when a desire or longing is strong enough that we cannot extinguish or change it, and we perceive (with or without awareness) that it might be rejected, ignored, or received as inappropriate, we have an automatic, biological way of counteracting its expression. This explains the more limited common sense notion of shame as a regulator of moral transgression. "You should be ashamed of yourself" means, in other words, "Pull back from your course of action, it is 'wrong.'"

Of course, if a longing or desire is weak or unimportant, we can simply extinguish it. Shame is necessary only when desires are strong enough to mobilize us to action. Ironically, this means that the only time that we are at risk of experiencing shame is when we care enough about something (Kaufman, 1980). But this also gives us some insight into why shame is so powerful, for it occurs only when our caring--our longing or desire -is met by an equally significant sense of danger in the social field. Thus shame is connected to hiding and hiding serves the purpose of protecting us from danger.

The Therapeutics of Shame

From a treatment perspective, paradoxically, it is often what is hidden that holds the possibilities for reconnection or connection in a different way. That is, what was perceived as inappropriate, rejected, ignored, or unsupported in the past might be received, supported in the present. In Kevin's family, I suspected that my observations--their collective loss of voice around expressing appreciation directly, the bursts of blaming anger to settle differences, and father's absence--might be signs of hidden shame. If true, I wondered, what were the underlying yearnings that were being hidden, and how had this family come to believe that these yearnings were shameful?

At my request, dad accompanied the family to the second session. Not surprisingly, he turned out to be as good at humorous putdowns as the others, except he displayed more acceptance of the others and a humility in the way he delivered his roastings. I again asked the family to tell me about themselves, but this time to do it nonverbally by creating family sculptures. I invited them, one at a time, to put all the family members in some sort of pose, including appropriate facial expressions, that would express some part of how each person experienced the family. They appeared to truly enjoy this experiment, seemingly taking it as an opportunity to more fully roast one another. Two common themes emerged from their sculptures. Mom was usually characterized as somewhat out of control, angrily ranting and raving at the kids. And dad was always placed outside of the family scene, at work, driving around town, or the like, and always facing away from the family. It was as if father had nothing to offer his family except his ability to earn a living. But reflecting on this later, I did not perceive this to be true. Among other things, he had an easy-going manner and soft voice that seemed to calm and stabilize the rest of his family.

It appeared that mother had responsibility for the kids while father had responsibility for earning money. This traditional division of labor seemed to leave both mother and father frustrated and overwhelmed, partially because they were both very alone with their tasks. As I learned later, Mother wanted help from father with raising the kids, but she also wanted the final say about defining what was important in that regard. It appeared that rather than fight, father withdrew and left this domain to his wife. On the other hand, mother wanted to help father with the troubles he encountered in his business. But here father wanted the final say and didn't want help that came with advice.

Shame and Support

With respect to Kevin, this parental division of labor seemed problematic. Mother complained that not only would father not help enforce the rules she laid down for Kevin, but would sabotage them. For example, mother said that one evening when she was out, Kevin called home and asked for permission to stay longer at a friend s house, which father gave him. Mother said she felt betrayed and was enraged when she learned what had happened. Father replied that he didn't realize mother's wishes; he didn't see at the time how a half an hour in Kevin's getting home would make that much difference. It was not clear to me whether dad was intentionally sabotaging mother's rules, but in the very least he was responding from a different sense of what Kevin needed. Mother tended to notice the places where Kevin might need more structure, limits, or watching; whereas father tended to support Kevin's independent exploring of the world. Both approaches seemed important. But even more important was that they both support some agreed upon plan.

I suggested to Kevin s parents that they come in for a session by themselves for the purpose of better understanding each other around what was important in setting limits for Kevin. In doing this I also wanted a safer, more appropriate atmosphere in which they could talk, if they wanted to, about why father was so little involved with his family. And in fact a significant new understanding of the family's belief system in that regard was uncovered in this session. But before proceeding let s review a little more of the nature of shame.

Shame and Support

If we view what the affect theorists tell us about shame from a Gestalt field theory perspective, we realize that shame is not just an affect that is important in modulating intrapsychic dynamics, but is *a major regulator of the social field*. The experience of shame signifies our assessment that our need, want, longing--perhaps some way of being in the world, some part of who we are or want to be--will not be received. In Gestalt field theory, the opposite of shame is the experience of support. By support we mean a connection in the field that meets and receives the yearning, hope, desire, etc. And support refers to both internal and external support (although internal support is often derived from some past connection in the field).

Now, an important characteristic of shame is its temporal quality. Shame can be an assessment in the present moment that no one is available to receive my desire. Shame can also be based upon my ground of expectations, generalized from a history of my desires not being received, having little to do with the moment. That is, if I have had recurrent or severe enough experience in the past that my needs and desires were not received, then any recurrence of the same needs and desires may trigger an experience of shame. Shame, in other words, will become indelibly linked to that yearning, in what the affect theorists call a "shame bind," causing me to pull back from action whenever that yearning is stirred. In time, or if my past experience has been severe enough, I will not experience my yearning at all; I will only experience the shame associated with it (Kaufman, 1989). And, as my shame persists, my belief is continually reinforced that there is no possible reception in the field for my shameful yearning. As a result I come to disown and lose voice for a piece of myself, my yearning, by shaming it. Thus important parts of the self--desires and yearnings and self-expressions--are chronically rejected in the field of our lives and go underground. Consequently, the self does not develop fully in these areas for lack of integrated contact in the field. What remains at the overt, interpersonal level, are often only tiny or masked signs, mere hints of the buried longing--longing that is "protected" from exposure by its linkage with shame. This is the basis of the formation of taboos as had come to be in place in Kevin's family.

The key to undoing such taboos rests in understanding the nature of shame. A linkage of shame only exists when there is an underlying yearning. Shame does not extinguish yearning; it only controls it. *Thus, where there is shame, there is yearning.* This gives us an extremely valuable tool in therapy. It means that following the signs of camouflaged shame will potentially lead us to hidden, disowned yearning. Thus, when signs of possible shame are noticed (e.g., a pattern of avoidance, deflection, angry outbursts, justifying, sudden politeness or quietness, humor or sarcasm, nervous laughter; in general, some change in the quality of contact), *listen for the yearning* that might be there.

The yearning will usually be guarded at first; you might only be afforded a quick glimpse of its existence--a look in the eye, a note in the voice, a gesture, a leaning towards someone. The yearning will only start to appear if the person perceives (with or without awareness) that there is at least the possibility that her yearning will be received. The problem is that as the person gets close to shame-linked yearning, she typically experiences shame to protect the yearning from exposure. What will then be seen is the behavior used to cover up the shame and the yearning.

Thus, an important first step of therapy is to provide an atmosphere that offers the best opportunity for people to feel safe with their hidden yearnings. This includes allowing people to go at the pace they need in exposing these yearnings, but also to notice the yearnings to the extent they are offered. An example of this occurred in the couple session with Kevin's parents.

The Couple Session

The meeting with Kevin's parents started with Kevin's mother complaining about how her husband would not join her in setting and maintaining limits for Kevin. At first she was angry, but before long, she became discouraged and started to cry. At this point Kevin's father, who had been quiet until then, said, "She does this every once in a while; she'll be okay soon." The way he said this caught my attention. His facial expression and tone of voice seemed to subtly indicate that he was attempting to care for his wife, but it did not appear that she experienced it as support. This then might be a yearning that would otherwise go unnoticed. I mentioned to Kevin's father that it looked to me as if he was trying to care for his wife with what he said, and asked him if that was true. Mild surprise appeared on his face that seemed to say, "Of course, what else would I have been doing?" and he nodded "Yes." I asked his wife how she experienced what he had said to her and she replied dejectedly, "He was just trying to shut me up; he doesn't like it when I cry." I said I could imagine that what he had said hadn't helped, but from the look on his face and his tone of voice, I believed that he was trying to help. I then asked Kevin's father what his experience was when his wife cried. He looked at me intently as if he was checking me out, and then he suddenly relaxed and said that he didn't know what to do when she cried. When I inquired what he meant, he continued, saying that he didn't have any prior experience to measure it against. It dawned on me that Kevin's father didn't know much about relationships at all.

When I asked more about this, Kevin's father confided that before he met his wife he hadn't let a relationship--friend or lover--last more than six months. When things got too serious, he would just move on. He had been on his own since age 13. His father was an alcoholic; his mother a compulsive gambler. After his father left the family when he was age seven, his mother would make frequent out of town, often out of state, gambling excursions with a boyfriend, lasting several days to a week, leaving him and his brother at home alone to fend for themselves. He said that as a result he didn't have any models for having a family. He loved his family dearly, but he never knew whether what he did with them was "right." In fact, he said that he imagined that what he did was often wrong, so he tried to stay out of the way.

He offered all of this relatively easily which surprised me. It brought back to me the way he looked at me before he started talking, as if he was checking me out. It seemed that in that brief moment he had decided he could trust me, had concluded there was a chance I would hear him. When he left the couple's session, Kevin's father said to me, "You are the first person who has understood. That other family therapist we saw just said I was a cowboy." I didn't understand the significance of the word "cowboy," but I did understand that he felt that I had received a part of him that he had not believed was receivable. The session did not provide the agreement between parents on appropriate limits for Kevin; that would come later. But it did provide valuable information about family beliefs and their possible roots, and it began the work of replacing this family's legacy of shame with the possibility of support.

A Start at an Understanding

I now had enough information to form a hypothesis on significant aspects of Kevin's family's belief system. In Gestalt therapy this kind of understanding is held as an ongoing experiment, rather than as an absolute. A hypothesis can then inform our interventions, the outcome of which can modify our hypothesis. This, after all, is the same human process that Gestalt theory contends we all use in deriving meaning from our experience (Wheeler, 1997).

Let's filter the information that we have gathered through the lens of our Gestalt field theory with its ability to appreciate how shame monitors connections and disconnections in the field. Kevin's father said that he had little or no experience of healthy relational interactions prior to his marriage. Thus, in order to build his confidence and skill in this area, he needed to know how who he is and what he does relationally was of value to his family. However, it appeared that he had a shame bind (again, an ongoing link between a part of self/other and shame) around his need for this kind of information. From what he told me about growing up, it was easy to imagine that this kind of information was not available in his family. It seemed very possible that he learned that he had to do without this information, and that he "shouldn't" need this kind of feedback, since this is the way shame works when there is insufficient support. This might have been Kevin's father's contribution to the family taboo against directly expressing appreci-

262

ation and fondness. If he had learned that one "shouldn't" need this kind of information, then open and direct expressions of this sort would certainly serve to trigger the experience of shame.

More generally, if my hypothesis was true that Kevin's father had developed an internalizes shame bind, then we would expect him to feel ashamed whenever he felt the need to know his value to his family. Presumably, in these moments, Kevin's father would experience a sense of inadequacy, perhaps tainted with shyness or embarrassment, and consequently pull back from contact, camouflaging both his need and his shame. Consequently, he never knew if his involvement with his family was "right," and so he tried "to stay out of the way." Kevin's father, in other words, used withdrawal (and perhaps other strategies as well) in an attempt to cope with and hide the shame he experienced when he got close to this need. It now seemed more plausible that "the demands" of his business helped provide some of the camouflage for his withdrawal. This enabled him to at least feel good about his economic value to his family. However, as with most strategies used to avoid shame, this strategy often left him feeling even more inadequate (shameful) around his shamed need (his need for information on his relational value). This, in turn, would inhibit him further from gaining a sense of relational competence, and in the process would counteract, even overpower, his desire to be more involved with his family.

It appeared that Kevin's mother did not usually notice her husband's need for positive feedback, even though she appeared to care about him dearly. (She did give him feedback when she thought his behavior was "not right.") It is quite possible she did not notice his need because his major shame avoidance strategy (withdrawing) inadvertently triggered her own sense of shame. Indeed, she acknowledged that his withdrawal left her feeling abandoned, and her reaction to this experience was to become enraged at him. How does this fit with shame theory? Abandonment is a loss of a needed connection and, as such, implies a sense of lost and insufficient support—the primary trigger for shame. The fact that she would fly into rage, focusing upon her husband's "bad behavior" rather than reporting her own experience of abandonment, further confirms that she was struggling to contain her own sense of intolerable shame in those moments.

In the couple session, she had reported that her own father was distant and that her mother had to yell at him to get him to do anything. Kevin's mother said that she had known growing up that she couldn't get anything relationally from her father. So maybe Kevin's mother's shame was what Fossum and Mason (1986) call "inherited shame"--shame that comes from living with a parent who has experienced abuse, neglect, loss, or other significant hardship. Possibly these experiences contributed to Kevin's mother's expectation that she would have insufficient emotional support from her husband.

At this point in my assessment, I had gained a beginning understanding of a major family dynamic and belief system, governed by shame, that held in place the couple's division of labor around their family in general and around Kevin in particular. A key missing element in this system was a means for Kevin s father to get feedback around how he was valuable to his family relationally. Being shame-bound in this way, he was too embarrassed to ask for this kind of information, and was most likely not even aware that this was his need. And since his withdrawing triggered his wife's shame, it was be difficult for her to notice his need, even though she cares about him.

Implications for Kevin and Treatment

What are the implications that this set of hypothesis holds for Kevin and how do they influence treatment interventions? If Kevin's father had a yearning to be more involved with his family, held in check by his sense of inadequacy and lack of positive feedback, then supporting his need for information in this regard might free him up to more fully support and enjoy his family. Kevin would benefit in several ways--more direct access to his father, support for his mother which might help her to keep her balance when Kevin made mistakes, and having a male role model in the family for getting affirmational needs met.

With this hypothesis, one task in therapy was to find ways of helping Kevin's father experience his relational value to his family in general, and to Kevin in particular. A second task was helping Kevin's parents develop awareness of their hidden code of camouflage for their respective shame and yearning. This meant helping Kevin's mother learn to see her husband's withdrawal as a cover-up for his yearning to know where he stood with his family, rather than an intentional, shaming, abandonment, as she had construed in the past. For Kevin's father, this meant helping him to see his wife's descent into criticism as a signal that she needed his companionship and soothing.

With these tasks as the experiments of therapy, family work became the main mode of treatment, augmented with occasional individual sessions with Kevin and couple sessions with his parents. Not surprisingly, the therapeutic tasks involving Kevin directly turned out to be variants of these tasks.

Attending to the first task, helping Kevin's father experience his value to Kevin and his family, was the easiest, and in retrospect the most pivotal for the success of therapy. As this was accomplished, it facilitated much of the other work in therapy. It was the easiest because Kevin s father s yearning in this regard was large and accessible, and because there were abundant concrete examples of his positive effect on his family in family sessions. Pointing out these examples allowed him to explore his involvement with his family.

One example of this exploration occurred early in treatment. Kevin and his parents came in and sat down on the couch with Kevin's mother between Kevin and his father. Kevin and his mother were in the middle of an argument; she was berating him over something he had done, and he was disdainfully stonewalling her. Both were agitated and stuck. Because I had observed Kevin's father's calming influence on his family in the past, I suggested an experiment. I asked Kevin s father if he would be willing to change seats and sit between his wife and Kevin, and I asked Kevin and his mother if they would be willing to have him sit there, just to see what might happen. They all agreed and changed seats. Kevin's father said a few soft words to the others as he sat down and, almost immediately, both Kevin and his mother relaxed and softened. Their interaction suddenly changed tone. Amazingly, they could now hear and respond to each other's concerns. Many times in therapy I have witnessed this kind of seemingly magical turn of events, when an underlying, shamed yearning finds a listener. Still, whenever it happens, I am in awe of the process. Not only did Kevin and his mother receive soothing and grounding from Kevin's father's presence between them, but this was then an excellent opportunity to give Kevin's father feedback on the positive effect he had just had on his family. (Of course, he at first put down the feedback with a humorous self-roast.) He said later that he would not have understood on his own that what happened between Kevin and his wife had anything to do with his presence.

Through experiences such as this, Kevin's father slowly started to understand his nurturant value to his family. As he did he started to use the family sessions and occasional couple sessions to process his doubts about how he related to his family and to hone his skill in doing so. This was not a linear process. There were times when he would withdraw from his family and/or miss sessions, sometimes because of the legitimate demands of his business, but other times because, as he acknowledged later, he lost a sense of his value. As he came to understand and be able to hold on to his sense of his nurturant value to his family, he became more consistently involved with his family. For example, he arranged to be home for dinner more often, and he made a point of being with Kevin in the mornings, several days a week, before Kevin went off to school and he went off to work.

And half way through the fall school term when Kevin's grades came home (all D's) and it was discovered that Kevin had not been turning in homework, Kevin's father was able to take an important next step. In the next family session, Kevin's mother was outraged, saying she felt betrayed by Kevin's lying to her about doing his homework. I was struck by her focusing solely on Kevin's "wrong doing" and her seeming inability to ask what Kevin's actions meant for Kevin. Could Kevin's mother's rage and sense of betrayal (another form of abandonment) be a sign that she had been shamed and humiliated by Kevin's actions? If so, what was the support that she needed? When I voiced these possibilities in the session, Kevin's father sat up in his chair and said compassionately to his wife that it was not her fault that Kevin did not do his homework. What was different here was that he intervened on his own initiative. Kevin's mother looked surprised and calmed by his comment, and he quickly turned to Kevin and gently asked him why he wasn't doing his homework. For the first time Kevin admitted that there were many times when he didn't understand the homework so he would just give up (essentially revealing his shame around getting help when he needed it). Kevin's father, with his wife's urging, then took over the role of problem solving with Kevin on how he could get help with understanding the material. In general this meant asking teachers for help, which Kevin was too shy to do without support. Kevin's strategy with teachers had been to camouflage his need for help--by acting cool, making wisecracks, being tough, and in several instances picking verbal fights with them. (One such fight revolved around whether he had the right to sharpen his pencil while taking a test for which he was ill-prepared.) On my suggestion, Kevin's father agreed to check in on Kevin each night to see how the homework was going, and to give him support if he needed to get help in understanding it.

As Kevin's father became more involved with Kevin, he began to speak more with his wife concerning his sense of what Kevin needed. This was important because Kevin's father had the better understanding of Kevin's need, in this phase of his life, to explore his world on his own.[3] Kevin s mother's approach had been to assume, when Kevin made mistakes, that he needed more supervision; a strategy that worked well when Kevin was younger, and which still had merit at times as exemplified by Kevin's problems with his homework. But there were many other areas--such as the degree to which Kevin wanted to share what was going on with him, whom he chose as friends, and what activities he got involved in--where Kevin's father brought a moderating influence on parental involvement, coming closer to the mark regarding Kevin's developmental needs. Interestingly enough, having greater involvement with his father supported Kevin to be less risky in his explorations in other parts of his life.

I finished seeing Kevin and his family the following spring. This was partially motivated by family financial concerns. However, it appeared to me that the family had gained a beginning ability for making connections in ways that would have been taboo in the past--including ways to have father's support and to expose their relational needs. This didn't mean that they didn't occasionally fall into their shame cycles; but now they understood it better when they did. Their parting words to me were a humorous roasting of my style, which I took as an expression of their appreciation of me. In June when the term ended, Kevin's mother called me and said that Kevin had received his first A ever, in a difficult science class no less. (He had also received a D.) She concluded that Kevin's problems were now merely normal adolescent problems; and she could handle that.

In Closing

We have seen how following the signs of shame can lead us to areas of insufficient support in the field, and how "listening" for the underlying yearning at such times can provide access to the otherwise hidden, often out of awareness, perceptual fields of our clients. In Gestalt field theory, chronic shame represents an ongoing emotional assessment, with or without awareness, of insufficient support in the field, a belief that a desired connection is not possible, and a consequent disowning of that sense of self/other. And as we have seen, shame is not merely an individual, intrapsychic phenomenon. Not only is shame a statement of the perceived quality of support in the field, but one person's attempt to camouflage his shame (e.g., with withdrawal, rage, blame, control, contempt, sarcasm, or so on), can trigger another person's shame, thus reinforcing a cycle of insufficient support. Moreover, a sense of insufficient support (i.e., chronic shame) in a dependent person (e.g., an adolescent) can reflect a sense of insufficient support (chronic shame) in the person or persons upon whom that individual depends. This means that treating an individual often means working with the field processes that co-construct that person's experience. In particular, restoring a sense of support (healing chronic shame) in an adolescent often requires restoring a sense of support (healing chronic shame) in his or her parents. (See Lee, 1997 for a fuller discussion of how this ethic can be derived from Gestalt field theory.) Shame and support are social variables that interdependently and intersubjectively regulate the fields of all members of a system.

With Kevin's family, several possibilities emerged early as potential signs of hidden shame--the family's inability to openly share direct expressions of appreciation or fondness of one another, the quick bursts of blaming anger used to settle differences, and father's seeming isolation. The key to learning more about the family beliefs driving these behaviors came in the first couple's session when I was able to hear and appreciate Kevin's father's desire to care for his wife, when she started crying. We can now see this as an example of his larger yearning to care for and to be more involved with his family--a yearning that he had learned to suppress, and that the family had not learned how to receive and confirm. My hearing his yearning supported the exposure of his sense of inadequacy and his dilemma around his need. This in turn was a key element in understanding the family belief system and providing a direction for treatment--namely to help Kevin's father explore his relational value to his family. The results of this exploration were that Kevin's father became more involved with his family in general and with Kevin in particular, which eventually provided the support in a number of ways that Kevin needed to expose his own sense of shame. Not only did noticing the possible signs of shame and listening for the yearning provide an entry into important aspects of the family's belief system and an overall direction for treatment but, in addition, these strategies refined that direction throughout the course of treatment.

References

Fossum, M., & Mason, M. (1986). *Facing shame: Families in recovery.* New York: W. W. Norton.

Goodman, P. (1951). Part two: Manipulating the self. In F. Perls, R. Hefferline, & P. Goodman.*Gestalt Therapy: Excitement and growth in the human personality.* New York, NY: Delta.

Jacobson, E. (1964). *The self and the object world.* New York, NY: International Universities Press.

Kaufman, G. (1980). *Shame: The power of caring*. Cambridge, MA: Shenkman.

Kaufman, G. (1989). *The psychology of shame*. New York, NY: Springer Publishing.

Lansky, M. (1985). Preoccupation as a mode of pathologic distance regulation. *International Journal of Psychoanalytic Psychotherapy, 11*, 409-425.

Lee, R. (1994). Couples' shame: the unaddressed issue. In G. Wheeler and S. Backman (Eds.), *On intimate ground: A gestalt approach to working with couples* (pp. 262-290). San Francisco, CA: Jossey-Bass.

Lee, R. (1995). Gestalt and shame: The foundation for a clearer understanding of field dynamics. *British Gestalt Journal, 4*(1), 14-22.

Lee, R. (1997). Ethics: A gestalt of values/The values of Gestalt. Unpublished manuscript.

Lee, R., & Wheeler, G. (1996). *The voice of shame: Silence and connection in psychotherapy*. San Francisco, CA: Jossey-Bass.

Lewis, H. (1971). *Shame and guilt in neurosis*. New York, NY: International Universities Press.

Lynd, H. (1958). *On shame and the search for identity*. New York, NY: Harcourt, Brace.

McConville, M. (1995). *Adolescence: Psychotherapy and the emergent self*. San Francisco, CA: Jossey-Bass.

Retzinger, S. (1987). Resentment and laughter: Video studies of the shame-rage spiral. In H. B. Lewis (Ed.). *The role of shame in symptom formation* (pp. 151-181). Hillsdale, NJ: Lawrence Erlbaum.

Tomkins, S. (1963). *Affect, imagery, and consciousness: The negative affects, vol. 2*. New York, NY: Springer and Company.

Wheeler, G. (1996). Self and shame: A new paradigm for psychotherapy. In R. G. Lee & G. Wheeler (Eds.), *The voice of shame: Silence and connection in psychotherapy* (pp. 23-58). San Francisco, CA: Jossey-Bass.

Wheeler, G. (1997). Self and shame: A gestalt approach. *Gestalt Review, 1*(3), 221-244.

White, R. (1959). Motivation reconsidered: The concept of competence. *Psychological Review, 66*, 297-333.

Footnotes

1 A handful of psychoanalytic theorists (e.g., Jacobson, 1964; Lewis, 1971; Lynd, 1958; White, 1959) first discovered the ubiquity and importance of shame in individual dynamics. And they identified that shame took many forms. Later affect theorists, whose theory contained a firmer platform for understanding the interpersonal nature of shame, contribute their own versions of the forms that shame takes (e.g., Kaufman, 1980, 1989; Tomkins, 1963).

2 More accurately, Tomkins called the positive affects interest-excitement and enjoyment-joy according to their extremes of experience.

3 Kevin's needs to explore his world more on his own might be thought of in the light of what Mark McConville (1995) talks about as a disembedding stage of adolescent development.

10

Anorexia and Contact

Nicole de Schrevel
Translated by Gordon Wheeler

I want to tell you something about Denise, an adolescent girl with a diagnosis of anorexia nervosa--how we met, how the contact between us took shape as I struggled to encounter her more fully and understand her, and then how I had to adjust my own style and approach, as we co-constructed together a different kind of contact, one that Denise might use in the service of a restoration and resumption of interrupted growth and development.

As I think about this experience, I organize the case in my own mind along three temporal axes or stages in a therapeutic cycle: (a) first of all, the context--the situation as I was given to understand it--and the initial overture to engage in some kind of therapeutic process; (b) a second stage in which I tried to engage Denise on the ground of what I imagined might be nourishing contact; and (c) how I learned from and with Denise to take a different approach, in the service of nourishment that she herself could find a way to take in, metabolize, and use for her own living--no matter how much that might go against my own notions of what was nourishing, or my own more accustomed personal style.

The first stage includes how the initial contact with me was made, what the therapeutic demand seemed to be and where it seemed to be coming from, as well as the organization of everything that took place around the transaction of this bid. The second is the stage of engagement, how the therapy began, and how that played out. The third is a period of adjustment, first and foremost on my own part, as I modified my initial hypotheses, and worked to modify my own manner of working. With this particular young girl, this third period stood out more clearly than in many cases, since I had a clear sense that Denise was telling me clearly how not to proceed, and thus to abandon the path I was embarked on. This "telling" was not yet in words;

rather, she showed me, with her body language, by not responding, by being monosyllabic, and by the fluctuation of one of her presenting symptoms, which was a recurrent experience of hallucination about her own body. Thus, the communication between us played out, as her life was playing out, through the mediation of her own body image and experience, and the therapeutic process consisted of working to take this communication *into the realm of relationship*. It was as if Denise were saying to me: "I present my physical body; I do not offer myself." This was the ground of our initial meeting.

My experience with Denise began, one day, with a phone call from her mother, who had gotten my name somewhere, and launched straight into the matter. She had spoken with her daughter, she told me--a young adolescent just about to turn 14--and her daughter had agreed to come to see me. The problem, she said, was that her daughter didn't eat: for a year now she had eaten "nothing at all." She was in the care of a physician, who was speaking of "serious anorexia"--the loss of some 25 pounds in the past year. The physician is gravely concerned, she told me--as she was, and Denise herself as well. Denise was willing to talk to me about her eating problem, and perhaps other issues as well, though, according to her daughter, she said, there were no other particular problems or issues. Might I speak directly with her daughter, I asked? Yes of course, was the response, but at the moment she was at school, and would come and talk with me directly, at an hour we worked out. I accepted this initial organization of the situation: that the mother was alarmed about her daughter, and was making this whole series of arrangements on her daughter's behalf. To know more, I would have to wait for the appointed day.

When the day came, Denise arrived alone at my office in the center of the city, at the correct time. Since they lived outside Brussels, in the suburbs, she had had to leave directly from school, take the train, and find her way to my office. All this she had managed quite competently, arriving with her bag of schoolbooks in her hand. The first impression I had, which still stays with me, was of a face that was small, narrow, and extremely white, extremely pale, and a long body form, made longer by legs so thin they seemed endless. As for the rest of her body, I got no impression at all, as if between the small head and the endless legs there seemed to be nothing significant, nothing that registered. In her manner, she had the air of a girl "of a good family," with conventional dress, and great politeness-- "Bonjour, Madame"--and socially formal manners, waiting for me to invite her to sit down, take off her coat, all with an air of perfect neatness and organization. These were my first impressions.

I began by asking her what brought her there. Her reply was to ask me in turn, very politely, whether her mother hadn't already explained that to me. She addressed me with the conventional "vous," and instinctively I replied with "tu," as to a child. Yes, I told her, her mother had told me some things, but I was interested in how things looked from her own perspective. Well, Denise told me, it seems that everyone is very concerned about me, because I'm so thin. It's true, she went on, that I don't eat, but that's because I'm not hungry. But that isn't my problem. It's not a matter of all that, but that is what is worrying everybody else.

Does it worry you, I inquired? No answer.

What does worry you? I tried again. And right away she plunged in. It seemed that her bedroom at home was on an upstairs floor, and on the stairway landing hung a full-length mirror, which Denise had to pass in order to come downstairs. And every morning, coming down, something very upsetting happened. As she saw her own image in the mirror, she would see her body starting to distort, the right half swelling and looming, her head detaching from her body--an utterly disturbing experience, of her own body in complete flux, without definite form or limits. "What worries me," Denise finished, "is that I'm starting to wonder if I'm going crazy. I'm worried about whether I'm insane or not, and that's why I'm here."

The image was powerful, and to me, hearing it, vaguely destabilizing. Perhaps to steady myself in the face of the disturbing word "crazy," I framed what I was hearing, provisionally at least, as a creative answer or representation of some constellation of fears, which were being expressed in a body image. Even so, I was aware of a certain sense of feeling lost, without bearings--and all the more so because having said that much, Denise fell into complete silence. It was as though, having deposited the thing that was frightening her, she immediately resumed her regular position as the good little girl, who waits for the adult to put the questions and eventually solve the problem.

Trying to sidestep that role, I simply said, "I see, there's all that. And is there anything else on your mind? What about the rest of your life, these days?" Her reply was to speak of her family--first of all of her mother, a remarkable woman, she said, always at home, always taking care of the house and family, "always perfect."

Anyone else, I asked? Yes, there were two other children, and then her father whom she "didn't see very often" because "He works all the time" so that she had "no contact" with him. True, he was there for dinner, but no one spoke of anything, just how are you, fine, how was school today, fine--things like that. And then a sister, one year older--but she was an "idiot." Her sister, she said, wasn't serious, she was only interested in boys and flirting, she used makeup, etc.--all this said with considerable contempt.

. So it's not just a matter of being different, I offered, but of really judging her for these things. This seemed to stop Denise. "Well, that's just how it is," she responded vaguely. "She's successful at it I guess--but she's an ass."

And then there was a brother, two years younger, "But he's a child, he's only interested in soccer, he's stupid. He's stupid, and my sister is an ass." Again I was struck by the contemptuous force of the word, which has stronger sexual associations in French than in English ("conne" can mean "cunt" as well as idiotic) and which stood out from the careful politeness of her general manner.

I considered this family's presentation: a "perfect" mother, seen always in role, not as a person herself; father with "no contact;" and a sister and brother described only in terms of themselves and their deficiencies, not in relationship with her at all. When I reflected to Denise that I couldn't get a picture of her relationship with her siblings, her reply was simply, "it doesn't exist."

And school, I asked? Oh, school is fine, no problems," Denise replied, as if back at the dinner table. "My grades are good." Friends, I asked--contact with the other students? Denise was vague: yes, she had friends, really it all depended, it changed from time to time. And again her energy was gone. Where school was concerned, she had no story to tell, beyond "everything is fine."

And psychotherapy--what did that mean to her, I asked? Her reply was that she didn't know. She had seen psychologists at school, mostly they asked her a lot of questions. (Like me, I thought to myself, having just asked a string of questions). They ask a lot of questions, but "I know it's in order to help me."

And do you have some idea of how I might help you, I asked?

"No," Denise answered simply. Either she had no idea, or--as I conceived it later--it was irritating to her that people were always trying to help her. "Help," I began to understand later, meant something like wanting something for her, and at the same time demanding something of her. As for curiosity about herself--she showed no sign of it.

And, of course, that was what I had been doing--asking questions, assessing her environment, with the idea of being able to offer her something. Either the gesture was simply too strong for her boundaries or else what I was offering was not something she could take in and use. And yet I did not yet have any clear idea of how else to proceed, almost as if something about her presentation were affecting me too strongly, in some way that destabilized me as well, and left me at a loss. In any case, I remember telling her at this time that therapy, for me, was a period of time--I didn't specify how long--in which two people would work together to understand what was causing the suffering of one of them--to put words on a suffering which was there--but had not yet found words, and was not yet really understood. I conceived my role, I said, as one of working with her, and with other people, in this way: listening, and putting words on the suffering that was there, in this way. I used that word--suffering. I didn't speak of talking about the suffering, but of finding the words to express it, putting it in words. This is all I remember saying to her at the time.

Did she understand, I queried? And as usual when I asked Denise a direct question, she answered in a good-little-girl way, "Yes," in a small voice. This I took to be a way of not engaging, and not entering into a more intimate discourse, which in any case she seemed to have no experience of, and no idea how to do.

I told her as well that I was paid for my work, and asked how we were going to handle that. "But Mama gave me the money," she said. "Oh really?" I asked--"How much did she give you?" And Denise named a substantial sum, saying that her mother hadn't known exactly how much it was, and blushing just slightly. I asked if the subject made her uncomfortable, and she replied yes, with evident agitation, because she wasn't accustomed to dealing with it, and didn't know how it was done. It was as if without a social form to fall back on, she was at a complete loss. For now, I accepted her answer without any further questions. It seemed too early to confront, or to go into the fact that it was of course her mother who was paying, and what that meant to her. I simply named my usual fee, and Denise gave me that amount. (I should mention here that it is a regular part of my practice to require clients to pay in cash, at the end of each session. Cash, not checks, because I find that the sense of the money is more real that way.)

I did not push the question, but I did note the two points so far that destabilized her: (a) when she lost her fixed reference points or guidelines around the money transaction, and (b) when she looked in the mirror and saw her body image lose its form and coherence. For the rest, she preserved the air of the well-brought-up young girl, completely integrated into the social world of rules and expectations for what "is done," and what "isn't done." Thus, the first session together with some of the background.

For my part, my response at this point was to begin reflecting on what I actually knew about anorexia. I set off looking things up in books and reading up on different approaches. In other words, I took refuge in an expert position. She was, after all, alarmingly thin. And in my mind I kept always that image, head and legs, with nothing significant in between. In retrospect now, I would say that the therapy at this point remained fixed at these two points: the head, in that we talked "about" things; and the legs in the sense of actions, of taking steps. For all her restraint, Denise was by no means passive. On the contrary, she was plainly acting out something--in the sense of action without full experience, without awareness. In Denise's own language, this was her wish to have will-power--which, to her, would be the opposite of her "light" and changeable sister. At this point, her relationship with her sister consisted in this stance, of "I don't want to be like her." Her sister flirted with everybody, had many boyfriends, and did whatever she felt like.

And what would Denise herself like to be like? "I want something unique, true, authentic--to be a "perfect being." But this more direct language only began to come out later.

And so Denise began to come to see me regularly, every week--except in school vacations. At the first brief vacation, in November, when I asked if I would see her the following week, she responded with surprise: "Oh no, next week is vacation" as if what we were doing was part of the regular school calendar. And where would she be over vacation? Nowhere in particular, was the reply, probably she would be working on her diving lessons, at the pool. In spite of her overall low energy, and despite the fact that she was terribly cold in the pool ("Because, you see, I'm quite thin"), she was determined to master this sport. But when I speculated that perhaps it was the challenge and heavy demand of it that she liked, Denise fell silent. Remarks of that kind always went nowhere. Whenever I made any attempt to put words on her experience, or to reflect the experiential words I thought were implied, she became vague and unresponsive. "Maybe..." she might offer and then just trail off in silence.

It was in this sense that I began to think of Denise as "anorexic" in relation to anything that *came from me*. Anything that I put out into our common field that had to do with her seemed to become something *imposed on* her. Little by little I began to understand--not that she took in nothing at all (she could reject or judge with great engagement)--but that very many things simply did not nourish her in contact. And at those moments she seemed unable to say simply, "I don't care for that." And so I said, with regard to her not coming to therapy during school vacations, "Well, I understand that you see it as something that follows a school schedule. That's not my usual way of working, but it's your point of view, and I'm willing to accept it, if we can agree to come back to this question when we get to the next vacation." Again, I had a keen sense of not wanting to push her further in the direction of my interests, my demands (to explore what it meant to her, for example, to think of therapy as part of a school calendar).

Meanwhile, she continued to arrive each week, with the fee in cash. On one occasion she asked, at her mother's behest, whether she might send a check. I simply said no, I preferred cash, and no more was said about it. Again, my thinking was that even though of course the money derived from her parents, there should be a concrete transaction of buying and paying for something, directly between the two of us. Otherwise, the therapy would risk becoming yet another of those things that took place around her, arranged by her mother, in which she took no active part. Likewise, I wanted some transaction around the money to take place between Denise and her mother, even if I didn't know quite what that transaction was.

Another time Denise arrived in considerable agitation because she didn't have the cash on her. It seemed her mother had forgotten to leave it on the table as usual. Could her mother send a check this once or remit it directly to my bank in some way? I could see that she was deeply upset by this irregular state of affairs. As usual, when I made some comment on that--nothing, no response. Still, I was left with the impression that what disturbed her was not the actual money transaction itself, in which she still was not taking active agency, but just the fact that there was no form for this particular contretemps, and she didn't know how to act.

Another time she arrived wrapped up in a warm scarf, suffering from a head cold. "I'm really sick," she offered, "but I came anyway." She had not gone to school, yet she had left her bed to go to therapy. I forebore to ask or comment about this.

And still she grew thinner--a body that was disappearing before my eyes; a head with no color at all other than a blush from time to time--and from what? Shame? Embarrassment? That's at least how I imagined it, but I couldn't be sure. Rather, I continued to leave the space open for Denise to speak if she chose. And she spoke a great deal--mostly about whatever had happened during the week. For a time, she continued to refer to her disturbing experience with the mirror, which was developing into a reluctance to come downstairs at all, since she would have to pass the mirror to get there.

On one occasion I invited her to draw for me what she saw in the mirror. She looked shocked. "But I don't know how to draw," she protested. When I said that didn't matter, that it was just to give me the idea of the image as it appeared to her, she seemed blank--as if the idea that we could then share that experience were completely foreign to her. In the end, she complied with my request. Taking a black marker (from the box I held out, which contained all sorts of colors), she traced extremely light lines on the paper, so faint that I really could make nothing at all of them, just a stroke here and there as if in a fog. "So this is how you see your body in the mirror," I commented as neutrally as I could. It seemed important to me that she had done this--and equally important that I not comment too much. I did ask her what she saw there: no response. And then, "I don't know how to draw." Once more she had an upset air, as if the whole episode had destabilized her.

On my desk I have a folder where I keep notes and sketches from my patients. I slipped this one in the folder with the others. At the end of the session I said something like, "Is it all right with you to leave the drawing with me or would you prefer to take it with you?" This was the sort of careful language I was learning to use with Denise, for simple transactions: first making my own desire plain, and then inquiring about hers. Her reply: "It can stay here."

And she continued to speak of her sister and brother, putting words here on an antipathy that never erupted into open conflict at home. She detested her sister cordially, yet avoided any direct confrontation. Here too she avoided the openly conflictual, speaking rather in terms of judgment and rejection. And yet it was plain that she thought about her sister, watched her sister, practically all the time. For Denise, her sister was a negative: what she insisted she did not want to be: her sister's open flirting and many boyfriends, for example. To me it seemed plain that sexuality frightened her and the idea of body transformations as she matured frightened her as well. At this level, Denise's problem was developmental: an inability to assimilate womanhood. Femininity and a woman's identity were experiences she could not organize other than to say, "I can't be a woman like my mother, I don't want to be a woman like my sister, and obviously I can't be a boy like my little brother. Therefore, I will be nothing."

This was my hypothesis at the start and I clung to it as something that could organize my own experience of Denise. I tried to conceptualize the case along the deeply individualistic lines of much psychiatry and classic psychoanalytic theory about anorexia: the problem was in her own relationship to her developing body. I conceived Denise as a girl unable to face womanhood and that was the key to her problem. At the age of 14, she was quite aware of still not having begun having monthly periods. Moreover, she was socially quite isolated. She did take some part in young people's groups around activities such as her diving lessons, but she found these events "boring." She had no appetite for any of the actual peer interactions that presented themselves--and yet she spoke of these things with some definite charge; she was not indifferent. This too I related to the idea of an adolescent girl caught in a developmental dilemma: on the one hand, desire to please and be popular like her sister; and on the other hand fear and rejection of her own pubescent development that that would entail.

I inquired more about things at home. Surely it wasn't simple for her, I said, to manage the situation with her sister and brother, given her strong negative feelings. "Not at all," Denise replied simply. "Everything is fine." The main occasion for any encounter at all was at the dinner table and there the exchanges were limited to the "everything is fine" register. As for herself, she was "different." She was made differently from these people, her family--yet was unable to specify the difference in other than negative terms, unable or unwilling to express any positive desire. You are different, I tried to mirror: you feel unlike them, which must mean you want something other than what they want, a desire of your own. Once more, as soon as I said anything along these lines at all, anything that might invite or assume some positive desire on Denise's part, she lapsed immediately back into silence. I realized more and more clearly that she was telling me--again with her actions, or inactions, not her words--*to stop doing that*, to stop any form of suggestion, in even a conversational way, of language that might apply to her experience. Her experience, we might say, was missing; I could not look for it in my usual active way. Even little comments about her clothing, her handbag, anything like "Oh, that's a pretty scarf," seemed to act on her like an aggression, and bring her to silence. I began to let our sessions begin with more and more silence.

This new passivity on my part was uncomfortable, I believe, for both of us. No longer did I make the small talk I might use to make an adolescent comfortable. I intervened less in general. Whole long stretches of our hours together were spent in silence. I frankly did not know what else to do; all my habitual moves were blocked. And gradually this silence, this inactivity on my part began to open a space for a different conception of Denise entirely, and of her life situation and dilemma.

I should tell you that in the waiting area outside my office there is a wardrobe where clients can leave their coats if they like, and on the door is a small mirror. I had wondered at times what it was like for Denise, facing that mirror as she came out of my door after a session. But I had never asked and Denise had never mentioned it. Nor had she ever used the wardrobe. In the beginning she had stayed enveloped in her warm coat, hands in her pockets, through the whole session, even when it was quite warm in the room. I had mentioned the wardrobe, in case she ever wanted to hang up her coat, but otherwise hadn't commented. Later, as spring approached, she would arrive in a jacket or sweater and sometimes take it off. When she did this she would spend an enormous amount of time at it, folding and smoothing the garment exactly right and then laying it just beside her, on top of her schoolbag. The mirror itself would become important only later.

In the meantime, along with my own sense of feeling lost, and the continuing precariousness of Denise's condition, slowly I began to be aware of a different conception, a different organization of my own understanding, as I sat at times in silence and mutual discomfort with her. This condition, this "disorder," her bodily symptoms and expressions, all of her stance and way of being--all of this was not just Denise's reaction to puberty, but was more than that. These things were Denise's way, her attempt, to *find a solution to a problem of contact and relationship.* Not that she was wrestling with an inner problem as *opposed* to being in relationship or instead of contact but rather that all these "symptoms" were her way of taking up relationship. That is, this negating or disappearing that was Denise's style was more than just a reaction or avoidance of contact as the psychosexual model would suggest: *this was the contact.*

This change in my own conception then changed a number of other things in my behavior and attitude with Denise. New paths, new hypotheses became open to me. That new path, essentially, was to see Denise with others in relational terms. And to see her as engaged in a process of self-affirmation, which however was failing to affirm her own difference, and above all failing to affirm the conflict she felt with others. In remaining a "good girl," she, in effect, disappeared by not showing herself. The image of others was quite strong and vivid for Denise; her image of herself, by contrast, remained vague and indistinct. Here I thought once more of the drawing she had made, of her own image in the mirror.

With this frame of mind, I left the classical conception of a purely "inner" or drive-based conflict clearly behind. To work in this new frame, it was plainly necessary for Denise to show herself in some way, and not merely answer or react to my initiatives. Rather than others always providing or imposing a form for her experience, she would have to begin to give her own form to herself and to who she was. As it was, her bodily form was slipping away from her--in the mirror and in life, as if in spite of her efforts. Socialization and education had given her the form of a "well-brought-up girl;" what was her own shape or form? So far she was able to say, I don't want this particular form, or that one, or that one--as if to say, "Everything you're telling me and proposing for me doesn't interest me." And to questions at that level, I of course had no answer. What did it serve for me to go on putting words on events and experiences with her? The meaning I was giving in doing that was my meaning, not hers. Rather, I needed to receive her meaning, however vague it might yet be.

And thus I grew even more silent, now passing three quarters of the session in silence. I sat in silence--and so did she. This was uncomfortable, again, for both of us, just accepting the idea of being present. Present to her, and present to myself, and my own experience--my bodily sensations, the images that might come to me. And gradually she began speaking of her diving, for example, in a new way. No longer was it only a supreme physical effort. Rather, she spoke now of a film, *Le Grand Bleu*, a love story, but also the story of two young men who have a diving competition, testing who can stay underwater the longest without breathing and survive.

Denise "adored" this film. I used all my efforts not to ask why, or indeed anything about it. If she was anorexic, I disciplined myself not to be "bulimic" with my words, not to spew out my own ideas and questions and curiosity. I did not demand her experience of the film. Rather, after a silence and a reflection, I might say for example, "Well, your experience of the film evokes some things in me." And from there I disciplined myself to remain strictly with my experience.

I should add that at the time, every adolescent I knew was deeply taken with this film. It was a touchingly romantic story, the story of a man who wants to win this diving competition one last time, really to go to the limit and beyond, before taking up an important new step in his new love relationship with a woman--before living out the relationship with another person. As if he absolutely must go all the way, as far as possible before the point of actual death, even almost beyond that point, in order to be ready to undertake something else, some significant new contact. As I think back on it now, the parallel to Denise's attitude is even more striking; but I said nothing of this perspective, which seemed to include all Denise's blocks and dilemmas in taking up new relationships--with her mother, with her sister, with friends, with her new womanhood itself. Certainly there was the question of femininity in the sense of sexuality in all that as well--but there was much more than that. And my role was to receive all this, let myself be touched by her experience, and not try to seize and impose form and meaning.

And gradually she began to speak more--of little things in the week, a boy she had seen, almost always in an ideal vein, or perhaps a theme having something to do with some challenge, a bit along the lines of the film, where some final test had to be passed. She made reference to the film as well, to the idea of a competition with oneself, and at the same time with an adversary. In the film, she told me, there were dolphins, who come as if to tell the young man that he has gone too far, to turn him back. And of course on the tip of my tongue were questions like, what test are you passing, how will you know when you have gone too far, who or where are your dolphins, and so on. But I said none of this.

And so we passed almost a full year in this way. The task, as I understood it now, was just to receive all this, to let myself be touched by it, by the vulnerability, the fragility of it all. I didn't know what it all meant, but as I sat, often in silence, I was filled with sensations and images--of things outside the confines of therapy, landscapes, for example. And from time to time I would offer these by saying for instance at the end of one session, "You know, I don't know why, but I have a vivid image of a distant landscape, with a little village, all the little houses, and a bell tower which I can hear very softly." Just that, without making any demand, as if to say, I'm here too, I too am a person with thoughts and images and sensations. I'm not necessarily giving them to you, but I'm putting them out, between us, just because they are there.

On the mantelpiece of my office were a great many small photos and postcards, many sent from distant places, by clients and others. Many of my women patients, it seems to me, send pictures with images of women in particular. And as Denise began to look around, to see her environment more, not just looking at me, one day she focused on one of these, saying, "Oh look, I like that a lot." It was a silhouette of a woman, dark, black against a gray background, but rather more distinct than her old drawing. I imagined a sort of continuity, something that was being constructed, taking form inside of her.

And then one day came the remark, "Oh, you know, leaving your office last week I felt less afraid of seeing myself in your mirror in the waiting room." In your mirror, I noted. Once more I had that sense of fragility, of a whole field of experience hesitantly being born. At the same time, I found this a good metaphor for therapy: seeing oneself, first of all, in the therapist's mirror. For Denise this involved seeing something that was part of her, that belonged to her--her own image--and was at the same time outside herself. And for her to actually be seeing it rather than seeing either a stereotype or a distorted fantasy.

Denise continued to be extremely, distressingly thin. She was in medical hands to monitor this condition, and I no longer thought of it as directly central to our work. Rather, I found myself thinking of "anorexia" in a different way, more in terms of the contact problem it represented and also solved. By not eating, Denise was saying that the food, the nourishment that the environment was offering her--metaphorically and literally--was simply not suited to her needs, not to her taste in a deep way. Thus, the statement becomes at the limit, "I want nothing of what's available from the outside, from the environment." Rather, she needed, for a certain time anyway, to suspend eating as far as was physically possible (and perhaps even farther, which was the medical risk of this approach, this solution). Therapy, then, needed to be the protected space where she could find out something, at least, about what her own nourishment, her own experience and choice would be. And for that she needed to construct and have an experience of her own, with enough form and force to hold up in the encounter with the environment, and with the experience of another person.

One day she arrived at therapy in a miniskirt, extremely short, almost to the point of an exaggerated provocativeness. She was showing her body in a new way--which had the effect of calling attention to her legs, which to me were shockingly thin.

I said nothing, staying with my own experience, with the kind of heightened presence I now felt in these sessions, leaving the space between us open. The challenge for Denise, as I understood it now, was to organize that space--eventually with a sense that her creation of her own experience, her way of organizing our shared field, would have some impact on me. Her organization of experience was ultimately a relational act, and must be solved or adjusted creatively or reorganized somehow in relational terms. The challenge for me was to remain available and involved without overwhelming the fragility of that delicate process, to be present in a real way, without imposing my presence so strongly that it left no space for some small, tentative attempt on her part to enter into that problem in a new way, and change her habitual way of solving it. Her "symptom" was a creation, in this conception, in relational space. To create something new, she needed a relational space of a very particular, very delicate kind. Thus I was changed in my work with this patient--a change that carries over in some way to my work with others.

Through the following sessions, as Denise continued to talk about the various concerns of the life of an adolescent, her discourse gradually grew less generalized, less abstractly categorical. She spoke of two boys in her class whom she found "really cute." She began too to make references to what she liked and didn't like, to something that touched her deeply in a television program about childrenn... She was not at all certain about wanting to have children of her own someday--"because you do have a lot of trouble with children." Besides, she added, she could never bear to see her own body grow that fat... "It's so disgusting..."

For my part, my interventions continued to be essentially all in the direction of receiving and supporting her expressiveness, without trying to find out more, without interpreting, and almost always without giving my own opinion.

One day Denise told me that she had found sanitary napkins in her bureau drawer, which her mother must have put there without mentioning it (at this point she was still not menstruating, because of the hormonal disturbances caused by her anorexia). Denise was extremely irritated with her mother about this: "It's intolerable how she's aways watching me, always with this attitude of expecting me to do something." With great pride she informed me that she had thrown the pads in the garbage, conspicuously, so that her mother couldn't fail to see them.

At this point I did permit myself to observe, as casually yet directly as I could, that she was acting not much differently from her mother: not communicating directly, not telling her to her face that she was perfectly capable of buying what she needed when she needed it, for herself. I also remarked that I imagined she was probably capable now of asserting herself with adults, when she felt ready. Denise said nothing, and to this day I have no idea how she finally resolved this with her mother.

At the same time, I deliberately avoided any mention of the subject of the body, much less sexuality itself. Obviously the theme was deeply relevant; yet I continued to stick with only those subjects brought in by Denise herself, their development, her own organization of her own experience, and of her relationships with others (including me).

Thus, the sessions we had together, over a period of some two years, became essentially a time in which we looked for and constructed a way of existing together, in relationship and yet separately, in therapeutic space. A time for Denise to try out giving voice to herself and her own modes of expression, without the intrusion of another voice seeking to correct her experience, or her way of putting it together

We parted for the last time just before one summer vacation. When I suggested setting another appointment for the fall, Denise replied that she wasn't sure at the moment whether she wanted to continue our work or not. She felt better, she told me, less afraid of herself.

I accepted this way of terminating, for now anyway. To me, this was Denise's way of doing what I had said some time before: asserting herself with an adult, maintaining herself in the context of a relationship with another person.

During the vacation I received a postcard, showing a painting from a museum of primitive art in Switzerland, with the note, "To decorate your desk--"

Today, I cannot say that all of Denise's problems were ever totally resolved--or resolved at all. Body image, the life of the emotions, self-nourishment and eating, intimacy, sexuality, perhaps one day motherhood--all these issues were still there, potentially anyway, or else somewhere on the horizon. What I can say is that the experience of becoming more able to maintain her own existence in some way, face to face with another person, gave her greater resources for confronting all these challenges, and perhaps others as well, that her life might bring.

11

Shame, Interiority, and the Heart-Space of Skateboarding: A Clinical Tale

Mark McConville

Introduction

The first time I met Jeff, he cut a profile almost tediously familiar to me, working as often as I do with youngsters diagnosed Attention Deficit Hyperactivity Disorder (ADHD). In tow of his parents, Jeff sprawled his gawky, developing thirteen year-old frame across the couch in my office, while they--his father in a business suit, his mother in tasteful Talbot's casual--thoughtfully recounted a year of academic disinterest and decline, punctuated increasingly by episodes of defensive, angry, impulsive reaction to their best efforts to help him learn and grow. As they recounted their tale of repeated confrontations and failed incentives and consequences, and confided their fears that he would not be allowed back to the private school he attended for his eighth grade year, Jeff shuttled between bona fide boredom and silent, eye-rolling irritation.

He had been through this drill--sitting in a room, outnumbered by judging, nagging adults--a number of times before. There was the meeting with the pediatrician, the intake at the Learning Center where his parents took him for assessment and study skills tutoring, and most recently, the conference with his teachers, principal, and parents at his school. He was tired of it all, "fed up to here," to borrow his words. For if he was familiar to me, I was also familiar to him: one more adult who would poke and probe, get on his case, and make him feel dumb.

The Heart-Space of Skateboarding

But in the end, some ten months later, there proved to be a great deal about Jeff that was not at all familiar. By the time we finished our therapy work together, he had taught me as much about development with its component threads of learning, connecting, and becoming at home in the world, as any adolescent client I can recall. I want to tell Jeff's story as an example of the secret pain and challenge of self-development for so many adolescents, and as an illustration of the power and utility of the Gestalt approach for understanding and supporting this development.

My therapy with Jeff was, by any objective measure, quite unremarkable. I first met with him and his parents in different configurations-- all together, Jeff by himself, his parents alone. I also had several teachers at school fill out behavior rating scales, and talked at some length by phone with his Principal. The picture that emerged was a textbook example of what is commonly called Attention Deficit Disorder with Hyperactivity, with prodromal signs of an Oppositional Defiant Disorder in the making. "I've known few kids who could generate so much anger from his faculty and fellow students," the principal confided. And indeed, one teacher wrote on the rating form that Jeff was "loud and obnoxious" in her classroom. Another said he was like "a bull in a china shop," moving quickly and impulsively, bumping into desks, tables, lockers. He couldn't pass a classmate without somehow encroaching on the other's physical space, poking or "goosing," and the like. And this spontaneous roughhousing virtually defined the label "impulsive," as it occurred with no apparent grasp of the propriety of time or place, and revealed his almost complete obliviousness to consequences in any given present moment.

When confronted about his behavior, whether it was thrusting out a foot to trip another student, or coming to class without homework, and regardless how measured and calm the confrontation, Jeff reacted defensively. Nothing was his fault. Teachers picked on him unfairly, played favorites with other students, made mountains out of molehills. During periods when adults supervised his schoolwork closely, either parents, or teachers, or both, he improved marginally. But the gains inevitably disappeared as soon as the supervision relaxed. And, when asked to account for his poor performance, he would cite the supervision as interference, complaining that he was never given the chance to do it on his own.

In his peer relationships, Jeff displayed many of the features common to ADHD students. He was socially unskilled, apparently unable to read and interpret the cues that ordinarily regulate interpersonal interaction. He was aggressive, often bullying or teasing other kids, and when taken to task for his behavior would regularly protest that he was only defending himself or responding to provocation. Even in football, where his aggressiveness and athleticism made him a standout player, he was eventually benched by his coach when his behavior at practice--riding and demeaning other players for their shortcomings and mistakes--was judged to undermine team morale. Jeff was, to quote again the confidential assessment of his principal, "a real piece of work."

There were a few other pieces of information that fill out the presenting picture, all of them common features in the psycho-social descriptions of ADHD children and adolescents. Conflict at home was a daily affair, focused primarily around schoolwork, but also around matters of limits and temper control. Jeff hated school, but was bright enough that, in spite of the considerable adjustment difficulties there, he always maintained passing grades. His passions in life were skateboarding and snowboarding, endeavors where his aggressive, impulsive style was rewarded, and where his considerable talent earned him the admiration (however begrudging) of his peers. And, one other thing worth mentioning, something I will come back to later because it played into Jeff's sense of being out of place in the world: Jeff was adopted.[1]

The overall design of psychotherapeutic intervention with an adolescent like Jeff is, as I suggested above, unremarkable. I assessed the field of his learning and behavior difficulties, and involved myself in various ways designed to influence Jeff's environment to become more consistently supportive of his development. I met with several teachers and school personnel, assuring them that their concerns would be taken seriously, working assiduously all the while to inch them away from their own angry, judgmental posture, toward a posture more compassionate and helpful. I spent a great deal of time with Jeff and his parents together, helping them to become less entangled, clarifying boundaries, supporting his parents being in charge, helping them to work through their shame at having "failed" to prevent his developmental difficulties. This "field work" was arduous and complex, and as the Gestalt approach tells us, absolutely critical to the ultimate success of Jeff's therapy. But it is not the part I wish to emphasize in this chapter. Instead, I want to focus my attention on the underlying phenomenology of Jeff's disordered behavior, his first-person experience of *being* ADHD, and on the role played by our individual therapeutic relationship in his eventual ability to transcend his clinical diagnosis.

boundaries within the field, his experience of differences become paramount. This development became apparent for Jeff during his seventh grade year, when he became sharply and self-consciously aware, overnight it seemed, of all the ways he was different from his peers. This same sort of boundary sharpening occurs during adolescence within the family field, and has the effect of disembedding the adolescent from his parents and from his historical relationship with them. In Jeff's case, this process became evident in the growing frequency and intensity of conflict with his parents, particularly his mother.

The net effect of this life space differentiation for the individual adolescent is a heightened sensitivity to differences within the field, and with this sensitivity, a heightened experience of his/her own interiority, which is to say, his/her own uniqueness and difference in the field. While some adolescents feel enough potential and actual support in the social field to reflect and develop awareness of this interiority, Jeff was one of those who could not. At least, not without paying the price of overwhelming shame. For Jeff experienced his differences, particularly the constellation of experiences to which the label ADHD had been affixed, as utterly unacceptable to others. His parents and teachers, for one thing, were always trying to change him. The impulses that bubbled up spontaneously--the touching and pushing and joking, whose fountainhead was a desire for friendly, playful connection--too often met with annoyance and rebuke.

He was humiliated by his parents and the school's continual efforts to get him "extra help," all of which testified to his unacceptability as he already was. Watching Jeff and his mother interact, particularly over the matter of schoolwork, was painful indeed. She could not so much as raise the issue of some assignment or project due, without his launching into a counter-shaming rebuke: "What, do you think I'm an IDIOT," he would shout; "You are such a PAIN in the ASS!" And it mattered little whether there was an audience around, for these scenes played out just as readily in my office, or at his teacher conference at school, as in the privacy of their home.

And as so often happens when children feel shamed at the hands of their parents, Jeff's parents seemed deeply shamed in their interaction with school personnel, and with me for that matter. "If only we had been firmer with him earlier..." or "If we'd put him into the private school right away in first grade..." And from his mother: "If only I was a stronger person..." In some unspoken way, they felt responsible for his learning problems; and they most certainly felt to blame when his behavior exploded across the lines of propriety, earning them a telephone call from the principal, and now this tour of duty with the psychotherapist. With children like Jeff, shame is never an isolated experience, nor the province of one person alone. Rather, it saturates the field, non-support breeding non-support, with each corner--his teachers, his parents, and Jeff himself--playing the deadly zero-sum game of "who's to blame." As I said, it was painful to watch.

With ADHD children, where the field dynamics of shame are often powerful, self-reinforcing, and well-entrenched, interventions in the social field (supporting teachers and parents to appreciate themselves and each other) are absolutely essential for therapy to be effective. But, by the same token, such field work can only take the adolescent client so far. At some point, an individual therapy relationship becomes an essential healing tool for neutralizing internalized shame dynamics and supporting emergent interiority. I had to find a way, in other words, to teach Jeff to live with himself. With boys like Jeff, who focus outwardly and launch so quickly into action, this task is challenging to say the least. Jeff's self-organization was dictated by a self-reinforcing outward orientation that mitigated against the development of a healthy interiority. And, of course, interiority--thought, awareness, reflection, sitting with experience--is precisely the antidote for impulsive action. But, in Jeff's case, interiority created a shame-bind (Lee, 1996), instantaneously triggering awareness of what was so unacceptable about himself to others. There was to be no reflective interior awareness for Jeff, not if he could help it. But this adaptation to shame of course perpetuates the problem of impulsivity and ADHD. For if the internal does not develop the capacity to form strong gestalts, then the stuff of interiority--ideas, plans, resolve, concentration, and so on--can be no match for the buzzing, bubbling hub-bub of the environment around him, particularly not a classroom filled with seventh grade boys.

The answer to this therapeutic challenge, in my experience at least, is nearly always the same. I must become an anthropologist of sorts. I must find a way to enter the adolescent's world on his own terms, via a path of his choosing, not mine, and certainly not a path awash with shame, a path where he knows for certain, regardless of anything I might say to him to the contrary, that I will only find him lacking. Such a path was school. The path Jeff opened to me was skateboarding.

The Heart-Space of Skateboarding

We got to skateboarding, or "skating" as Jeff called it, through schoolwork, which we both understood to be the problem for which he was referred. Jeff didn't like this, of course, and he didn't hesitate to tell me that he didn't need my help, though to his credit, he was fairly polite about it. Mostly, he seemed on guard, placing his focus immediately onto the incessant nagging of his parents and teachers, and carefully monitoring me for signs of accepting or rejecting his views. Skating came up incidentally, when he re-drew, at my request, a pie chart of "skateboard preferences" that had been part of a science project earlier in the year. He had researched the project, he informed me, by interviewing salespeople at several stores that sold skateboards. This conversation led us away from schoolwork per se, and onto more comfortable territory as evidenced by the dramatic shifts in posture, tone and demeanor as the conversation progressed. "So, skateboarding it is," I thought to myself, and off we went.

First, we explored his developmental history, wrapped of course around a timeline of his development as a skater--when and how he first began, how his skills developed, how peer relationships evolved in concert with this activity, how his parents had and had not supported his interest as it developed. The conventional wisdom in individual psychotherapy with adolescents is that topics such as this--hobbies and the like--are of value primarily for building rapport, as a prelude for the "real," problem focused work which is to follow. But this is not the case. As Wheeler has pointed out (1996), "rapport building" activities are contact episodes in their own right, and as such have the potential for going immediately to the heart of the therapy work. In Jeff's case, this work had to do with difference, interiority, and connection, those dimensions of contact that define the self. And of course, shame, and the question of whether contact was possible without this price to be paid.

For three weeks, we talked about virtually everything there was to talk about in Jeff's life, all of it through the lens of skateboarding. Skaters are different, Jeff informed me, sort of the cowboys of adolescent culture. They're rebels, always pushing the envelope of adult tolerance, especially since their playing fields are often the ramps and railings of strip malls and public libraries, (and indeed, in my own home town, some merchants have "No Skateboarding" signs posted in their shop windows, and the police confirm an ongoing campaign to keep skaters away from public areas.). Jeff reported this with undisguised pride for it elevated his underlying sense of being different, an outlaw or an outsider, to moderately heroic status.

The same tension existed between Jeff and his parents, who found skateboarding a less than desirable preoccupation. There's no team to play for, they pointed out, and its dangerous, what with all the bumps and bruises and Jeff often neglecting to wear his helmet and pads, and how many times have we told you to stay out of the street! "They don't get it," he complained, "They don't understand skateboarding at all." And he was right, they didn't. But this is part of the function of disembedding from the family milieu--pulling out and taking ownership of those parts of self that feel unsupported or unsupportable by parents. And in this sense, skating mimicked much of Jeff's experience in other areas of his life, like learning and school, except that here his unacceptability was ennobled, and since it found support in other quarters of the environment, could be carried without shame.

Skateboarding, in short, supported the development of interiority. As a theme of therapeutic discourse, it tapped a rich inner world, a world of feelings and dreams, of goals and plans, of self-assessment, including self-criticism, and esteem--in short, an identity, a supportable crystallization of an experience of authentic selfhood.

I, of course, knew little about the world of skateboarding, and so had little choice but to become the willing student, which included learning the names of various tricks and maneuvers, leafing together through trade magazines, and a near disastrous skateboarding lesson in my building's parking lot. But by the same token, as an outsider I could see things about this world that Jeff himself had not really noticed. I could see, for example, that skateboarding required sustained attention and self discipline; that mastering a new trick required careful intuitive assessment of possible outcomes and dangers; that knowing about equipment required reading and study; that improvement required honest self-assessment and openness to feedback from others. Skateboarding, in other words, was a world like any other world, a place of challenge and commitment, an arena for testing out and learning, a venue for organizing the relationship of interiority and environment. In short, it was Jeff's preferred arena for doing the work of organizing a sense of self.

For some reason, this fact is often lost to adults--namely, that interests like skateboarding are often attempts to integrate a viable self, to bring interiority into the world, to work out an inter-penetration of the inner and the outer. That is, they are efforts to bring the inner world of desire and interest into a workable relationship with the outer world of challenges and supports. And the response of so many adults of dismissing such endeavors, usually in favor of more "serious" things like schoolwork, contributes to the cycle of shame that drives youngsters like Jeff farther and farther away from the business of academic learning.

In working with clients like this for whom contact with adults is fraught with shaming and counter-shaming possibilities, the essential work is to build a field of dyadic contact where shame is no longer the organizing principle. Jeff and I did not conspire to avoid the business of his difficulties at school. On the contrary, once I had learned to see his skateboarding for what it really was--an important expression of self--school, impulsivity, anger, parents, and peers, all became topics of conversation, topics that could be picked up and put down without any special press to give them identity defining status.

Adoption and Shame

It is well documented that adolescence is a time of unusual fertility for adoption fantasies. Wondering, "Who am I really?" and "Could these people really be my parents?" are commonplace experiences at this time in life. And why is this? Certainly it reflects the developmental phenomenon of disembedding, the growing sense of a boundary and of difference, the palpable experience and dawning realization that "I am unique; I'm not the same as them."

Every adolescent who has found himself launched on this journey of disembedding, of disengaging from the familiar bed of family and childhood identity, has had some version of this adoption-fantasy experience. What then of the adolescent like Jeff, who is in fact adopted, who has felt forever that he is different, and who now begins to understand that difference in ways that leave him feeling disconnected and unknown? For these youths, like Jeff, adolescence and disembedding can become a grotesque caricature if itself. I recall one client of mine, a quiet, reflective, cerebral boy of sixteen who had been adopted into a family of gregarious extraverts. By their reckoning, he was depressed, and indeed he displayed many classic clinical signs of this disorder. But more fundamentally that that, he was different in a way that was so much a part of ground that it defied definition, his nervous system cut from, quite literally, a different cellular cloth. What was missing for him was the experience of being recognized, of being found, in however penumbral and inarticulate a fashion, *familiar* by others in his social field.

This was very much Jeff's experience as well, although like most adopted children, he had no one to say it to, and therefore no way to say it. In our conversations about skateboarding, I had stumbled into a language domain where words were not so alienating for Jeff, and he could allow him-self to be known. What his parents and teachers called "impulsivity," we labeled "quickness." Quickness, it turns out, is an essential component of becoming a competent skater. It meant acting without stopping to think, reacting instantaneously yet intelligently, sometimes in mid-air, without conscious regard to consequences. New tricks were sometimes identified after the fact, with Jeff asking himself, "How did I do that?" as he dissected and attempted to reconstruct an unexpected move.

And so, when I asked finally, "How does your quickness play out in school?" Jeff was ready to talk about his experience of being in a class-room. And not unexpectedly, this experience revealed itself to be deeply sat-urated with shame. One interchange in particular stands out in my memory. We were talking about how Jeff's feet could think by themselves. On a skateboard ramp, this was a distinct advantage. In a classroom, it got him into trouble all the time. Jeff related an episode when he was asked to leave the classroom by a teacher he particularly liked, a man who was funny in a wise-guy sort of way, and who managed his students in a fashion that earned their respect and trust.

Jeff had just tripped another boy who was approaching the black-board, much to his own surprise since it was the third time he had done so in that single class period. With a knowing smile, the teacher said, "Okay Jeff, out in the hall. That's where we put future serial killers." The comment was such an absurd overstatement of the crime, that it lightened the situation even as it exacted a consequence for the behavior. Everyone chuckled, including Jeff. "But it really bothered me," Jeff confided. "I just kept think-ing, maybe he's right; maybe there's something *really* wrong with me."

After relating this incident, Jeff grew silent for a long time, sever-al minutes. "You're thinking about something," I suggested. He nodded, maintaining his silence. Finally, he spoke, slowly, with evident pain. "Do you have to report me, like if you think I'm dangerous or something like that," he fumbled. "No," I answered. He then told me a dark and horrible secret, a story that contained the awful, dangerous truth of being "impul-sive." The previous summer, he had been at camp. One evening in his cabin, he had confronted another boy who had been picking on him and putting him down throughout his stay. It turned into a verbal equivalent of a back-alley brawl, each boy shouting insults and taunts at the other. The victor in such verbal brawls was determined by who got in the last word, and who succeeded in drawing the other cabin-mates onto his side. As the other boy laughed to himself, and received the supporting laughter and admiration of the other boys, Jeff knew that he had lost the confrontation. He stood there, spent, speechless, humiliated. The other boy turned his back, bowing to his admiring audience. In that moment, Jeff's eyes lit on his Swiss army knife, lying on the shelf near his bunk. "I wanted to stab him," he said. "I'm sure you did," I replied. "No," he said; "you don't understand. I mean I could feel my hand going toward the knife, and I felt like it was just going to happen, and there was *nothing* I could do to stop it." "And..." I said? "I dunno..." he answered, "it just stopped. I don't know how."

For the first time, I felt a glimmer of understanding of what it felt like to Jeff to be "impulsive;" what a horrific curse this was, and what danger it carried for him. Now I was speechless. And then, something happened to me, in me, something that I have experienced only a few times in all my years as a therapist. A memory came back to me, something I had pushed out of my conscious mind many years ago, and which now brought with it a surge of shock and shame. When I look back on this moment through a lens of psychological theory, I see it as a revelation of what we mean when we use the term "field" in describing shame. For if Jeff had found in me a potential node of receptivity, a person who might understand, in some unexpected sense I had done the same with him.

At the time of this interchange, I attempted to be supportive to Jeff, but said nothing of my own experience, in part because it was too surprising and raw, and in part because I felt at that moment unsure concerning the propriety of sharing the experience with a thirteen-year-old client. But by the time of our next meeting, I felt settled about it, and decided to tell Jeff my own story. "When I was a kid," I began, "a few years younger than you are now, I did something really awful, something really impulsive that I've been embarrassed about ever since. There was this girl who lived behind us who I couldn't stand. She was always taunting me because I was overweight. I was out back one day with a bunch of other kids from the neighborhood, and she was there, saying stuff to me. I had been in the woods earlier, and so I had this bow and arrow with me, not a real one, but the kind little kids play with. Only I had taken off the rubber tips, and had sharpened the tips to a point. She was saying stuff, and I told her that if she didn't stop, I would shoot it at her. I notched an arrow and pointed it at her; she was no more than twenty feet away. She just laughed, and when I heard her laugh, I shot the arrow. It hit her on her cheek bone and glanced off. She had a small cut. But that cut was no more than an inch from her eye."

I shudder even now as I type these words. The sense of what was possible turns my stomach; the fact that that angry, hurt, impulsive, dangerous boy was me is still something I can't quite integrate. But Jeff understood. He nodded. And then he simply said: "You *know*."

Conclusion

I continued working with Jeff and his family and his teachers for the duration of the school year. But it was clear Jeff had turned a corner. Or perhaps more accurately, we had all turned a corner--his parents, his school, and me, included. I worked with his parents on stepping back and letting Jeff experience greater ownership of his behavior and its consequences. I met with his teachers and did some reframing for them of Jeff's behavior, talking to them about the nature of shame and face-saving defensiveness. It was striking how readily they accepted this more humane and sympathetic way of understanding Jeff's behavior, and how much more responsive he became to their educational interventions in response to this field shift. And Jeff's work in our individual meetings shifted more and more to the concrete business of staying out of trouble, getting along with other kids, and managing the boring but necessary business of school work. I met with Jeff several times during his eighth grade year, each time at his request and only for a single visit. When last I heard, Jeff had moved on to ninth grade--playing football, doing well enough in his schoolwork, challenging his parents in ordinary adolescent ways, spending time with friends. I would venture to say that by now, shame has lost its grip on Jeff's developing self, and that his interior world, once dimly illuminated, even avoided, now anchors a vital and emergent identity.

What did I learn from my therapy with Jeff? Many things. I learned that the "under-developed cognitive skills" of ADHD children--the poor memory and concentration, the weak cognitive focus, the paucity of forethought and prediction--are deeply intertwined with a sense of shame about the self. This shame, I believe, shuts down the developing interiority of adolescence, since getting to know oneself, forming clear figures about one's private feelings and intuitions, heightens the fear of disconnection and nonsupport that accompanies all periods of personal change. For these youngsters, the classroom, or any social situation for that matter, amounts to a bubbling, buzzing distraction, an environment filled with energy, noise, and solicitations of all kinds. But for these youngsters also, shame has conspired with neurological function to inhibit the development of internal resource, the thoughts and plans, the concentration and focus, the resolve and good intentions that anchor us in our environments, that most of us take for granted. And without these elements of interiority for ballast, the Jeffs of the world bounce around these environments like so many human pin-balls, unable to contain themselves, unable to focus, unable to learn.

The Gestalt model of development, with its attention to the field nature of developmental delays and progress, and particularly with its understanding of shame as a developmental variable, is an indispensable guide for working with adolescents like Jeff. It serves to remind us that, however symptomatic or provocative their behavior, they are managing the best they can. And as a compass, the Gestalt model orients us toward the relevant regions of the therapeutic field--toward parents, and peers, and teachers, and culture, and not least of all, toward ourselves.

Footnotes

1 I do not mean to suggest here that all adopted children feel traumatically disconnected during the time of their adolescence. Indeed, in my experience the vast majority of adopted children move through adolescence with a ground sense of deep connection and belonging to their families.

12

Sex, Lies and Audio Tape: A Conversation about Adolescence with Sonia Nevis

Mark McConville, Mary Ann Kraus, and Gordon Wheeler

Sonia Nevis has worked in therapy with children, adolescents, and their families for over forty years, and is the co-founder and director of the Center for the Study of Intimate Systems of the Gestalt Institute of Cleveland. On March 18, 1997, Gordon Wheeler, Mary Ann Kraus, and Mark McConville met with Sonia in her Brookline, MA apartment. A month earlier, we had met to discuss the development of younger children and the family field, and convened on this second occasion to explore the subject of adolescence. The result was a delightful amble through a variety of connected themes, ranging from the developmental issues faced by the parents of adolescents, to emergent adolescent sexuality, to the meaning of lies, truthfulness, and privacy in the developing family field.

Anyone who has spent time with Sonia Nevis has experienced her remarkable ability to see directly to the heart of complex issues, and to capture those issues with a clarity, a simplicity, and an elegance that is truly compelling. This occasion was no exception. In the conversation that follows, we think you will appreciate the penetrating insight, as well as the warmth and wisdom, of Sonia's thoughts on adolescent and family development.

… "mattering," "storm and stress," and the family field…

Sonia Nevis: So, where were we?

Gordon Wheeler: Well, we were talking about childhood, before adolescence, and how the child's experience of the family field influences development. The whole question of what the child needs in the family field in order to develop, to become a self, and you introduced the word "mattering"--the child coming to experience herself as mattering, counting for something. And then the quality of this mattering; not too much, not too little. And the other thing I recall was your talking about how important it is that other things also matter to the parents, how important this turns out to be for the child's development; things like the parents being interested in community, or politics, and their own work, and other aspects of the field.

Sonia: And each other.

Gordon: And each other. We were talking about parents who are very focused on their child, but then as their attention turns outward, the developmental field changes for the child. It's like when in infancy the parent's gaze carries the child's visual attention out to other things. And this is especially true as the child gets older, and certainly in adolescence, with the parents shifting to other parts of the field that matter to them, beyond the child, and this supports the child or adolescent to move beyond the family. It's the whole business of education and peers, the world beyond their parents and their family.

Sonia: Yes... good... so it's no small thing how the parents having things to care about makes room for development. And of course, what matters to them changes over time.

Gordon: Those were two things that stood out for me, the word "mattering," and the fact that there needs to be other things that matter to the parents, and these two things are part of a field that develops over time.

Mark Mconville: So, adolescence. We'd like to get your thoughts today on adolescent development, and especially from this perspective of a field that is evolving, and how field conditions play into development.

Gordon: I have a question for you, to help us get started. Authors like Peter Blos take the classical view that adolescence is a time of storm and stress, particularly for boys, in the tradition of the male model, in part because of hormones, and also because there's a breaking of the connection to parents.

A Conversation with Sonia Nevis

The classical view is very much interested in this whole business of breaking ties, becoming free of the tie to parents.

Mark: Breaking the "libidinal attachment."

Gordon: Coming out of the old model, it's much more a pre-supposition of breaking contact than in your work with adolescents and their parents. I'm re-reading Olga Silverstein, *The Courage to Raise Men*, and she takes a vehement stand in direct opposition to that. She says that that's not what it's about, and it doesn't have to be that way. So, there's these two opposing positions on this question. What do you think?

Sonia: I think a third thing. I think that the difficulty in adolescence, at least one way to look at it, is much more on the parents' side than the children's side. I think that the feelings aroused by seeing a younger version of one's self, be it male or female, with insides, especially with the awakening of sexuality---these feelings aroused in the parents are most often where the trouble begins. I believe that a careful study would show that if you have parents who are getting along pretty well together, and are happy with their work, their adolescents do not have such a stormy transition. If they're satisfied with their own lives, then it's not so hard to be happy that their children are turning away, happy that they're getting older, and so they can support that growth. But if there are feelings of regret, or jealousy, or maybe projections of their own unfinished business of growing up, unresolved sexuality for instance, I believe this is where the storm and stress originates.

Now obviously, the adolescent has something to do with it. I mean, they're making their own choices, and not always such good ones. But I think the bigger factor is the parents getting stuck in their own emotional business, more so than the child, the adolescent causing the trouble. In adolescence, the child is getting ready to go, and of course they're scared because it's a big step and they're really not grown up yet. So they vacillate, they act little, then they act big, you know, but not in such a crazy way. I mean, naturally there's some push and pull, but it doesn't need to be problematic. So, adolescence got a bad name as if the trouble were inevitable.

But it's really a question of what gets stirred up in the parents, that's how I've seen it in families I've worked with again and again. So, that's the theory I've been working with all these years, and have found very useful. When I'm referred an adolescent, I always look for the ways in which they're unable to tolerate the changes taking place, how the parents' field gets stirred up by a growing adolescent, and I pay attention to that. I can remember when my own children were at this point, struggling with my own feelings as I watched them growing up. First of all, seeing them tells me I've aged, and who doesn't have feelings about that? I mean, we make jokes about it, but there are a lot of factors that enter into it. I look at them and they're *free*, they're having a good time, while I'm working, with numerous responsibilities. They're having a great time, while I'm financing it, so there's a lot that adolescence stirs up in us.

Gordon: I know it, I'm wincing with recognition.

Sonia: They arouse *feelings*, and most parents don't have much awareness of those feelings. You don't want them to just have a good time; you want them to work harder, you know, get out there and *earn*, and to pay attention to the world, to learn how it works. Or else you want them to do what you did *not* do in *your* adolescence.

Gordon: Particularly if you're not happy with your life…

Sonia: If you're not happy with your own life, you'll not be happy with *them*.

Mark: I think too, adolescence triggers a lot of anxiety in parents. It's the age when you look at your kid, and you see his or her future, and you measure everything against "how is this helping them prepare for adulthood?" So it's easy to scare yourself. If they watch cartoons on Saturday mornings when they're eleven, it's no big deal, it's expected. But at fifteen or sixteen, you tell yourself it's slothful, it's regressive, and get yourself all worked up.

Sonia: Exactly. Do you remember any of the feelings in yourself as your kids went through those stages?

Gordon: Certainly the part about, they're just lying around, and here I am working my tail off. I can certainly relate to that one. You're saying, "Get out and earn!" but I'm just thinking, "How about just pick up your dishes!"

Sonia: Even though another part of you knows that it's your job to be doing that, and it's their job to be kids, to be adolescents. But it doesn't matter that you know this; the head gets over ruled very quickly by the feelings.

A Conversation with Sonia Nevis

Gordon: The other thing is, as a parent your feelings get hurt, to the extent that you're susceptible to that. And I know I certainly am. The parent thinks, "I *told* them to pick up the dishes, and if I have to tell them again, they're not listening, and that means they don't care." The same parent would never put that meaning on their six-year-old's behavior. But with adolescents, some parents end up feeling that way. I never said to my little kids, "Hey, where do you get off? I'm working my butt off here!" But to my teenagers I have certainly said that.

Sonia: The issue of whether they *care* or not--you don't have that with a six-year-old. You know they care. Actually, they're so attached, you can't keep them from hanging on to you. But with an adolescent who really is turning away from you suddenly you really want them to care about what you say, suddenly it *matters* to you. And the truth is, they *do* care *less* about you, which is very, very frightening to some parents, maybe to everybody. How aware you are of it, and how you handle it, whether it's okay that they care less about you, is the *key* to turbulence in adolescence. But they *do* care less about you; that's the truth.

Mark: The word "matters" really jumps out as central to the experience of parenting an adolescent. You discover that you matter less than before, and then your management of this fact becomes a critical dimension of the adolescent's developmental field.

Sonia: That's right, you discover that you matter less to them. And if development goes well, you also discover that they matter less to you, or at least that they matter in a different way.

Gordon: So now we're really talking about the *field* of the child's development, part of which is the parents own field of experience, where the child matters, but other things must matter as well.

Sonia: Right.

Gordon: Now we're saying, to get through adolescence as a parent, you must have other places where *you* matter.

Sonia: I think that's right. You've got to matter elsewhere and other things have to matter to you. Otherwise, your field narrows, with an adolescent, to searching for signs of their caring for you. Your birthday, Mother's and Father's Day, and so on, become too significant.

Gordon: And then the battle begins.

Sonia: Well immediately, as soon as you want all those things, you'll be embattled. You've got the adolescent on the other side, with their different issues, and they don't know exactly what they want, and they don't know how to handle the confusion of their parent's wants. They get it that their parents are in trouble. I'm sure you run into this with the families you see where the issue really is how the parents are managing.

Mark: I have a question related to this. You have always worked more with families, and less with the adolescents themselves. For myself, I think the balance is reversed. I often work with families, but also quite often with the adolescent individually. It depends on where, on how tangled up I see them being with the family. How do you decide whom to work with?

Sonia: The first important assessment we make is whether this family needs to learn to let go of the adolescent and the adolescent let go of the family, or does this family need to get closer, to learn to connect more powerfully? This assessment directs the therapy. Another way to say this, I need to determine is if this person, this half child, half adult, is more adult than child, at which point I work with them alone. That's what I think each of you do, especially in these situations where the family is not going to let go. In these cases the adolescent has got to be able to do it, unfortunately, without the support of the family. So, I have to support them. With any number of kids, I've said, "Look, you know in two years you'll be out... think wise, don't make it worse now, nothing will stop you in two years." They had figured out by that time that their parents were not going to let go, that they were going to have to wrench themselves out, and eventually they could do it because as therapists we give them support. But if this child is really still a child, and has unfinished business that *can't* be finished with a therapist, then I don't want to see them alone, because their business is with their family. I'm not so sure we do it differently.

Mark: Your reasoning feels familiar.

A Conversation with Sonia Nevis

Sonia: I'm more apt to see the family, watch them interact, and then have a few sessions with the kid, in order to support him to find a way to stay in the family. After all, at their age they *have* to stay and it's not a good situation when the battle escalates.

Gordon: Because in some sense they are ready to leave the family or at least ready to be ready to leave.

...separation, connection, and culture...

Mary Ann Kraus: I am curious about some of the ways that we organize ourselves in this culture around the importance of independence and separation, particularly for boys--boys separating from mothers. And I'm curious if you have any comment about that, about working with that particular bias in this culture.

Sonia: Well, I imagine that's something we all think about. I can remember one of my children saying to me, "I *like* it here." I liked it also, everyone was happy. She said, "*Why* do I have to leave?" and I said, "Because, in this culture, you *have* to. If you don't leave home, you'll be looked at as somehow under-developed, so you *have* to. And besides, you're not going to grow without other adventures. This adventure is finished, in a sense," I said. "It's now time for other adventures."

Now, is it necessary to have other adventures? That's really the question that I think you're bringing up. What's the matter with family life? Lots of sub-cultures have just exactly that. They live two blocks away. They don't separate; they get together for Sunday dinner every single week; they call each other every day, and so on. That's their life. Now, what's the matter with that? What's wrong is that in our culture, it's not viewed as mature. Is that right? Is that wrong? I mean, I see the lack of maturity in the sense that the experiences are repetitive. But the experiences are *deep* in terms of being together in a nurturing context, assuming it's all nurturing.

As you know, you get the same kind of thing with abusive families that hold together. They all act the same way. They can't let go of one another and often they just don't have a sense that there is another way of doing things. So their experiences are repetitive; there's no support for adventures beyond what's familiar, and they get stuck. There's an old, old joke about the social worker who had to check on this family where they'd heard there was incest. He goes to the neighbors, and the neighbor said, "Ah! That's the nicest family, they do everything for themselves." The question is, what does the culture support: holding on or letting go? Either can be nourishing; either can be abusive.

Mary Ann: So, in terms of your own parenting, it was a matter of preparing your children for this culture, where they have to separate in order to achieve.

Sonia: That's right; they *are* in this culture, so that's what they have to learn.

Gordon: Do you have to leave home in order to have adventures?

Sonia: Well, yes, I lean in that direction. I think that leaving home helps you break the frame of your family life. Now, leaving home isn't necessarily the whole story, because in my case I began to break my frame, not by leaving home, but through books. I read about other lives. And every time I read about another life, I was stunned. How could anyone think this? I'd say to myself. To some extent I broke my frame *this* way, so clearly there's more to it than that.

Gordon: In fact, I left home and went two thousand miles away, and even so *didn't* break the frame for quite awhile. I carried it with me.

Sonia: Yes, well, I wanted to add that I'm not sure books truly broke the frame for me. Intellectually, perhaps, but it wasn't until my first workshop experiences that I could break it emotionally. Intellectually, I broke the frame, but it took more before I had the courage to live that difference. Maybe that's a whole different thing. The lucky kid has the support in the home to break the frame by getting out, and the emotional support to get new experiences, but I think without these two things, adolescence have a hard time.

... "attractiveness" and support...

Mark: Where did the support come for you?

Sonia: Nice question. I had a hard time as an adolescent and a young adult.

Mark: That's a question I'd like to raise, whether in this culture it is necessary to find other adults, outside the immediate family--uncles, teachers, coaches and so on.

Sonia: I don't know about "necessary", but it certainly makes adolescence easier. Lucky kids attract supportive adults. There is the sad statement, but probably true, that attractive kids do better in the world because adults gravitate toward them. It's not their attractiveness that leads to an easier existence; it's the support they get that the unattractive don't get.

Mary Ann: That really fits the profile of the "transcendent child," those kids who come from horribly emotionally abusive or neglectful situations. Researchers have looked at the kids who have been able to survive these circumstances, kids who actually made it. One of the characteristics of these kids was a quality of being what they called "adoptable." They were very bright, very intelligent socially, and this enabled them to find a meaningful, even if somewhat marginal place in the world.

Sonia: That's what it is, and they do all right, but it's not their brightness and their sociability per se that makes them survive, *it's that adults come and I and give them support.* I love that phrase, "adoptable."

Mary Ann: They get mentored.

Sonia: Yes.

Gordon: But we've got to be careful here. I mean attractiveness is a very shifty concept.

Sonia: Well, of course I don't mean prett, or handsome. I always go back to the basic research I did on infants years ago. I started to test newborns one half an hour after they were born, and the difference in what I'm calling attractiveness was there, immediately, half an hour after they were born. One of the things I did was to hold them by their ankles. One baby would hardly notice me or care; another one would struggle maybe for ten seconds, or twenty seconds, and then, to heck with it. And another one was going to fight me right down the line. And you know the attractiveness of that baby that was forming a real relationship with me, and not leaving me, right then, a half hour after birth, was amazing.

So, "attractiveness," I said to myself, maybe it goes back further,

307

maybe these babies were nutritionally better. I was trying to understand how far back to go, where did this come from? But I think it's genetic, whatever that means, and we don't know exactly what that means. We have another mystery now, genetics. But within a family, you'll get one attractive kid, and two non-attractive kids. Now, we know that the relationship of each one is different with the parents, but I think that one of the reasons their relationships are different is that they're attractive to begin with, and the parent gets drawn to them. Okay, so it's a chicken-and-the-egg kind of thing; you can't tease it apart real well. But a parent loves a kid who makes life easier for them, in some way. Now, some parents like the kids that don't do much, they think they're wonderful, they think they're good, they call them, you know, "little princess," or "the professor," or "the thinker;" they give them all these positive names. If the parent doesn't like that kind of kid, then they're "lazy," or they're "dumb," or they're "sullen." So much depends upon the interaction of the parent and the child, what's attractive, and what isn't attractive, what's "adoptable." I love that word, *"adoptable."*

Mark: You said a few minutes ago, if they don't get it at home, then they go and get it out in the world. *Can* they get this same thing at home?

Sonia: I think, definitely, most kids get it at home. All a child needs is a "good enough" home. Kind of nice, happy to have you around. They get support, you know, to go out to the world, to go to nursery school, to kindergarten, to have friends, to play. I think most of the time they get it from home. But if you can't get it from home…

Mark: But let me take it to the extreme. What about the child who gets plenty of support at home, her parents think she's wonderful, but is not very attractive to the outside world, to other kids and teachers? This sort of child seems encased in the family, and doesn't find much welcoming beyond the family.

Sonia: Any number of kids that I work with that are just like that. They're often kids whose parents appreciate them, but the world, certainly their peers, have trouble with them, and the school system often has trouble with them as well. In fact, I think that those kids, when they get to adolescence, find it harder and harder to leave home. Often, the families I see are parents who need help to help their child get into the world. Usually, they come out okay. They have a harder childhood, but if their parents are supporting them to get out, and to find something they're good at, whatever it might be, they do okay.

...what about sex?...

Gordon: So, what about sex?

Sonia: Well, Gordon, what about sex?

Gordon: Well, it wasn't so much there before, and then adolescence happened, and then it's there. And so, what about the family field?

Sonia: So much depends on the family's habitual response to growth--to each developmental lurch. I think it often is experienced as a lurch. I doubt if any development is smooth. Has growth been celebrated or has it been seen as a problem? The onset of signs of sexuality is a big change for the family. If they have learned to ride these turbulent change times out then the adolescent feels supported and with the adults can learn to manage it.

Mark: Are you talking about the family making some sort of space for your sexuality, so that in effect there is a place made for it? I'm thinking of my growing up in an Irish Catholic family, there was no space made for sexuality, or maybe a sort of negative space. So, I think I was *required* in adolescence to differentiate from my family if I was going to develop a sense of being sexual, or at least a sense of being sexual without being ashamed.

Sonia: It's a delicate question, because most adolescents, the kids in the hormone stage, or whatever you want to call it, want to be told "Yes, go do it; yes, be sexual," but they also want to be told "Don't you dare be sexual." They're afraid of it, so they want to be told no, but it's attractive, and they want to be told yes; so, there we are. You can't say yes, and you can't say no, or you're going to get some backlash. You must say yes *and* no; you must be very skilled at saying yes and no, *both* at the same time. This is what I mean by saying it's a delicate question, and everybody has to manage it.

Mark: Absolutely, and those are parents who indeed are very skilled, I agree; I've never heard it put quite so clearly.

Sonia: I remember with my own children having to find a way to say both yes and no at the same time, because otherwise they were going to go out of balance. They were either going to go too slow or too fast; either be cata-pulted into it, which is not any good, or be held back, which is not too good for most of them either. So, it's a very complicated question. *(Turning to Mary Ann)* You're learning what you're in for?

Mary Ann: I sure am, and I'm saying, *Ohhhh!*

Gordon: You've been talking about how the child, in order to develop, needs to have a field in which they matter, but also in which other things matter to the parents as well. We've been saying how parents need to be happy, in their relationship, hopefully, but at least in their lives, and how this provides a field support for children to be turned outward, beyond the family. Now, this same thing must in some way be true sexually.

Sonia: Well, on the one hand, one of the supports is that the parents them-selves are sexual. That's a support, right there. And then the other thing is, parents' sexuality makes the statement as to why teenagers shouldn't be sex-ual quickly. You see, you're still holding out that they're going to be sexual, so they're getting support to get there, but they're getting told why they need to go slowly. So, who the parents are, in themselves, is the major support.

Gordon: That must somehow be true

Sonia: I think it's true.

Gordon: One of the greatest disagreements I ever had with my oldest daugh-ter was about this, though displaced; it had to do with the sex life of her friend.

Sonia: *(laughing)*

Gordon: She was about fourteen, still pretty young. But her friend was six-teen, from New Hampshire, and she was coming to visit for a weekend, and bringing her eighteen-year-old boyfriend with her. At that time, my daugh-ter's room and the guest-room were up on the third floor. So, I'm getting everything ready for this visit, making up beds and so forth. And I'm mak-ing up the bed for the boy in the guest room, and for the girl, the guest bed in my daughter's room. My daughter sees this and says, "Why are you making up separate beds for the two of them?" And I said, "Well, I'm sorry, I'm making up a bed for your girlfriend in here, and for her boyfriend in there." "Well, that's *ridiculous*! You *know* that they sleep together," she says to me. And I said, "Well, I know that you've said that, but it's not really my business, so as far as I'm concerned, they're two friends of yours visiting in our home, and they'll each need their own place to sleep." And she said, "Well, at her parents' house, they sleep together!" And I said, "Well, I guess that's their business," but my personal thought was, this girl's parents were over involved in her sex life, probably through having no sex life of their own. That was my diagnosis of the situation.

Sonia: Yes

Gordon: And from comments my daughter had made, I guessed they had been over involved for some time, pruriently, possessively involved. I think this was one of the cases you're talking about where we find parents either promoting sexuality, or else holding them back too much, but in either case because of not having their own sexuality. And I'm not talking about the parents' sexual behavior per se, I mean they could be living celibate, but still living a sexual, erotic life in their own experience.

So, back to the story. I said "Well. I understand that may be what they do at her parents' house, but I don't want to be involved in their sex life, so here they get separate bedrooms." To which she said, "Well, then in other words, this is just *complete* hypocrisy!"

Sonia: Well, that's what you're going to get.

Gordon: Well, you know, I stammered a little. I thought, "Well, I don't *think* it's hypocrisy, but I see her point. But if it's not hypocrisy, what is it exactly?" So, I tried to defend my position, but I stammered, and she pressed her point. She said, "You know the minute you go downstairs, she's just going to get up and go into his room." And I said, "Frankly, *that's their business*. It's not hypocrisy. It's that I think they ought to have the *decency* to sneak around!"

Sonia: With my children, my version of this message was "you want to learn about sex ?"--I wouldn't advise any parent to do this--"You go out with your peers to learn about it. It doesn't belong in the house, because it's your business; it's not mine to get involved with your sex life." I think I have my ver-

311

sion of that same story. I know I was groping for some truth that was difficult to articulate precisely. I was trying to establish the boundary of what I
approved of and what I didn't approve of. But I think the biggest thing I told
them was this: you want to have sex with anyone you please, you go ahead.
It's your emotional life, granted; but I told them, if you want a cluttered,
chaotic, emotional life, that's the way to do it. If you choose to manage your
sex life that way, that's what you'll get. So, my message really was: "Plan
your life, pay attention to your choices." But you see, the delicate part here,
the challenge, is how to find a way to talk to them that isn't "do it", or "don't
do it."

Mary Ann: That's interesting, that very frank way you put it. You really went
to the heart of the matter, the dangers of experimenting, but in a way that a
kid might be able to grasp the real danger of it, without having to have the
unfortunate experience of littering their life so much. That's one way to
learn about it, I suppose, but the cost is a little too much.

Sonia: A little bit too much, that's right, you want enough that they can
know the experience, but not so much that people have become just objects.

Mark: I'd like to bring you back to your statement of "you must say yes, and
you must say no," which I think is a uniquely Gestalt way of looking at
things. You're describing the ambiguity that is part and parcel of a boundary
where differentiation and growth are supported. As I was listening to your
story, I was remembering parenting my kids when they were teens, saying
to them, my job is to make sure that you know where I stand, and that there
are consequences for going over the line; your job is different from mine.
Your job is to watch out for yourself, and to make sure you don't get caught.

Sonia: That's it; that's what the tension in adolescence is. Adolescents have
to keep wanting to go faster; parents have to keep them going slower.

Mark: And one way to describe that, as a parent, is to say that I'm organizing a *contact boundary*; contact in the sense of allowing for differences. We
have a boundary here, between the two of us, and I have a strong want or
desire or position. But I am treating our field precisely as a contact field,
where your wants may be different from mine, and as a parent I'm implicitly supporting that you have business that's your own business.

A Conversation with Sonia Nevis

Sonia: And visa versa that the parents have their own business too. That's why I would say yes to the word "hypocrisy," at least from the kid's point of view. It's not their business why I say no, really. I'll explain it once or twice, but I don't *have* to explain it to them. That's what I meant when I said to you, yes, I'm a "hypocrite." I don't have to have their approval.

Mark: If we look carefully at this word, "hypocrisy," we can see that if speaks more of the child's experience than the parent's. You can only have true hypocrisy in a field where it's assumed everything must be consistent, where the correct position is either yes *or* no, not yes *and* no. And in a way, I think the adolescent would find it easier if everything were consistent, if we either approved of or prevented their behavior.

Sonia: That's it; that's right.

Mark: So, the developmental work is extending the field precisely so that that transaction becomes non-hypocrisy. That would be a way of describing what the growth is.

Gordon: The way this comes together in the anecdote about my daughter and her friends, is that what was *not* alright with me was to be involved. *That's* what felt like a boundary transgression. If they wanted to "steal" some sex, then they would be doing it on their own, without pulling me into the experience. I couldn't help feeling that that would be better for this girl than sleeping in her parents' bedroom with her boyfriend. I couldn't see how it would ever be hers.

Sonia: But that's what we're saying, they need adventures outside of the family, independent of the parents' approving or disapproving.

...truth and lies...

Mary Ann: This has always been the dilemma for me. What is the place of truth and honesty in raising an adolescent, just at the time where you're beginning to have and value these differences. You don't want to know everything, because you don't want to exert control over the boundary. To the younger child you were saying, "Let's have a relationship based on truth and honesty." But to the adolescent now, you're saying, "I don't want to know, and better you don't get caught." For me, this presents a dilemma,

313

how to handle this transition.

Sonia: I can answer it for me. Am I lying when I say to a child, "I'll take care of you, I won't let anything happen to you"? Am I lying or am I telling the truth? The fact is, it's a lie, but it's also the truth. So, I'm going to say what the child can understand, which is why I would say, yes, from the adolescent's point of view, it's hypocrisy.

Mary Ann: What about the discontinuity? Early on, you attempt to help them to learn about their process of telling their truth, and now you get to a place where you give them the messages saying, there are times when it's your job to not tell me the whole truth.

Sonia: The problem with the word "lie" is it's an absolute, with the connotation of "bad." When you think of "lie" rationally, you realize that we gauge what we say according to what a person can understand and even to how much time we have. So, you say, "There is a Santa Claus" and "You will be okay" and so on. It all depends on the psychological age of the child. Mary Ann, when do you tell your children "the truth?"

Mary Ann: When they ask

Sonia: Yes, because they're ready to know that you've been lying to them. You see, you're always gauging what they can assimilate.

Gordon: I never wanted to lie to my children. I always turned the question back to them because I wasn't comfortable telling an outright untruth.

Sonia: Alright, that answers your question in a sense. Parents lie all the time and the child needs the lies to develop a sense of security--what we adults know is a false sense of security, since we know we can't really protect them from most things. Somewhere maybe between eight and ten, kids get a little suspicious and start to ask, "Are you sure there is a Santa Claus?" You say "yes," and they want to and do believe you for another year. But they continue to develop and finally they perceive the "truth." They know you have been lying. They are at a new stage of development.

Gordon: I never wanted to lie to them.

A Conversation with Sonia Nevis

Sonia: You lied when you told them there's a Santa Claus

Gordon: I never told them

Sonia: But did you ever say to them, "I'm going to kiss you and make it better"?

Gordon: Uh, yeah… yeah

Sonia: Think of all the lies, all the lies we tell children: "Nothing bad will happen to you."

Mark: I used to leave my daughter a letter each Christmas, on old, charred parchment, from Santa Claus. And what the letters said always came from Santa Claus's heart, so I always thought of it as the truth, not as a lie. Once, when she was thirteen or fourteen, she said something about the letters, and I said, "I don't know what you're talking about."

Gordon: But she knew that you…

Mark: Of course, she knew. She's grown now, but it remains unspoken between us, and we both enjoy the lie, I think because it was the vehicle for so much truth. Those letters were one of the ways I told her how I really felt about her.

Sonia: I told each of my girls when they were very little that they were my favorite, and don't tell the other one. And I asked each of them when they were grown up, did they know I did that? Yeah, they knew, but they *liked* the lie.

Mark: Because the lie carried a truth

Sonia: That's right.

Gordon: Yes, but then in adolescence, you were talking about something different, right? A lie takes on different meaning. I'm not talking about truths you don't tell…

Mark: The alternative is that you're using the word "lie," but you're really

315

pushing the meaning of it, because a lie is something that damages.

Sonia: The word lie still has another meaning--again, it relates to the stage of development of a child. My grandson, about six, told his parents that his friend had asked him to take care of his gerbil. He said he went to his friend's house and no one was home, but the door was open. He went in, took the gerbil. Later his friend came and took it home. Turns out, the whole story was untrue. He told a lie. But is that a lie? I don't think so. He was so deep into his imagination that he believed it.

Mark: We're talking about the figural level of communication, which is the truth or untruth of a statement. But really, what matters developmentally is the ground condition of the relationship, whether the whole think is based on lies, or whether there's a value for what's true and real.

Mary Ann: This is getting me clearer about the difference between childhood and adolescence as far as this issue is concerned. At ages five and six, I wanted my kids to get the difference between what is considered the truth and what is considered a story or fantasy. I wanted them to get that distinction so that they really knew it, and I really would work on that sense of true and not true, real and not real. But when they reach their teenage years, what I might be saying is that for them to have privacy, they may be to tell me something that's not true, or not tell me something that is true. Privacy seems like a larger developmental issue during adolescence. So, in one developmental phase, I want to push one side of this issue, and have them be able to be really clear with themselves and me, and at another developmental time, to be still true to themselves but not to necessarily have to tell the full truth to me.

Sonia: Yes, with adolescence the issue of privacy comes in, and that changes the meaning of truth and lying.

Mark: Adolescents routinely do the sort of lying where they say, "I'm going here," but they're really going somewhere else. And in my experience this sort of deception has a lot to do with their losing faith in the relationship's capacity to tolerate the truth of what they're experimenting with and discovering. I say to them "so, talk to your parents about that," but they have lost faith that such a conversation will get them anywhere.

A Conversation with Sonia Nevis

Sonia: It's a continually changing picture. The struggle adolescents have whether to ask permission for something or to go ahead and do it heralds a new stage. Parents have learned that when an adolescent asks whether or not he can do some forbidden thing--drink at a party, smoke with his friends-- then the answer has to be no. When an adolescent is getting ready to be a young adult, she doesn't ask--she just does it and manages the family situation. If they ask, they are not ready. The asking is to stay engaged with the family. So, they innocently announce their developmental stage.

Gordon: Right. To me it's indecent to mix up the generations.

Sonia: Don't ask me to say yes to you or no to you; go and do what you need to do, and don't ask for permission, just do it. That's an adult act. They'll slide back and be a child again, because we know these transitions are hard. But if they've had "good enough" support earlier it's a quicker, smoother transition.

Gordon: I have a friend who quite inadvertently ruined her son's first intense sexual relationship. He was eighteen and was quite involved in this steamy relationship, and my friend commented on it in an indulgent, joking way that somehow involved her in it, and that ruined it for him, broke it up.

Sonia: I understand that. It was no longer just his experience.

Gordon: It was contaminated. She was divorced and he was her oldest son, and, after the divorce, had gotten very close to her. I know her intentions were good, involving herself innocently, giving the love affair her blessing, but that was *not* what he wanted.

Sonia: That's right.

Gordon: Well, she was complaining to me about this, claiming that she was being unjustly taxed; and I said, no you're not, you're being justly taxed!

Sonia: But you can't come down too hard on her.

Gordon: Right, but if you have to choose, a tad of disapproval would be about right.

317

Sonia: yes, because they needed to feel their separateness.

Gordon: Then it's fine.

Sonia: (*To Mary Ann, speaking playfully*): With your children's adolescence still to come, this must be very hard for you.

Mary Ann: Oy vey!

Sonia: I don't see why you should make any fewer mistakes that we did. We all do the best we can, Mary Ann... the things my kids forgive me for are too numerous to mention.

Gordon: Hopefully.

Sonia: I keep hearing stories from my kids, "Did you know...?" Of course not, because they were healthy adolescents doing all sorts of things I didn't know anything about. That's what it was: I really didn't know. That's where they were successful.

Mark: In psychoanalytic language, for adolescents to be able to maintain the connection with their parents, and yet to be able to keep them out of their business, requires a healthy degree of ego development.

Sonia: They are becoming adults; they really are turning into interesting people, and thank god.

...age, and the stages of parenting...

Gordon: Now, let me ask you about another issue that seems to be surfacing more and more. A lot of people are having children much later in life than they used to, 35, 45, sometimes in second marriages. And when those children get to be adolescents, instead of having a parent who is 38, they will have one who is 55 or 60. My youngest, Alex, will have a parent who's 58 when he's 17, and I'm concerned about quitting too early. I getting near the point of feeling like I've kind of had it.

Sonia: It's an issue. I've heard you speak about it.

A Conversation with Sonia Nevis

Gordon: I've been doing this for 25 years!

Sonia: And you're tired of being a parent.

Gordon: It's not quite that so much, it's that I want to go out and live. I want to go out myself and have other adventures. It's developmentally the right time for me, but too soon for him.

Mark: I grew up on the other end of that dilemma. When I was 15, my father was 60, and he didn't have a lot left for me.

Sonia: Sad for you.

Gordon: Well, in my particular case, I think it's because I've been doing it so long, and doing it by myself. But there are a lot of people, men especially, who have children in their second marriage, and that's where their energy is.

Sonia: They want to parent.

Gordon: Maybe they missed it the first time. But also a lot of people have children at 38 or 40, and it's their first family. They're good for the whole stretch.

Mary Ann: They had their adventures before they hit 38.

Gordon: For myself, particularly as a single parent, I'm feeling the urge to push the horizons of my own life. I've been parenting pretty intensely for a long time. Maybe that's just my issue, but I think it's broader.

Sonia: I think it's not only your issue. Taking it to a broader picture, some parents are most attracted to their children when they are infants. They adore little babies. Other parents are more attracted to their children as they grow older. I was surprised to find that I did not adore little babies---and I liked my children more as they got older. They began to grab my interest at about three years old. I had to work to be a competent parent to my babies, but after three years it was a cinch. I know it is the other way around for some parents. I wonder how all this affects children.

Gordon: Well I also love them older. It's not that I don't enjoy them and don't have contact with them, but I'm beginning to feel kind of *in loco parentis*.

Sonia: Sure, but what I'm saying is that there are lots of parents we encounter in therapy who are *enthralled* with parenting up to a certain age. Their age, or the child's age. Then they lose interest and want to give the child to you, so that you can make them better in therapy.

Gordon: Yes, but I believe that if they have a really good base by the time that happens, they can probably all weather that transition.

Sonia: That's what I'm saying. If they have to, they grow up sooner, and the fact is it can work out decently. If there has generally been "good enough" parenting, then the stages at which children have been under-protected and over-protected may not make much difference. There is a lot of room for mistakes. All we want is "good enough."

Mary Ann: *(laughing)* Yeah, my own family of origin was really great with little ones, but really tired of us as we got older.

Sonia: I think it's not such an uncommon thing. You had the good first years, which gave you the support to go out and have the adventures you needed to have.

Mary Ann: I see, I never quite understood it that way.

Sonia: Okay, are we done?

Mary Ann: It's such a pleasure, to be with all of you, and *(to Sonia)* especially to hear you again. I was just saying to Mark how much I miss the meetings we used to have together, you, Mark, Jim (Kepner), and me. I never see you anymore. But for so many years what you've said has stayed with me. For years, I could hear your voice, kind of know your perspective and response to things, and it's been so long now that your voice has faded into the background. It's just a pleasure to hear you again.

Sonia: Thank you.